EX LIBRIS

COLLEGII DAVIDSONIENSIS

Given in memory of

ALBERT WERTHEIM, Ph.D.
Professor of English
Indiana University

by his wife
Mrs. Judith B. Wertheim

# British Theatre
## 1950–70

# Drama and Theatre Studies

GENERAL EDITOR: KENNETH RICHARDS
ADVISORY EDITOR: HUGH HUNT

*Also in this series :*
Theatre in the Age of Garrick
CECIL PRICE

A Short History of Scene Design in Great Britain
SYBIL ROSENFELD

The Theatre of Goethe and Schiller
JOHN PRUDHOE

Theatre in Ireland
MICHEÁL Ó hAODHA

# British Theatre
# 1950–70

ARNOLD P. HINCHLIFFE

BASIL BLACKWELL · OXFORD
1974

ISBN 0 631 14810 8 (cased edition)
    0 631 14820 5 (Blackwell Paperback)

Printed in Great Britain by
Alden and Mowbray Ltd at the Alden Press, Oxford
and bound at the Kemp Hall Bindery

for Jim

# Contents

# List of Plates

Guildenstern in *Rosencrantz and Guildenstern are Dead* by Tom Stoppard
The National Theatre production was directed by Derek Goldby with scenery and constumes by Desmond Heeley, 1967

15. The Royal Court Theatre in Sloane Square

16. 1956 production of Osborne's *Look Back in Anger*
Left to right: Mary Ure as Alison, Alan Bates as Cliff, Helena Hughes as Helena, Kenneth Haigh as Jimmy Porter

17. The 1965 production of Edward Bond's *Saved* at the Royal Court with Ronald Pickup, Dennis Waterman, John Bull, William Stewart, Tony Selby

18. *Serjeant Musgrave's Dance* by John Arden, revived at The Royal Court Theatre in 1965.

19. The *Hair* tribe. *Hair* opened at the Shaftesbury Theatre, London, in September 1968

20. Peter Brook's production of *A Midsummer Night's Dream*, Royal Shakespeare Theatre, Stratford 1970

21. John Geilgud and Mona Washborne in *Home* at the Royal Court Theatre, 1970

22. A scene from the new 1950s Rock 'n' Roll musical *Grease* at the New London Theatre, 1973

# Acknowledgements

Permission to quote from the following is gratefully acknowledged:

From *Serjeant Musgrave's Dance* and *The Business of Good Government,* by John Arden, by kind permission of Methuen & Co., Ltd., and Grove Press, Inc., copyright © 1960 and 1963 by John Arden.
From *The Confessions of St. Augustine,* translated by Dr. Pusey, introduction by A. H. Armstrong, Everyman's Library Edition, by kind permission of J. M. Dent & Sons and E. P. Dutton & Co., Inc.
From *Waiting for Godot,* by Samuel Beckett by kind permission of Faber & Faber, Ltd., and Grove Press, Inc., copyright © 1954.
From *The Messingkauf Dialogues,* by Bertolt Brecht, translated John Willett, by kind permission of Methuen & Co., and Pentheon Books, a Division of Random House, Inc.
From *the empty space,* by Peter Brook, by kind permission of MacGibbon & Kee.
From *The Cocktail Party,* by T. S. Eliot, by kind permission of Faber & Faber, Ltd., and Harcourt Brace Jovanovich, Inc., New York.
From *The Lady's Not For Burning,* by Christopher Fry, by kind permission of Oxford University Press.

ACKNOWLEDGEMENTS

From *Venus Observed,* by Christopher Fry, by kind permission of Oxford University Press.

From *The Philanthropist,* by Christopher Hampton, by kind permission of the author and Faber & Faber Ltd.

From *Notes and Counter Notes,* by Eugene Ionesco, translated by D. Watson, by kind permission of Calder & Boyars, Ltd.

From *Look Back in Anger,* by John Osborne, by kind permission of Faber & Faber, Ltd., and S. G. Phillips, Inc., Copyright © 1957.

From *The Entertainer,* by John Osborne, published by Faber & Faber, Ltd., by kind permission of David Higham Associates Ltd., and S. G. Phillips, Inc., copyright © 1958 by John Osborne.

From *Luther,* by John Osborne, published by Faber & Faber Ltd., by kind permission of David Higham Associates Ltd., and Abelard-Schuman, Ltd., copyright © 1961.

From *Inadmissable Evidence,* by John Osborne, published by Faber & Faber, Ltd., and Grove Press, Inc., copyright © 1965 by John Osborne Productions, Ltd.

From *The Birthday Party,* by Harold Pinter, by kind permission of Methuen & Co., Ltd., and Grove Press, Inc., copyright © 1959 by Harold Pinter.

From *Tynan Left and Right,* by Kenneth Tynan, by kind permission of the Longman Group, Ltd.

From *Chicken Soup With Barley, Roots* and *I'm Talking About Jerusalem,* by Arnold Wesker, by kind permission of Jonathan Cape, Ltd.

From *Saint's Day,* by John Whiting, by permission of A. D. Peters and Company.

# Preface

The dates 1950–70 seem neat enough to suggest the arbitrary rather than the significant, but they were chosen with care. Twenty years is a good span, large enough to show developments but not too large to be lost in panorama; and these twenty years have been particularly interesting. No one, surely, believes that everything changed on a certain night in a certain place in 1956 but something became clear, asserted itself more impressively at that time, confirming what had hitherto been circumstances full of promise. The theatre is so precarious an institution that it is permanently renewing itself, and must do so or it would become a dead thing. About 1956 British Theatre enjoyed a strong sense of renewal. That it seemed to happen overnight only suggests the longer period of germination.

1970, as the date of writing, was, inevitably, some kind of end and although I have allowed important plays and their dates to slip into the text and added to the bibliography, I have kept it as the end. 1970 seemed a time when what happened in 1956 had the appearance of being exhausted yet was compelled to go on happening in ever new and elaborate ways. The result is that theatre is far from being a museum, is, indeed, more like Pope's moving toyshop. There has been a great deal of talk about preserving the theatre from becoming a museum, although museums do have a place in our cultural lives and some may think them better institutions than the present boutique where everything is desperately eccentric. At least if the theatre in 1950 lacked passion (which is now dangerously equated with political content) it knew what it was doing and it was momentarily relevant to a post-war world. In 1970 the cry about making the theatre relevant leads to the question: relevant to what? In that sense this work may be seen as a valedictory to British Theatre.

Obviously in so synthetic a history the acknowledgement of debts would occupy a great deal of space. The major debts are recorded in the bibliography and as frequently as possible in the text. I am most deeply in debt to Eric Bentley, Martin Esslin and John Russell Taylor but many others have helped. I am grateful to my editors, and to Prue Wintrip who coped with the final typescript so valiantly. For all this assistance, insights and criticism I am most grateful; the prejudices are, of course, all mine.

A.P.H.

From a critic's point of view, the history of twentieth century drama is the history of a collapsing vocabulary.

Kenneth Tynan

The Theatre is the Public Art of Crisis.

Herbert Blau

# CHAPTER ONE

# European Influences

British theatre in the years 1950–70 showed a growing awareness of and response to what was happening in the theatre of Europe, and particularly the work of two dramatists: Beckett and Brecht. During the summer of 1955, a young director, Peter Hall, put on a play called *Waiting for Godot* written by an Irishman in exile in Europe who used the French language. This play became the talk of town and country while London audiences at the Arts Theatre could see a production of *The Lesson* by Ionesco and *The Balcony* by Genet—plays which were later given the label Absurd. Meanwhile, over in East Germany, a Marxist poet, dramatist and director was, according to rumour, reviving Epic Theatre, and such rumours were confirmed in 1956 when the Berliner Ensemble visited England. Although obviously different, indeed opposing, views of the theatrical art we can detect anger in each, anger at society and at the conditions in the theatre which mirrored that society.

The influence of Brecht has proved to be the greater, not because of the slogans—Epic Theatre, Alienation, Commitment—but because the tendency over these last twenty years has been to shift the emphasis from actor to writer and finally to producer and Brecht has more to offer the producer than Becket.[1] James Agate once said that an

[1] There is some confusion between the words 'producer' and 'director'.

imaginative producer was a luxury only the best plays could afford and only the worst plays needed. If this remains not without truth it is not in keeping with the tendency of the times which has been towards the Gesamtkunstwerk in which the producer clearly plays the most important part. Brecht, of course, was in the privileged (and fairly rare) position of being both dramatist and producer and this eliminates possible conflicts. But it is this authority rather than the theory of Alienation which accounts for his importance. Most people do not need Brecht to tell them that they are in a theatre and undergoing a complex double experience. St. Augustine, long ago, mused on the curious nature of that experience, and his rejection of theatre and Aristotle is more fundamental than most of the Christian Fathers. Where Aristotle had advanced a theory of therapeutic imitation Plato had banished drama from his well-ordered state, although, admitting his own pleasure in the theatre, he allowed the dramatist and audiences the right of appeal. It is Plato's view that persists in the thinking of the Christian Fathers but nowhere so completely as in St. Augustine who saw the analogy between suffering and the suffering of spectators at a play as both false and dangerous:

Howsoever, when he suffers in his own person, it uses to be styled misery; when he compassionates others, then it is mercy. But what sort of compassion is this for feigned and scenical passions? for the auditor is not called on to relieve, but only to grieve: and he applauds the actor of these fictions the more, the more he grieves. And if the calamities of those persons (whether of old times, or mere fiction) be so acted, that the spectator is not moved to tears, he goes away disgusted and criticising; but if he be moved to passion, he stays intent, and weeps for joy.[2]

Much of Elizabethan and Jacobean theatre appears to have

The word 'producer' is now commonly associated, through film and television practice, with management rather than artistic direction. Old habits die hard and the word 'producer'—meaning the man who is in charge of artistic direction—comes most naturally to me and has, therefore, been used; although on occasion the word 'director' slips in.

[2] *Confessions of St. Augustine,* Book III, Everyman (1949), p. 33, translated by E. B. Pusey.

rested on alienation and when the child actors were making free use of painted scenery in the Franco-Italian manner—the latest, trendy thing—the playhouse builders rejected this in favour of medieval symbolism: a roof to shelter them also became the heavens so that Shakespeare's Globe was aptly named containing as it did the heavens, an earth platform and hell beneath. This must have been a deliberate choice rather than economy since they were at the same time prepared to purchase the richest costumes and stage properties. The Athenian mechanicals rehearse and perform *Pyramus and Thisbe* according to rules which suggest that they, rather than Brecht, had written *The Little Organon for the Theatre*. Even Coleridge's famous phrase for the condition of empathy, 'the willing suspension of disbelief' insists on a willingness which makes all the difference between a trance which ignores all problems and the more complex, because willed, belief which has been led to the problems, informed about them and is now part of an 'enlightened complicity'[3] between author and audience. In Brecht's own work we frequently have the impression that the actors are pretending that they are not pretending, while any producer will tell you that Brechtian economies are very expensive. Both Martin Esslin and John Willet[4] agree that Brecht modified or jettisoned his theories whenever it suited him and yet rather than looking at the plays interest has focussed on the theories. Since those theories involve a serious examination of theatrical conditions such a preoccupation is not entirely vain.

Brecht (1898–1956) wrote *Baal* in 1918 (although it was not performed until 1923) and this play, with other early works, could be classed as Theatre of the Absurd. In 1928 Brecht turned Gay's *The Beggar's Opera* (1728) into *The Threepenny Opera* using Gay as the basis for an attack on bourgeois society and making clear his Marxist commitment. Brecht left Germany for Scandinavia in 1933 moving on to the United

---

[3] The phrase is from Damian Grant, *Realism* (1970), p. 70.

[4] Critics like Esslin and Willett have, however, been attacked as saving Brecht for the West.

3

States in 1941 where he wrote solidly until about 1945. After that date his important work finishes and he devoted himself more and more to poetry, theory and the direction of his own plays returning, in 1949, to run his own company, the Berliner Ensemble. With the appearance of *Mother Courage* (1949) (with his wife, Helene Weigel, in the title rôle) he began to be recognised as an important influence through his theories and production methods.

He explained his theory in *The Messingkauf Dialogues* (1963) substituting an Alienation Effect for the customary Empathy. Because of this effect events were reproduced on the stage to underline their causality in the spectator's mind:

He [i.e. the actor] must give up his *complete conversion* into the stage character. He *shows* the character, he *quotes* his lines, he *repeats* a real-life incident. The audience is not entirely 'carried away', it need not conform psychologically, adopt a fatalistic attitude towards fate as portrayed. (It can feel anger where a character feels joy, and so on. It is free, and sometimes even encouraged, to imagine a different course of events or try and find one, and so forth.) The incidents are *historicized* and socially *set*.[5]

Brecht is asking the old question: how can theatre be both instructive and entertaining. His attitude shows respect for the audience which is asked to think for itself and become more responsible for accepting what is seen only if it is convincing. Empathy is something which applies to both audience and actor: the audience weeps for the tragic hero that the actor is striving to become. For Brecht this identification with and acceptance of that rôle means that both audience and actor unquestioningly accept a certain view of life. In Greek drama human suffering springs from Fate which usually reflects the rule of Gods who need no justification and who cannot be criticised. This kind of tragedy is characterised by a sense of inevitability which appears also in, say, the plays of Shakespeare. Here the Gods have been replaced to a large extent by the awkward but useful mistranslation of hubris as a

4      [5] *The Messingkauf Dialogues,* translated by John Willett (1965), p. 104.

fatal flaw. The end of Shakespearian tragedy is a restoration of order but this presupposes that there is a sense of order that can be restored and leads to an unquestioning acceptance of the catastrophe. Catharsis may purge but it does not cause questions to be asked and it is this which Brecht attacks.

One simple method was to remove the natural development of the play by breaking it up into episodes, putting in songs and music *outside* the action, getting actors to pretend to be actors and showing the scenery and lighting as obviously only scenery and lighting. Such devices are there to keep people awake, to shock us into bringing our best reason to the play. Thus Joan Littlewood dressed her First War soldiers as Pierrots to prevent conventional responses or thoughtless sentimentality, and Peter Brook brought the house lights up before the blinding of Gloucester in his production of *King Lear* to make the audience take stock of the scene before the curtain fell and they awoke to clap. Clearly such interferences can be dangerous but they reflect a thoughtful concern for what is being played and remind us that what we watch is not inevitable but, since the situations are created by humans not Gods, avoidable. In this sense Brechtian theatre cannot be ideological theatre or committed theatre since the audience must be left at the end of a performance questioning the action and the choices made during it. Brecht, of course, reduced the tragic hero to a ridiculous example of self-sacrifice. The nobility of individual suffering is seen as perverse because the tragic hero neglects the possibility of changing the world and dies. Such a theatre must be described as dialectical, and for it Brecht chose the epic form.

He took this form from Erwin Piscator who claimed to have invented it in 1924 with a production which used films and placards as well as actors in a kind of didactic, political theatre allied to the Marxist cause. Critics have noted, however, epic theatre before Piscator (for example, Hauptmann's episodic *Die Weber*) and point out that he did not go very far. Piscator did insist on the supremacy of the producer and complained (it is to become a familiar

5

complaint) that he could find no good dramatists for his theatre. At the same time Piscator refused any completed scripts and handed out material to authors for completion with him at the theatre. This can work well unless the dramatist happens to be good. But, more significantly, the idea of doing away with dramatic illusion, making a direct appeal to the audience and abandoning artistic wholeness in favour of moral or didactic results tended to rule out both pleasure and entertainment. Brecht himself got to the point of abandoning audiences and using plays to educate the actors morally and politically as they learned not to act in them. Fortunately the idea of delight as well as profit was readmitted as a proper function of theatre.

The term 'epic' is wider in German than it is in English and goes back to Goethe and Schiller who distinguished between the dramatic and the epic, the latter representing everything through the medium of a narrator. This outside focus gave Brecht the perspective he wanted. An example would be Mother Courage who is intentionally created as a contradictory figure with whom we should not try to identify. She is a helpless victim but she is also a willing accessory and the lesson she should teach us is not how nobly she suffers and endures but that she belongs to a state of society in which the individual is alone. Her society exhibits no sense of solidarity between the victims of oppression. The historical setting puts the action at a distance which helps the spectator to compare her situation with present conditions: she could not be part of a movement but we can. Thus while the spectator of a Beckett play can estrange himself by laughter there is no possible alternative to the action, but with Mother Courage we can recognise the pathos of her situation and ways of altering a position that for her is inevitable. Like Shaw before him, then, Brecht intended a drama of ideas to unsettle the audience and shatter the theatre of trance. There is little point in mounting a theatre of ideas in a form which dulls the mind and when we have a theatre that offers easy sentimentality there is a strong case for a theatre of reason. But such a theatre appears to be

6

fighting a natural and irrepressible urge towards shared feeling. Empathy may prevent an audience from thinking but alienation robs them of feeling and since feeling is usually instinctive the theory tends to become gratuitous in our response to the plays. The methods then become another convention to be absorbed through familiarity and, finally, overlooked.

The actual influence of Brecht on dramatists is hard to assess. It is recognised that he influenced Auden and Isherwood, and Martin Esslin suggests[6] that since 1956 he appears as a greater influence than Pirandello. There has certainly been a great deal of lip-service paid to him and what he was thought to stand for but few valid productions of his plays, little genuine knowledge of his work and, not unexpectedly, scant evidence of direct influence. Tynan, the dramatic critic of *The Observer* in 1954, was first impressed by the Theatre Militant through the Berliner Ensemble and rapidly made the name of Brecht his trademark. He might have been influenced in this by the fact that the Berliner Ensemble seemed to refute those critics of a National Theatre who suggested that such an institution must become sterile, like the Comèdie Française. In late August 1956 the Ensemble came to the Palace Theatre and made a considerable impression in spite of a lukewarm critical reception. Significantly this impression was most evident in those spheres unhindered by a language barrier: stage design, lighting and music. Subsequently we can point to Sean Kelly's set for *Oliver*— flexible, mobile and using textures—and a rash of socially-oriented musicals. It is likely, however, that Joan Littlewood would have done her work anyway, and produced, say, Behan's *The Hostage* (1959) which has many parallels with *The Threepenny Opera*. By avoiding style of delivery Brecht seems to have been left with uncontrolled roaring strongly reminiscent of the days of Kean and Irving and seen in William Gaskill's production of *Mother Courage* at the National Theatre in 1965. On the other hand it was Gaskill

[6] See *Brief Chronicles*, pp. 84 ff.

who did the very successful production of *The Recruiting Officer* at the National in 1963 (Brecht's version had been brought to London in 1956). Peter Brook insists that his *Marat-Sade* production could not have existed without Brecht and cites as devices for alienation the ending where the asylum goes berserk until the stage manageress walks on and blows her whistle, when the lunatics become actors and the stage image only a stage image. At this point the audience applaud but then the actors applaud back and the audience stops clapping. Brook describes this as 'a momentary hostility' but it might be plain embarrassment.[7] Certainly if we look forward to *US* where alienation was supposed to make us readjust our positions there were moments when the production also seemed to take advantage of our good manners, and this tendency to insult audiences can be seen in the later antics of the Living Theatre. Among producers Peter Brook and Joan Littlewood must be regarded as the most positively influenced of stage directors.

In 1965 the Berliner Ensemble made their second visit to London and by now critics had learned to be unanimous in their praise. But whereas Brechtian methods can influence producers his effect on dramatists is obviously much more difficult to trace. Brecht seems to have been attractive to both Osborne and Wesker. Osborne, for example, has used historical subjects in *Luther* and *A Patriot for Me* and his treatment is epic in scope and uses Brechtian techniques. On the other hand the plays show little feeling for social, cultural and political background and finally look like psychological problems tricked out in costume. Wesker's use of cinematic techniques is probably the result of his early training, although they might not have been so confidently used had Brecht not already familiarised the theatre with them. Bolt claims an influence in *A Man For All Seasons* but that is a trivial if pleasant play. Peter Hall, who wanted to work on the epic scale but in plays by someone other than Shakespeare, persuaded Whiting to write *The Devils* (1961) and Shaffer *The*

8

[7] Peter Brook, *the empty space* (1968), pp. 74-5.

*Royal Hunt of the Sun* (1965)[8] but neither play justifies the description Brechtian. John Arden would probably be the truest parallel in England. A left-wing writer, Arden's plays actually remain neutral (unlike Brecht's!), use Brechtian techniques and show that a major poet can still write drama. But in the climax of *Sjt. Musgrave's Dance* Arden is more a dramatist in the tradition of the Absurd, a tradition he seems to espouse fully in a play like *The Happy Haven*. In brief, Brecht influences producers rather than writers. This is reasonable, for whereas producers can borrow techniques and use them as part of their own style a writer who is too influenced loses, or risks losing, his individual voice. Any influence from abroad will be naturalised and writers (as creators) as opposed to producers (as interpreters) resist fundamental influences.

Moreover, writers for the British Theatre lack commitment in the sense that we seem to find it in the European theatre. In England the word 'committed' means, not inaccurately, left wing and propagandist. As a slogan it harks back to the world of postwar France when Sartre wrote *What Is Literature?* (1947). The Occupation compelled thinking Frenchmen to reconsider their values and commitment, as much as Absurd Theatre or the impersonality of a Robbe-Grillet novel, was a response to the extreme pressures of the time. As J. H. Wulbern points out in his study of Brecht and Ionesco (1971) the two dramatists share a common view of the incapacity of man to control his own destiny and each responded in his own way to the political and social conditions existing in his own country and the world at a decisive time in his career, conditions—as between post-war Germany in 1918 and post-war France in 1945—which were strikingly analogous. Both writers are fundamentally solitary but Brecht was able to transcend this condition first by his dedication to Communism and secondly by life in the theatre. Ionesco, far from innocent of political views—as *Rhinoceros* and *The Killer* show—refuses to provide an alternative and fails to work

[8] Shaffer's play was finally produced by the National Theatre.

successfully within the theatrical situation. This, unlike other art forms, is specifically a shared experience.

The difficulty with Brecht is to reconcile a commitment to Marxism and a devotion to art, but Brecht insists that there will be no contradiction 'provided that the artist is talented, honest, and *cunning* enough to couch his perception of the truth in terms which have some appeal to the regime'.[9] The italics are mine and catch the word—cunning—which appears in Brecht's pamphlet of 1934, *Five Difficulties in Writing the Truth*. This pamphlet, written for underground distribution in Nazi Germany (but applicable to any totalitarian regime[10]) lists courage, wit, know-how, judgement and cunning, and Brecht devotes half the essay to this last quality. Brecht embraced communism as the only solution to the problems facing Germany at that time; he laid down his priorities in *The Threepenny Opera* (1928): eats first, morals after. But far from restricting him, communism alleviated his basic loneliness and nihilism. Cunning, to the western mind, is opposed to honesty; but here it means playing dumb like the Good Soldier Schweyk. Brecht recognised the dangers of accepting the only possible solution, but he also accepted that for him and his situation, it was the only possible solution.

Commitment is frequently criticised because it gives great importance to politics but, to echo Napoleon's comment to Goethe, politics have replaced destiny in modern life. The committed writer can justly say that the political crisis is the most acute expression of our contemporary crisis and that few, if any, aspects of our private lives are not in some way bound up in politics.

Politics should be a major theme, for an individual does not achieve freedom outside or against society and society is a political structure. The most serious charge that can be levelled against political writing is that it is propagandist, but all art, since it is a criticism of life, is in a sense propaganda. The case for being committed rests on two factors. Creative

[9] J. H. Wulbern, *Brecht and Ionesco: Commitment in Context,* p. 27.
[10] Brecht went to neutral countries, *not* Russia.

10

freedom must be inseparable from a sense of social responsibility. Thus a writer is entitled to expect freedom to write but society is entitled to expect social responsibility in what is written. Secondly, commitment is inescapable. According to Sartre to write is to talk and to talk is to reveal an aspect of the world in order to change it. But if Commitment is inescapable why waste time writing about it? Sartre here distinguishes between the lazy writer who is inevitably involved and the committed writer who is not only involved but seeks to write about it *lucidly,* who is involved with awareness. Sartre would not insist that his is the only way of writing, only that it is the *honest* way of writing. His challenge to show him a good novel written against the Jews will probably never be answered. Goodness is, of course, a debateable term. When Sartre argues that art cannot have real value unless it carries good ideas and makes us rethink things, the word 'good' remains (for a philosopher) vague. Sartre gives commitment atheistic content but, as Peguy demonstrates, it can have, though this is rarer, Christian content.

All of this, like Absurdity (and Sartre confusingly figures in both) is very French, very cerebral and seductive. Should we, for example, see Genet as a committed playwright? Probably not since his plays are not intended to improve conditions for maids, blacks or Algerians but to put a halo on the oppressed and so on Genet himself, making his rituals, like his novels, masturbatory. Sartre insists that each writer must discover and work within his own historical situation and in England the historical situation is different. John Mander, in his study *The Writer and Commitment* (1961) points out that the Left in England—Raymond Williams, Richard Hoggart, John Berger, Arnold Wesker, John Osborne and Lindsay Anderson—were more sociological than political in their aims and if we take two heroes who make a plea for caring—Jimmy Porter and Ronnie Kahn—we get some idea of the English quality of commitment. Jimmy, according to his creator, is so vehement as to be almost non-committal and the play itself does not add up to a clear statement of commitment. There are

11

no alternatives to Jimmy which makes it difficult to take him seriously and his tirades become monotonous and finally suggest little more than private neurosis. We are left in doubt as to whether his creator recognises that he is a phoney or not. Wesker, on the other hand, with the benefit of Jimmy before him, draws Ronnie more ironically and takes care, in *Roots,* to keep him off-stage all the time. Mander overlooks this strategy. Nor is *Roots* exactly that breakthrough into the working class and the documentary that Mander suggests it is. He sees *Roots* as an allegory: Beatie (Social-ism, *i.e.* Education/Enlightenment) versus Family (Working Class = Inertia). Because Ronnie is kept at a distance and quoted we can recognise him as a phoney and cope with his anger while accepting his image of bridges of communication (which, at the simplest level = love). But in the famous moral fable the bridge becomes a ferry showing us, through Beatie, that communication is more difficult. And at the end, when Beatie recognises that she has no roots, family or community Mander feels that her stamina is sufficient to convert this into socialist action. This can depend on the actress, and in any case is questionable, as is Mander's description of *A Taste of Honey* as a play lacking sentimentality in its treatment of the working-class dilemma. All three plays present, surely, extreme cases of unusual individuals seeking feeling, and even Wesker, the most politically-oriented of British dramatists finds his solution in terms of education: a Burns poem rather than Top of the Pops. That these personal documents are presented through naturalistic techniques that appear to be social comment and invite social criticism should not hide their crucial identity as essays in personal feeling.

The main value of the term 'committed' is that at least we know, roughly, what plays are meant by it: Brecht, Sartre, Osborne, Wesker, Arden, and more recently Peter Weiss and Hochhuth. The alternative would be Absurd dramatists: Beckett, Ionesco, Genet and Pinter. Of course, no playwright actually fits the label. Moreover, to each his own historical situation, for, as Jan Kott reminds us, in his country when they want fantasy they put on Brecht, but when they want realism they perform *Waiting for Godot*!

It was Beckett's *Waiting for Godot* rather than Ionesco (although Ionesco has been the polemicist of Absurdity) which introduced into England what Martin Esslin has called the Theatre of the Absurd. His book, or at least its title, *The Theatre of the Absurd* (1961, England 1962) has been a mixed blessing for its author. Dr. Esslin modified his position in the introduction to *Absurd Drama* (1965) where he suggested that the term was still critically useful, even though there was no school or movement, to describe a number of plays which reflected certain moods, ignored the usual requirements of the theatre and yet managed to be successful. The phrase was to be regarded as intellectual shorthand for 'a complex pattern of similarities in approach, method, and convention, of shared philosophical and artistic premises, whether conscious or subconscious, and of influences from a common store of tradition' which is certainly vague enough to disarm opposition. In *Brief Chronicles* (1970) Dr. Esslin is still defending the label as a working hypothesis and suggesting that the Anti-Theatre of the Absurdists was not a deviation but central to the main tradition of theatre and that it was the brief period of photographic realism that constituted the deviation.

What, then, consciously or not, characterises these dramatists and their plays? They reflect a sense of wonder, incomprehension and despair at the lack of meaning and coherence in the contemporary world and eschew the well-made play because it rests upon assumptions about character, motive and value which are no longer tenable. Dramatists like Sartre and Camus had, in fact, chosen to represent this philosophy in perfectly regular plays but the Absurd dramatist sought a form organic to his themes, questioning the possibility of communication (*i.e.* language) and the idea of plot or character (both of which predicate order and consequence). They are to be seen as part of a long tradition but reflecting disorder rather than translating it into drama. Whereas their immediate predecessors—such as Dada—were 13 deliberately shocking and limited in scope and appeal, contemporary Absurd Drama has received a wide response from a broadly-based public.

Kenneth Tynan, converted to militant theatre, raised obvious objections. He suggested that reading Dr. Esslin's book gave the impression that the whole of dramatic literature had been 'nothing but a prelude to the glorious emergence of Beckett and Ionesco'.[11] There is the further problem of reconciling the view that these plays are a particular response to a peculiar contemporary crisis with the sense that they are part of a long tradition. But Tynan's basic objection was Brechtian:

Brechtian drama puts first things first, and insists that mankind must be raised to the same level of opportunity before one starts worrying about whether equality of opportunity means anything more than an equal chance to be spiritually unhappy. In any society, says the Ionesco supporter, misery is constant. Certain kinds of misery, argues the Brechtian, are curable; as to the rest, let us postpone judgement until we have built a new society.[12]

Thus Tynan pointed approvingly to Adamov who turned from the incurable ( = Death) to the curable ( = social ills). Tynan was also irked by what he called the Absurdists' 'pervasive tone of privileged despair'.[13] The argument came to a head in 1958 when Tynan, who had battled for the recognition of Ionesco in England suddenly had doubts which he expressed in an article called: 'Ionesco: Man of Destiny?'[14] Ionesco replied and it is a great pity that this debate on the two attitudes to theatre is not better than it is. Unfortunately it tells us more about the personalities of the debaters than theatrical practice, resembling a debate in an Osborne play in which each states a case and does not appear to hear the other side.[15] Ionesco has expressed his views at length, making him very

[11] *Tynan on Theatre* (1964), p. 190.
[12] *Ibid.*, p. 189.
[13] *Ibid.*, p. 191.
[14] Published in *The Observer*, 22 June.
[15] See 'The London Controversy', *Notes and Counter Notes*, pp. 90–112.

much the spokesman for Absurd Theatre. Basically he insists that the twentieth century is too various for didacticism, that things are only simple and clear to, as he puts it, Brechtian boy scouts. He suggests that Pirandello, unable to make drama out of a bourgeois society had turned to the dramatisation of the artist's relationship with that society and its theatre. *La Maschera e il Volto,* produced by Luigi Chiarelli in 1914 became the battle cry for a general movement to pull off masks and reveal the reality beneath. This theatre was called Teatro del Grottesco and drew heavily on the techniques of the native tradition of commedia dell'arte. In so doing Pirandello freed the stage simultaneously from the demands of modern realism (a literal copy of scenes *off* stage) and the Wagnerian demand that the theatre should be an artist's obedient instrument of hypnosis. Nowadays Pirandello's theories about personality and the multiformity of truth seem rather simple, and are inadequate. It is necessary to insist even more than Pirandello on the stage as a stage, and, ironically, achieve even more completely the alienation claimed by Brecht:

It was not for me to conceal the devices of theatre, but rather to make them still more evident, deliberately obvious, go all out for caricature and the grotesque, way beyond the pale irony of witty drawing-room comedies. No drawing-room comedies, but farce, the extreme exaggeration of parody. Humour, yes, but using the methods of burlesque. Comic effects that are firm, broad and outrageous. No dramatic comedies either. But back to the unendurable. Everything raised to paroxysm, where the source of tragedy lies. A theatre of violence: violently comic, violently dramatic.[16]

When Ionesco heard an audience laughing at *The Bald Prima-Donna* he was amazed because he thought he had written a tragedy, the tragedy of language. John Styan, in *The Dark Comedy* (revised 1967),[17] has shown that a mixed form is not exactly a twentieth-century phenomenon. There have always been disturbers of the neat critical division between

[16] *Notes and Counter Notes,* pp. 24-5.
[17] See also Marvin T. Herrick, *Tragicomedy* (1955).

comedy and tragedy, including Shakespeare, but what makes the mixture particularly disturbing now is that we lack confidence in conventions. In previous times society understood that there was an order outside the drama on the stage. A glance at the critical studies which purport to tell us what tragedy or comedy is suggests that the division has never been as neat as critics desire, but possibly at no time has an audience been so totally abandoned to individual judgement. Now there is no sense of what a collective judgement would or should be. Ionesco writes farces (but they are farces such as remind us that the genre can be serious) and drawing-room comedies (but the drawing-rooms shrink, and from *Huis Clos* onwards are prisons, dungeons, torture chambers). Even more confusingly illusion which has always been an element of dramatic action has now become the expression not of reality but only of illusion, protesting against those very conditions by which it threatens to become real. Amidst such general doubt the only certainty is death and this, significantly, is usually violent and arbitrary.

Ionesco challenges the theatre of Brecht in a comparison with Beckett. If theatre is old-fashioned (in style, psychology and realism) it is because it is held in the grip of two dangerous forces: the mental sluggishness of the bourgeoisie and the tyranny of political regimes.[18] Ionesco sees the plays of Beckett as *essentially* tragic, posing 'the problem of the ultimate ends of man' and giving a more complex and soundly-based picture of the human condition than Brecht since, for Brecht, there is only one social problem, the struggle of the classes which Ionesco suggests is a limited and prejudiced view of the world. Ionesco's own play *Rhinoceros,* for example, is an anti-Nazi play but it is also, and primarily, an attack on collective hysteria and epidemics that lurk beneath a superficial reasonableness, against, in short, the serious collective diseases which masquerade as ideologies.[19]

Absurdist themes occur first in novels and in novels written

[18] *Notes and Counter Notes,* p. 84.
[19] *Notes and Counter Notes,* p. 206.

by writers like Malraux and Sartre who have decided political commitments. But the novel form permits a leisurely description of those everyday acts by which man is distinguished, and the sum of which makes up his character until the moment of death. Even in novels it was, however, death and the violent act which most crucially defined a character, and in the economy of a play the dramatist is obliged to choose the particularly intense or momentous act since the more horrible the action the more a spectator is compelled to question. Both Sartre and Camus, as committed writers, brought the central issues of Malraux's novels into the theatre: war, oppression and revolution. They did not follow Giraudoux and Cocteau in using ancient myths. Sartre uses myth in only one play (and that was probably a reply to Giraudoux's *Electra*) and Camus only comes near myth by using a historical character, Caligula. Subsequently Ionesco, Adamov and Beckett move deliberately away from culture and if they use myths at all they are drawn from the modern mythology—such as Charlie Chaplin or the Marx Brothers.

Sartre saw man as an eternal play-actor who is free because he has no character. Although he exists in a certain situation man is nothing in the way a stone is hard or soft or black or white. Man is simply the sum of his acts which, despite morality, conventions or other protective rationalisations, are invented freely as he goes through life according to the view of himself which he wishes to project to others. Since others are doing the same thing we can understand the basic situation of Hell in *Huis Clos*. Because they are dead the characters are final (they have no more choices available) and because there are three characters no agreement on that finality is ever possible. This new intensity, however, was achieved by strictly classical means: three characters in a single action in a single place lasting for one and a half hours.[20]

Ionesco and his contemporaries sought, apparently, a more appropriate form. In rejecting the validity of language,

[20] For a fuller treatment see R. F. Jackson, 'Sartre's Theatre and the Morality of Being', *Aspects of Drama and the Theatre* (1965), pp. 35 ff.

character, plot and even meaningfulness we are surprised to find that they write plays at all. But if Ionesco implies that Absurd and Meaningful are opposites and irreconcilable he misleads. The plays depend on the destruction or questioning of all that we take for granted as meaningful, necessary or normal. They suggest matters which cannot be described by words or gestures: Nirvana, which is to be defined in terms of what is not.[21] There is the difficulty, however, that such definitions ultimately work in terms of what is. This, however, is the philosophy of the Absurd, not the plays. When a play repudiates the absurd and becomes reasonable it repudiates drama. There is, after all, little point in writing a play about a crisis in life which can be resolved by two or three pages of reasonable argument.

Absurd Drama is open to two objections, both closely linked. *Waiting for Godot* clearly presents the image of a meaningful world in a compelling way and more so than a play by Sartre or Camus. But if choice is arbitrary, choices must be made, and therefore Sartre and Camus move on to political or moral drama whereas Beckett and Ionesco remain with choices that are both arbitrary *and* pointless. Thus their plays raise the question whether or not the essential nature of man can be explored in solitude rather than through his relationships in the physical world. Moreover, such plays are self-limiting and shrink into silence. The absence of character means no development. The absence of plot leaves the dramatist with only situation which, if the basis of drama, accounts for the fact that most Absurd Drama is restricted to one act. The rejection of language, or at least an insistence on its unreliable and arbitrary nature, throws out a main tool of drama: words. Having admitted this it must also be said that these plays are, at their best, blatantly theatrical. They can be great entertainment and take in social comment on the way. But they operate mainly behind the proscenium arch, and their explicit stage instructions and effects leave little scope for

[21] For a fuller treatment see R. N. Coe, 'Eugène Ionesco: The Meaning of Un-Meaning', *ibid., pp. 3 ff.*

a producer. It is, therefore, the theatre of Brecht which has been more influential, since it offers great scope to a producer. For over the last twenty years it is the producer who has emerged as the major rôle in that polygon of forces we call the theatre.

# CHAPTER TWO

# 1950–1956

In 1950, Kenneth Tynan published a book on the theatre with the revealing title: *He that Plays the King*. Tynan is now noted for his association with militant theatre in *Curtains* (1961) and productions of the controversial *Soldiers* and *Oh! Calcutta!* but this volume is frankly introduced as a book of enthusiasms for the heroic theatre written at a time when Tynan thought criticism had forgotten about excitement and taken a wrong turning into imperturbability and casualness. He records the big, unique occasions in the theatre of 1944–8, performances by Olivier, Richardson, Gielgud, Wolfit, Vivien Leigh, Alec Clunes, Redgrave, Alec Guinness and Paul Scofield, productions like Peter Brook's *Loves Labours Lost, The Brothers Karamazov* and *Huis Clos* in 1946 and *Romeo and Juliet* in 1947, and the memorable appearance of Jean-Louis Barrault at the Edinburgh Festival of 1948.

This was a period of great acting when stars like Olivier, Thorndike, Richardson, Gielgud, Ashcroft, Redgrave and Edith Evans chose the right part, played heroic rôles and created memorable if ephemeral occasions. It was a period when the speaking of the words was at least as important as the sense and when actors had entered an institution that was not merely the most powerful form of entertainment but, as far as they could see, offered them a lifetime of playing before live audiences. Such actors replaced a generation probably best represented by Gerald du Maurier, a generation noted for its sophisticated acting in comedies largely without serious intellectual content. It is ironic that these actors are now regarded, by post-1956 standards, as mere purveyors of elegant escapism, since they were responsible to a large extent for bringing back some intellectual rigour into the theatre. It was Gielgud with his *Hamlet* (1930) and *Romeo and Juliet* (1935) who brought Shakespeare back to the West End. And, offering a different kind of challenge to an actor, Chekhov, too, was restored so that Olivier's *Uncle Vanya* (1964) was in direct line from Komisarjevsky's *The Seagull* (1936) and Michel Saint-Denis's *Three Sisters* (1938).

A theatre-goer in 1950 could see Edith Evans in *Daphne Laureola;* Gielgud at Stratford in *Measure for Measure, Much Ado, Julius Caesar* and *King Lear,* and elsewhere as Thomas Mendip in *The Lady's Not For Burning;* Olivier as director and Duke in *Venus Observed;* Ashcroft in *Much Ado* and *King Lear* at Stratford and playing Viola in *Twelfth Night* at the Old Vic while Redgrave was Hamlet at Elsinore and the Old Vic. In 1951 the cast of *The Waters of the Moon* included both Edith Evans and Sybil Thorndike while Gielgud could be seen as Leontes, Richardson as Vershinin, Olivier as Caesar and Antony, Ashcroft as Electra and Mistress Page and Redgrave as Richard II, Hotspur, Prospero and the Chorus in *Henry V.*

So, if looking back to 1950 is to enter a world innocent of either Beckett or Brecht, it is by no means an empty world. The regular patron of the St. James's Theatre in 1950 would have seen Olivier in Fry's *Venus Observed,* Dennis Cannan's *Captain Carvallo* and in subsequent years Giraudoux's *The Mad Woman of Chaillot* (with Martita Hunt), the Oliviers in both *Caesar and Cleopatra* and *Antony and Cleopatra* (when, with the backing of the Arts Council money was spent as if Irving himself had returned),[1] Jean-Louis Barrault, Orson Welles in *Othello* (an early example of treating the text as a starting-point rather than the final thing), Clifford Odets's

---

[1] Barry Duncan, *The St. James's Theatre* (1964), p. 339

*Winter Journey*, Pirandello's *Enrico IV* and *Tutto Per Bene*, the Comédie Française, *Pygmalion* (with John Clements and Kay Hammond), *Six Characters in Search of an Author*, Terence Rattigan's *Separate Tables* and Ruth Draper. That same patron would also have noted that in 1954 a speculator had obtained official permission to build an office block on the site. In spite of public protest, parliamentary questions, an offer from Winston Churchill to start a fund to save the theatre and a demonstration by Vivien Leigh in the House of Lords the theatre closed in 1957, the year after *Look Back in Anger* heralded the renaissance in English theatre.

There would be no regret at the Royal Court or out at Stratford East, for faded elegance has no place in the living theatre. The decorum established by Sir George Alexander (with carpets back-stage and stage-hands in white overalls and cotton gloves) belongs to what was increasingly seen as the deadly theatre, the museum. European influences were, by 1957, working to transform enchantment into democratic intimacies: the new slogans were 'relevance' and 'participation'. Seen in perspective the theatre of the 1940s and 1950s required little participation and was not stridently relevant. It was still very much the theatre described by R. C. Sherriff in his autobiography, *No Leading Lady*: People went to the theatre for clever acting, an intriguing variety of scenes, fascinating actresses in eye-catching clothes; they expected fine speeches, witty dialogue, a story to excite them with unexpected twists and turns.[2]

It was, undeniably, conservative, which is hardly surprising since it followed a long period of dramatic experimentation and coincided with the austerities and exhaustion of World War II. The period 1880–1930 had been an exciting period as can be detected from the large number of 'isms' and the extensive use of technical devices which have since been 'discovered' by young producers.

When war was declared in 1939 the Government closed every theatre in the country and with large cities threatened by

[2] *No Leading Lady* (1968), p. 57.

bombing there could be no question, except at *The Windmill,* of business as usual. In fact a large amount of acting was done up and down the country with London as a touring date until May 1941 when she once more became the home of the long run. Writing after this period, W. A. Darlington, in *The Actor and His Audience* (1949), describes the theatre as going through a period of happy post-war convalescence after a long and serious illness. There were actors, audiences and enough old plays on the shelves to tide the theatre over until new writers should appear. Even in 1949, however, Darlington noted that rising costs were making managers reluctant to risk failure with an untried author. Nevertheless he saw a chance of moving into a great theatrical period. Short, in *Introducing Theatre,* also published in 1949, was equally optimistic, listing the number of theatres alive and well in London and the suburbs with provincial and civic repertory theatres at Birmingham, Stratford, Manchester, Bristol, Leeds, Glasgow, Farnham and Norwich. This theatre had its own kind of glory. As Peter Brook reminds us in *the empty space* (1968) it was the theatre of Jouvet, Bérard, Jean-Louis Barrault, *Don Juan, Amphitryon,* Gielgud's revival of *The Importance of Being Earnest, Peer Gynt* at the Old Vic, Olivier's Oedipus and Richard III, *The Lady's Not For Burning, Venus Observed* and Massine at Covent Garden: a theatre of:

colour and movement, of fine fabrics, of shadows, of eccentric, cascading words, of leaps of thought and of cunning machines, of lightness and of all forms of mystery and surprise—it was the theatre of a battered Europe that seemed to share one aim—a reaching back towards a memory of lost grace.[3]

A theatre of escape and nostalgia but also, as a glance at the reviews of, for example, T. C. Worsley shows, a lively theatre. We must avoid thinking that literacy in characters debars them from membership of the human race. During 1950–1 Worsley writes about *Venus Observed, Ring Round the Moon* and *John Gabriel Borkman* at the Arts, new plays by Bridie and R. C. Sherriff, a second production of *The Cocktail Party* at the New Theatre, *The Little Hut, The Second Mrs.*

[3] *the empty space,* p. 43.

*Tanqueray*, Hugh Hunt's *Twelfth Night* at the Old Vic, George Devine's *Bartholomew Fair*, Pirandello's *Six Characters in Search of an Author*. He also records the death of George Bernard Shaw.[4] In 1951 Worsley mentions *The Merchant of Venice* at the Old Vic, *Hedda Gabler* at the Arts, *A Penny for a Song*, the Oliviers at the St. James's Theatre, Wolfit's *Tamburlaine, Saint's Day, A Sleep of Prisoners*, more Anouilh (who was very much *the* popular dramatist of the early fifties), the Renaud-Barrault Company, Orson Welles and the death of James Bridie. 1951 was, of course, a holiday for a nation weary of austerity, war and the disillusionments of peace. It was Festival of Britain Year and between May and September three theatres were constructed in the Festival Pleasure Gardens. Individual managements arranged their own contributions to the Festival and there were no less than five Hamlets including the notorious flop of Alec Guinness. Tynan did a short season of Grand Guignol at the Embassy, Swiss Cottage and anticipated the later Theatre of Cruelty. The deaths of Bridie and Shaw were balanced by the arrival of a new dramatist with a play called *Saint's Day* but audiences were happier with N. C. Hunter's *The Waters of the Moon* or, if they must have social comment, with plays like *Cosh Boy, Women of Twilight* or *Iron Curtain* which made that comment entertainingly. Noel Coward's play *Relative Values* is typical of the kind of play that could still be produced. It deals with what happens in a stately home when the son decides to marry a common film star who turns out to be the disreputable sister of his mother's personal maid! There was also religious drama in theatres, churches and cathedrals including the York Mystery Plays and works by Fry, Charles Williams, Eliot and Ronald Duncan. Foreign theatre was mainly French, and mostly Anouilh, or American musicals, as *Kiss Me Kate* and *South Pacific* took over from *Carousel*. On 13 July the Queen Mother laid the foundation stone for a National Theatre (in the wrong place as it turned out) while Sybil Thorndike recited an

[4] After an absence of ten years Shaw returned to the theatre with *Bouyant Billions* (1948) and *Far-Fetched Fables* (1950).

ode by the Poet Laureate, John Masefield. The age of innocence was ending, although 1952 saw the first performance of a new play called *The Mousetrap*.

But what is suggested by such lists? We can see that there were actors, producers and audiences and sufficient plays, but relatively little new drama. J. C. Trewin in *Dramatists of Today*, published in 1953, listed James Bridie, T. S. Eliot, Fry and the professional writers for the West End stage: J. B. Priestley, R. C. Sherriff, Noel Coward, Emlyn Williams, Clemence Dane, and Terence Rattigan, while under the heading of future hopefuls he included Peter Ustinov, Wyngarde Browne, Roger MacDougall, N. C. Hunter, John Whiting and William Douglas Home. Ten years later his list, admittedly in an essay for a volume called *Experimental Drama*, contains only three of these names, suggesting that something has happened between 1953 and 1963.

John Russell Taylor, in *Anger and After* (1962), was clearly interested in beginning at 1956 but writes, in a preliminary chapter, on Coward, Priestley and Dennis Cannan who is remembered now for his vaguely defined role in writing for the Vietnam show *US* (1966) rather than for *Captain Carvallo* (1950).[5] The theatre-goer, then, could see Priestley off-form, Coward saying nothing in his usual brilliant manner: or Terence Rattigan's *The Deep Blue Sea* (1952) with Peggy Ashcroft and Kenneth More, described by Tynan as 'the most absorbing new English play for many seasons'; or Graham Greene's *The Living Room* (1953) which launched Dorothy Tutin, and was described by Tynan as the work of a 'potentially great dramatist'. In 1954 Rattigan produced *Separate Tables* and Aunt Edna, that universal middle-class playgoer whose tolerance of sexual abnormality and such matters had to be kept in mind by any would-be successful dramatist. The major theatrical dispute was over the relative merits of two verse dramatists although T. S. Eliot's *The Confidential Clerk* (1953) and Fry's *The Dark Is Light Enough* (1954) (with Edith Evans as the Countess) suggested that verse

[5] Cannan reappeared at the Royal Court in 1971 with *One at Night*.

drama had spent itself. Reading through Tynan's judgements on the period they now sound very charitable but already, by 1954, he is beginning to sound the alarm and in 1955, in 'Notes on a Dead Language', he pointed out that no play had been written by an Englishman since the third decade of the seventeenth century and that the legend of English drama springs from Shakespeare, our luminous accident, and an Irish conspiracy to make us ashamed of our weakness. The leading dramatists of this period, like Priestley, Rattigan, Coward, Greene, Hunter, and Ustinov were writing well-constructed plays on familiar themes whose main fault, but it was a serious one, was that those themes did not correspond with the mood of frustration prevalent in the 1950s. Individuals sensed that they were caught up in some action where the causes were too large or remote to be useful either in life or the theatre. And yet there was a strong need for involvement summed up by Arthur Miller in *Death of a Salesman* (1949) where the audience was asked to pay attention and also shown a new kind of set—a whole house with non-existent walls and acting areas that were lit only when needed. In some ways this production was quite prophetic. T. C. Worsley noted that the production—lighting, grouping, stylised action, timing and set—all aimed at achieving a poetic approach to everyday life without using either poetry or heightened language. He concluded, however, that none of them was an adequate substitute for the words which just were not there.[6]

The well-constructed play was usually innocuous in form and content, requiring conventional staging and providing suitable rôles for the actors. If serious topics were to be discussed audiences preferred them gift-wrapped, as, for example, by Graham Greene who stuck closely to the rules of West End Naturalism. Since Greene combined a traditional play, eminent author and uplifting theme he was even more welcome to theatre managers than T. S. Eliot. Coward and Rattigan continued to write, adjusting to the times in subject matter but changing the manner of their plays very little.

[6] 'Poetry Without Words', *The Fugitive Art* (1952), p. 93.

Coward in 1924 was a young revolutionary who threw out everything Pinero would have thought necessary. *The Vortex* now looks very dated but it was a shocking play, and Pinter, Livings and Jellicoe have all acknowledged his importance in the history of the drama of the unspoken. But if Coward and Rattigan can now introduce such themes as homosexuality openly into their plays the plays remain well written, well made and untouched by what has happened in the theatre recently.

In Trewin's list of 1963 three dramatists were already on his list for 1953: the two verse dramatists, Eliot and Fry, who are a special case, and John Whiting. John Whiting (1915–63) is a lonely figure and his place here demonstrates this. He was most unfortunate in his relationship with the theatre. *A Penny For A Song* (1951) produced by Peter Brook soon died at the Haymarket and the revised version at the Aldwych in 1962 fared little better.[7] *Saint's Day,* it is true, won the Arts Theatre Club Prize in the competition run to celebrate the Festival of Britain but it was hardly the play to match the spirit of the South Bank and Battersea Pleasure Gardens. The judges (Alec Clunes, Christopher Fry and Peter Ustinov) chose three plays out of a thousand entries and pronounced this the winner. It was puzzling to both audiences and critics, defended in *The Times* by Tyrone Guthrie, Peter Brook, Peggy Ashcroft and John Gielgud, and not revived until 1965. *Marching Song* (1964) ran for about three weeks and still awaits revival as does *The Gates of Summer* (1965) directed by Peter Hall at Oxford which did not even survive its pre-London tour. It was only in 1961 that Hall tempted Whiting out of retirement to write *The Devils* which had some success with the Royal Shakespeare Company at the Aldwych.

*Saint's Day* was written in 1947 when audiences were flocking to *Oklahoma* and *Annie Get Your Gun*. The play concerns the birthday of a great rebel writer Paul Southman who lives, with his daughter Stella, her husband, Charles (a painter) and an enigmatic servant called John Winter, in exile

[7] It was turned into an opera by Richard Rodney Bennett in 1966.

from society and at odds with the near-by village. They are waiting for the arrival of Robert Procathren, a young poet and critic, who is to drive Southman to London for a dinner held in his honour. The first act ends with the sound of a distant trumpet but no Robert. This trumpet and the death of a dog prepare us for the rapid violence that follows Robert's arrival in Act 2. The local parson, Aldus, comes to ask Southman's help against four soldiers who have escaped from prison and taken over the village but Southman refuses to help, saying that he is on the side of the attackers rather than the defenders. Stella is accidentally shot by Robert, the village set on fire (so that the women and children have to take refuge with Southman), Aldus loses his library, his church and his faith while Robert, converted by the accidental killing of Stella, takes command of the soldiers and revenge on society by ordering the deaths of Southman and Charles. As Robert says in the speech which is the climax of the play:

I thought the power invested was for good. I believed we were here to do well by each other. It isn't so. We are here—all of us—to die. Nothing more than that. We live for that alone. You've known that all along, haven't you? Why didn't you tell me—why did you have to teach me in such a dreadful way. . . .[8]

Unfortunately this speech, like much of the play, is confused. The title obviously refers to Southman (a saint's day is his death day) but the conversion takes place for Robert[9] and is certainly ironic. But the play was Whiting's first full look at the problem of violence, war and suffering, raising questions but offering no solutions. Written a few years after Hiroshima (1945) it discusses the responsibility for violence through three examples: fooling that accidentally ends in disaster (the shooting of Stella), the intentional action (the breaking of Aldus) and the soldiers who stand ready to do whatever someone orders them to do. The disaster that comes

[8] *Saint's Day, The Collected Plays of John Whiting*, ed. R. Hayman (1969), vol. 1, p. 164.
[9] Southman's birthday, 25 January, is the Feast of the Conversion of St. Paul.

to this small group of characters reflects what might happen to the world. Whiting asks what are the sources of destruction, and self-destruction and what are the uses of compassion and the wisdom that comes too late. He also looks at the position of the artist in this society. Clearly *Saint's Day* is a play of ideas but it started in Whiting's mind from an image—a mural seen in a derelict house—and it is this image, aided by symbolic objects and apparently allegorical names which is the strongest impression of the play. Whiting calls his use of symbols and images resonances to produce a 'density of texture' and this density avoids being mechanical because his characters are neither stock nor allegorical but portrayals that invite both sympathy and distaste.[10]

Tom Milne, reviewing *Saint's Day* in *Encore* compared it to Pinter's *The Birthday Party* (1958) and Arden's *Sjt. Musgrave's Dance* (1959).[11] All three examine the nature of violence and all three were damned on their first production. But the failure to recognise Whiting was more understandable in 1951 when seriousness in the theatre was measured in terms of Eliot and Fry. The theme of violence was new and difficult if remarkably topical. All three plays have a particular quality: they create the image of a disintegrating society which you must accept on its own terms or not at all. Plays by Osborne and Wesker offer an essentially familiar world from which the mind can take easier matters than the main theme; but these three plays will not permit such sidetracking and the price of their relentlessness would seem to be commercial failure. Significantly Whiting admired both Pinter and Arden because they refuse to provide answers or believe in ideas; Wesker he described as a child carrying a bomb. The morality which Whiting feared was not that of the middle classes but 'that immense new morality which has emanated from the Royal Court'. He did not crusade for the working classes or against the Bomb. He remained obstinately old fashioned, in a

[10] For a fuller treatment see E. R. Wood, introduction to *Saint's Day* (1963).
[11] *The Encore Reader* (1965), p. 115.

tradition of writing for an intellectual élite; difficult plays for discriminating audiences.

They were not to be found. Even his comedy *A Penny For A Song* written in 1949 and based on Carola Oman's *Britain Against Napoleon* had little success. Yet it is a happy play, full of charm, wit, incident and thought—celebrating life in an English summer. Whiting himself disliked his next play *Marching Song* describing it as a play without private parts. He is probably recognising that the extreme concentration—as if rhetoric would loose too much feeling—has eliminated feeling too completely. It takes up once more the theme of self-destruction and borrows the form adapted by Shaw from Chekhov in *Heartbreak House,* and, to a lesser extent, used by Fry in *The Dark is Light Enough.* Through a house party of representative characters society can be examined and a crisis of conscience explored. The action and the marching song are clearly contemporary but Whiting once more includes images and names (like Cadmus, de Troyes and Dido) which suggest historical overtones. The action shows that what a man does makes him what he is so that this is one of the best examples of existential drama in English. Whiting, of course, does not give his characters the particular political beliefs that would have *been Sartre's method and intention.*

*The Gates of Summer* (1953) first performed in 1956 is Whiting's most bitter play, again about a house party set above a capital city. After the failure of this play Whiting turned away from the theatre to writing film scripts including revisions for *Cleopatra* and work with Fry on *The Bible.* Peter Hall who admired Whiting and had produced him got him to write a sketch *No Why* for the Arts Theatre and later, in 1960, as director of the Royal Shakespeare Company, asked him to write a full-length costume drama for the first Aldwych season suggesting an adaptation of either Huxley's *The Devils of Loudun* or Rolfe's *Hadrian VII.*[12] Although *The Devils* was more successful than any previous Whiting play even this production was dogged by ill luck, and the play itself is not

[12] Later dramatised most successfully by Peter Luke.

entirely successful. It shows Whiting's usual capacity for eloquent dialogue and intelligence but his choice of Grandier as central character, although continuing the theme of self-destruction, was not entirely successful. There is a considerable amount of material that looks as if it is there to distract from the emptiness of the central action.

In *Saint's Day* and *Marching Song,* as in Miller's *Death of a Salesman,* we can see the plays of a private man calling attention to the suffering of private men. The new dramatists would soon be writing similar, highly subjective plays about despair, doubt and failure, about individuals for whom personal relationships would be the only value left and a refuge from that despair and futility. Jimmy Porter judges people by how they *feel.* Yet critics writing about Whiting and his plays frequently use words such as 'cold' and 'remote'. He makes enormous demands on an audience and really needed audiences trained on Beckett and Pinter. The central figure of his tragedies is always a man who cannot or will not respond to social or emotional commitment. Such a man, by his isolation, gains in honesty and can see the self-deceptions practised around him but he is also like Meursault in Camus's novel *L'Etranger*—he is remote from us. Perhaps he embodies Whiting's own predicament. To write before your time and then die just when the times seem to be catching up is a sad thing. Whiting anticipated the New Wave without living long enough to benefit from it. And the New Wave would not have recognised him. As Ronald Hayman says, we can use the word 'tragedy' of his plays. In a time of relative values he insisted on absolutes, believing that life is lived always on a tragic level: the Gods are there and they do not have to be just.[13] Although not indifferent to social and economic pressures he could not accept the view that man can alter his destiny. He made his own saints rather than borrowing a historical figure, and required these characters to cope with elaborate language and imagery. We have become accustomed, particularly through the plays of Osborne, to long speeches and find Whiting's

[13] See Ronald Hayman, *John Whiting* (1969), pp. 95-8.

31

language less difficult now. But Whiting did for prose what Eliot and Fry, whom he admired, failed to do for verse. His career, therefore, is significant in more ways than one. It points to a drama of intensity in prose rather than verse, and illustrates the need for a theatre that could take risks and train audiences. His isolation reminds us how little the theatre of the late forties and early fifties was a writer's theatre. For Aristotle the actor was more important than the poet, and he would have felt at home in the theatre of 1950–6. What we remember of those years is not the names of dramatists so much as the roll-call of performers: Olivier, Gielgud, Wolfit, Edith Evans, Peggy Ashcroft and, occasionally, producers like Peter Brook and Peter Hall.

# CHAPTER THREE

# Verse Drama

In 1901 Sir Walter Raleigh wrote that poetic drama had died in England with the disappearance of the boy players and had enjoyed no second life. Yet around 1950 verse drama looked like the only lively thing in the British theatre. It was, of course, entirely suited to that theatre. It was produced by men like Peter Brook, Olivier, Gielgud and Jack Hawkins. It was spoken by such great performers as Olivier, Gielgud, Alec Guinness, Rex Harrison, Richard Burton, Paul Scofield, Michael Redgrave, Margaret Leighton, Sybil Thorndike, Claire Bloom, Edith Evans and Pamela Browne in beautiful sets by designers like Oliver Messel. It met the post-war desire for colour, fancy and escape. But looking back it is difficult to understand how verse drama, as opposed to poetry of the theatre, could have cast such a spell. Nowadays it is a matter of either defending it or, as John Russell Taylor does, dismissing it as modish and parochial.[1] The term 'verse drama' rather than 'poetic drama' is used because Denis Donoghue, in his study *The Third Voice,* assures us that it is entirely neutral, a technical description with no implications as to quality. In literature poetry precedes prose and the idea of a prose tragedy is very modern. Not all situations are suitable for poetry and modern life seems curiously prosaic, or at least not consonant with blank verse. Ibsen thought that verse had been most

[1] *Anger and After* (1962/69), p. 20.

injurious to the dramatic art and considered that it was highly improbable that it would ever be used to any great extent in the future. It should be remembered that this decision was clear and deliberate and entailed laying aside a considerable reputation for verse drama when, in his fiftieth year, he took up prose. It was a decision which pleased his English apologist William Archer who suggested that drama written in verse, even by Shakespeare, only encouraged the dramatist to substitute rhetoric for human speech. This argument on the difficulties of representing human speech in verse is neither new nor recent. But if we are to estimate the success of Eliot and Fry we should do so in the light of their predecessors. A glance at Wordsworth's *The Borderers* (1795–6). Tennyson's *Queen Mary* (1875) and Masefield's *The Tragedy of Nan* (1908) should qualify our judgement on their failure.

Donoghue, writing what was in effect a post-mortem account of verse drama significantly defines the poetry of verse drama, in 1959, as 'not necessarily or solely a verbal construct; it inheres in the structure of the play as a whole'.[2] Cocteau had made some such definition in his preface to *Les Mariés de la Tour Eiffel* in 1921:

The action of the play is in images while the text is not: I attempt to substitute a 'poetry of the theatre' for 'poetry in the theatre'. Poetry in the theatre is a piece of lace which it is impossible to see at a distance. Poetry of the theatre would be coarse lace; a lace of ropes, a ship at sea. *Les Mariés* should have the frightening look of a drop of poetry under the microscope. The *scenes* are integrated like the *words* of a poem.[3]

Behind this replacement of words with scenes is the real battle, the battle between writer and the theatre. Arthur Symons's statement that the probable words of prose talk can only render part of what goes on in the obscure imageries of life is persuasive but it can be countered with Gordon Craig's statement that the poet has no place in the theatre, that even the dramatist has only a slight birth-claim to the theatre. This

[2] *The Third Voice* (1959), p. 6.
[3] Jean Cocteau, *Théâtre* I, Paris, Gallimard, 15th edition, p. 45.

is the old argument between Ben Jonson and Inigo Jones, between writer and producer, and it is not confined to verse, although verse intensifies the conflict. Henry James complained that writing for the theatre meant having to do everything 'between dinner and the suburban trains'.

The Irish and English poets in the theatre were unquestionably poets first and dramatists later, using the stage for their own ends. W. B. Yeats was fortunate in having a stage for his plays and yet his most important work occurs when he had turned over the management of the Abbey to Lennox Robinson and begun, around 1915, to work with Pound on the Fenellosa papers. Yeats claimed to have invented a form of drama 'distinguished, indirect, and symbolic, and having no need of mob or press to pay its way'. Such plays were, however, to require the specialist services of musicians, mask-designers and Dame Ninette de Valois but it is possible to see in some of them—for example *Purgatory* (1938)—the tradi-tion which fostered *Waiting for Godot* and *Fin de Partie*. Yeats was creating drama for 'a few people who love symbol, a play that will be more ritual than play, and leave upon the mind an impression like that of tapestry where the forms only half-reveal themselves amid the shadowy folds'.[4] This may be a long way from Cocteau's coarse lace but it does insist upon the spectacle element as much as the words. For the Nō plays provided Yeats with three things: a theatre form of proven worth (and as exotic as Artaud's Balinese Theatre), a theatre which presented more than the surface of life, and which gave him an elaborate store of non-verbal expression. But it was very much drawing-room theatre.

The English verse dramatists sought to restore verse plays to their central place in the English theatre. T. S. Eliot began with certain advantages over poets like Claudel and Yeats because he had already brought back ordinary words and situations into poetry. Even so he experienced the inevitable difficulties of getting modern characters to speak verse

[4] Programme note on the play *The Shadowy Waters,* quoted Donoghue, pp. 33–4.

convincingly. In drama there is a tacit agreement that characters can speak in a way which is not a faithful mirror of life but which allows the scope of drama to be enlarged. Naturalistic drama cannot allow this convention to include verse because the obvious organization of verse distorts the reflection of life's surfaces and though most, if not all, great dramatists have evaded the exact limitations of naturalism they have done so without using verse. Eliot saw immediately that verse should not be merely decorative; it was, he wrote to Pound, a medium to look through not at. What was to distinguish verse drama from prose was a kind of 'doubleness of action'. By this he explicitly did not mean either allegory or symbolism but a kind of under-pattern, possibly related to the imagery or at the deeper level of myth[5] which is the basic unity of the play and to which all parts must be subordinated. This leads to certain losses, particularly in characterisation, since although the character is an individual he is primarily typical of some aspect of mankind and his stage presence is drawn only with reference to that typical aspect. On the other hand Eliot believed that the play would gain richness because it operated on more than one plane. Eliot saw his task as twofold: to overcome the prejudice against verse in the theatre and to prevent the enjoyment of verse for itself. Such enjoyment would distract the audience from the serious purpose of the plays, for Eliot had turned to the theatre to gain a wider audience for the ideas in his poetry.

Because of his great authority as poet and critic, Eliot strengthened the impression that the problem of verse drama was, simply, to find a type of verse that would work on the stage. It has always been a convention of verse drama that there was an agreed type of verse, as the Elizabethans used blank verse or French classicism the alexandrine. Given this basic premise and the dramatic quality of his poetry, Eliot's move into the theatre is extremely logical. *Murder in the Cathedral* (1935) was, in context, very successful but the context

[5] Eliot's use of myth has been seriously, and persuasively, questioned in Hugh Dickinson, *Myth on the Modern Stage* (1969).

was not the world in which his audience lived and to which they returned at the end of the play. And Canterbury Cathedral was not the commercial theatre; it had a congregation rather than an audience. Eliot passionately wished to avoid the côterie drama of Abercrombie, Drinkwater, Flecker and Masefield. Looking at the many parts of Shakespeare's audience he envisaged a drama which would have something for everyone and not merely serve the minority who enjoyed verse and who would anyway read his poetry. Because he suspected that this wider audience would have a largely unthinking familiarity with theological matters he decided that such matters, which were the substance of his plays, would have to be presented in secular terms. He therefore modelled his plays on Greek myths which had provided the form for *Murder in the Cathedral* and now provided matter. He may have been influenced in this by the French dramatists although he works in a different way to them. Rather than rewriting the myth with modern characters he starts with modern characters and filters the myth through them and their actions. *The Family Reunion* (1939), as Eliot himself recognised, was not successful in adjusting Greek myth to a modern situation and ten years later he corrected this mistake in *The Cocktail Party* (1949). If the opening of the play reminds us of Noel Coward the basis of the play is the *Alcestis* of Euripides. Eliot has also removed the exceptional person from the centre of the play, although she still makes her choice and accepts the consequences in a way that suggests existential drama. The verse is largely the poetry of statement and critics have already begun to object that the verse is very nearly prose. Eliot, writing on the poetry of Dr. Johnson, had suggested that the minimum requirement of good poetry is that it has the virtues of good prose. But it is not easy to create a verse which is flexible enough to cover making a telephone call and the crucifixion of Celia. At high moments the verse works:

When I first met Miss Coplestone, in this room,
I saw the image, standing behind her chair,

37

Of a Celia Coplestone whose face showed the astonishment
Of the first five minutes after a violent death.
If this strains your credulity, Mrs. Chamberlayne,
I ask you only to entertain the suggestion
That a sudden intuition, in certain minds,
May tend to express itself at once in a picture.
That happens to me, sometimes. So it was obvious
That here was a woman under sentence of death.
That was her destiny. The only question
Then was, what sort of death? *I* could not know;
Because it was for her to choose the way of life
To lead to death, and, without knowing the end
Yet choose the form of death. We know the death she chose.
I did not know that she would die in this way;
*She* did not know. So all that I could do
Was to direct her in the way of preparation.
That way, which she accepted, led to this death.
And if that is not a happy death, what death is happy?

But the verse is also required for domestic chatter:

I flew over from New York last night—
I left Los Angeles three days ago.
I saw Sheila Paisley at lunch today
And she told me you were giving a party—
She's coming on later, after the Gunnings—
So I said, I really must crash in:
It's my only chance to see Edward and Lavinia.
I'm only over for a week, you see,
And I'm driving down to the country this evening,
So I knew you wouldn't mind my looking in so early.
It does seem ages since I last saw any of you![6]

Moreover, Celia's death seems more appropriate to verse than does the equally important relationship between husband and wife, so that the play is split between the terrifying journey of the exceptional person, Celia, and the common routine. Nor is it entirely a happy thought that the building up of Christian society rests on what Arrowsmith has justly called a Christian conspiracy!

Many critics feel that after *The Cocktail Party* there is a

[6] *The Cocktail Party* (1948), p. 179 and p. 164.

general loss in matter and verse. *The Confidential Clerk* (1953) showed Eliot moving towards comedy as a means of examining the choice between the ordinary routine and the dedicated life that leads to beatitude. Donoghue loyally suggests that what Eliot has achieved here is not anaemia but *sostenuto* and by shifting the division between spiritual and secular to one between commerce and art Eliot has solved the division that threatens the unity of *The Cocktail Party*. But even his sympathetic critic D. E. Jones places this play 'just across the border from prose'.[7] Eliot's last play *The Elder Statesman* (1958) shows a return to tragedy and a new version of *The Family Reunion*. The issues of guilt are reconsidered but contrition seems very easy and the pain is spoken about rather than made felt, while the verse is scarcely recognisable as verse.

Nevertheless T. S. Eliot made verse in the theatre a commercial proposition. He believed that 'the craving for poetic drama is permanent in human nature' but, as a poet, did not foresee that such drama might not have to be in verse. However secular his plays contrive to appear that all fulfil his maxim of religious usefulness. His plays were supposed to surprise people into the meanings and implications of Christianity but audiences could feel that they had not been to the theatre so much as tricked into attending church.[8] Salvation presents the dramatist with difficulties as a theme since it is far less dramatic than damnation and does not lend itself to action, which, after all, is the mainspring of drama. Tynan was probably accurate when he pointed out that Eliot could lower the temperature but never raise it. The theatre loves strong emotions and will ultimately reject him however noble his attempts to be serious, in verse, in a play.

The difficulty with Christopher Fry (b. 1907) is that he exists in any discussion as a rival of T. S. Eliot with whom he is compared, usually to the disadvantage of Fry. Donoghue, for example, in *The Third Voice,* a book entirely about verse

---

[7] See D. E. Jones, *The Plays of T. S. Eliot,* chapter 6.
[8] Donoghue, *The Third Voice*, p. 158.

drama, finds his reputation as a dramatist 'one of the more disquieting facts about contemporary theatre' and goes on to suggest that the early comedies refer to nothing but 'their tenuous and precious selves'.[9] When Fry has something to say it is very simple but tricked out with an over-abundance of style. It is not until *The Dark is Light Enough* where there is a decided lessening in verbal virtuosity that Donoghue will concede substance to a play, and his conclusion is that Fry's permanent contribution to the theatre will probably be slight. Fry, in short, is blamed for excess where Eliot is damned for poverty. Eliot came as a poet to the theatre in search of a wider audience for his religious ideas, and the austerity of those ideas was appropriately, if barely, expressed through severely limited images and vocabulary. The deliberately prosaic style rises at certain moments to a solemn richness. But Fry came to the theatre in the capacity of actor and producer and his choice of poetry as a medium was deliberate and not inevitable. He avoided some of the more obvious theatrical deficiencies that can be felt in Eliot's plays. Verse drama before 1930 had become an esoteric cult, and now it was enlarged. None of Eliot's plays aroused the excitement that accompanied the six plays by Fry between 1948–51; and if delight at his verbal fireworks soon palled there was undoubtedly delight; what a wonderful thing is metaphor, says Thomas Mendip and proceeds to prove it. For Fry, verse was there to renew wonder:

Poetry is the language in which man explores his own amazement. It is the language in which he says heaven and earth in one word. It is the language in which he speaks of himself and his predicament as though for the first time . . . and if you accept my proposition that reality is altogether different from our stale view of it, we can say poetry is the language of reality. . . .[10]

Fry's work in the commercial theatre is all of a piece, asking about the nature of existence and illustrating the mixed nature of life in which characters not qualified for tragedy have no

[9] Donoghue, *The Third Voice*, chapter 9.
[10] BBC talk, printed in *The Listener*, 23 February 1950.

place. Fry believes that there are times in the history of men when comedy has a special worth and the present is one of them. Certainly *A Phoenix Too Frequent* (1946) with its insistence on life brought back wonder and colour to the drab world of post-war London. If Fry saw it as one of the necessities of the time to redeem joy at least at that moment he was right. His attempt to do this was by writing a comedy of seasons. In 1950 Fry wrote that *Venus Observed* was planned as one of a series of mood-comedies. He defined mood comedy as a play in which scene, season and characters share the same climate. Thus *Venus Observed* is autumnal, the characters middle aged (and being replaced by the young), the house just beginning to decay. *The Lady's Not For Burning* (1948) thus became spring and *The Dark is Light Enough* (1954) winter. In this last play the poetry of inner life begins to displace the more decorative exteriors: a winter scene, a rather dark plot and sparse diction. Then Fry turned to writing film-scripts (including *Ben Hur*). The plays, in spite of their great energy and entertaining plots spoke, finally, only of wonder at the obvious which is a limited source of drama. Possibly it was the self-limiting quality of the plays as much as the new kind of drama which caused Fry to withdraw from the theatre until 1961 when *Curtmantle* was published. Writing about this play Fry still insisted that the appeal of the inarticulate and the pleasure of hearing the speech of the streets, however brilliantly recorded, was not the whole duty of man as far as language was concerned.[11] Certainly the theatre would be poorer without the light touch of Thomas Mendip:

Your innocence is on at such a rakish angle
It gives you quite an air of iniquity.
By the most naked of compassionate angels
Hadn't you better answer that bell? With a mere
Clouding of your unoccupied eyes, madam,
Or a twitch of the neck: what better use can we put
Our faces to than to have them express kindness
While we're thinking of something else? Oh, be disturbed,

[11] 'Talking of Henry', *Twentieth Century*, February 1961, p. 190.

Be disturbed, madam, to the extent of a tut
And I will thank God for civilisation.
This is my last throw, my last poor gamble
On the human heart.[12]

Jimmy Porter in *Look Back in Anger* and Ronnie Kahn in
*Roots* ask people to care with greater vehemence and, perhaps,
on more relevant matters; although a witch-hunt is not exactly
an unserious subject. There is also the danger that a love of
words can seduce the dramatist from his function as action-
maker as well as word-maker. Consider Hilda talking in *Venus
Observed*:

I know I have
No particular heights or depths myself;
No one who thought me ordinary or dull
Would be far wrong. But even I despair
For Roderic, my husband, who really is
The height of depth, if it doesn't sound unkind
To say so: not deep depth, but a level depth
Of dullness. Once he had worn away the sheen
Of his quite becoming boyhood, which made me fancy him,
There was nothing to be seen in Roderic
For mile after mile, except
A few sheeplike thoughts nibbling through the pages
Of a shiny weekly, any number of dead pheasants,
Partridges, pigeons, jays, and hares,
An occasional signpost of extreme prejudice
Marked 'No thoroughfare', and the flat horizon
Which is not so much an horizon
As a straight ruled line beyond which one doesn't look.[13]

*Curtmantle* (1961) was not the expected summer comedy.
Thematically it showed a return to the subject-matter of *The
Firstborn* (1946) and discusses the problem of authority, how
to use it and remain human, how to cherish both the state and
the individual. It is written in a mixture of verse and prose and
the verse was spare enough to disappoint many although still

---

[12] *The Lady's Not For Burning* (1949), pp. 12–13.
[13] *Plays* (1970), p. 193.

giving in at times to the temptations of its own cleverness. Beckett the saint is of only limited interest to Fry beside the many-sided king, and the message is once more the mystery of a multidimensional universe for which verse is needed if ambiguities are not to be lost. The summer comedy finally appeared in 1970. It was called *A Yard of Sun* and its action appeared to take place in our own post-war world (albeit in Italy and during a medieval pageant). The critics were kind to it but there were objections, once more, on the matter of the refusal of verse to be domestic (*i.e.* real).

Fry took the comedy of manners and added wit, fashionable conversation and verse but: 'the colour and richness were fairly obviously external'.[14] Raymond Williams has pointed out that Fry's effects are achieved technically by refusing the noun and using adjectives or adjectival phrases to usher objects in. This produces a relaxed and not unpleasing music but April and November, for example, *sound* very much alike. The mannerism of his plays helped to brush aside verse drama in favour of stronger dramatic forms. Tynan, writing in 1952, agreed that Fry had performed prodigies of artificial respiration[15] but compared the result to the painting of American morticians.

It is natural for a writer—be he poet or novelist—who comes to the theatre to trust words and forget that they will not be enough. Drama is a sequence of acts indicated by words but also by gesture, scene and situation and it is foolish to ignore any part of this complex. No one thing can carry everything, particularly in a society which lacks codes of behaviour or manners by which behaviour can be tested. The desire to resurrect verse drama, with its attendant paraphernalia of chorus, soliloquy and myth was a symptom of other things, not least the desire to write modern tragedy; as if the parts we conventionally associate with tragedy could of themselves compel it to exist. Here Fry with his mixture of

[14] Raymond Williams, *Drama from Ibsen to Brecht* (1968), p. 208.
[15] *Tynan on Theatre,* p. 36. The review is called 'Notes on a Dead Language'.

tragedy and comedy was nearer what was happening in the theatre than T. S. Eliot. But today we lack that shared morality on which tragedy rested. We ask questions; indeed, Brechtian theatre obliges us to ask questions. The Elizabethans would never have thought of asking whether or not Romeo and Juliet died a worthwhile death but we wonder whether Celia could not have sacrificed herself less wastefully. For that matter we can ask why Jimmy Porter does not get a better job. The idea of the death of tragedy is prevalent in our times, and George Steiner buried it handsomely in 1961.

For Steiner verse drama was a series of essays in archaeology. When Eliot noted effects in Ibsen and Chekhov which he thought only poetry was capable of achieving he makes the concession in terms of good luck or momentary success. But in rejecting 'the flat cabbage-smell realism' the verse dramatists turned to a ghostly past rejecting 'the imaginative richness and relevance to modern life of the dramatic tradition that leads from Büchner to Strindberg'.[16] In meeting the challenge of the novelists and trying to restore poetry to the centre of linguistic expression they overlooked the fact that poetry's relationship to the everyday world grows more and more precarious. There are exceptions but a play like Yeats's *Purgatory* is only briefly sustained over a single scene involving two voices. Verse drama, which seemed to have triumphed over realism, enjoyed only a small victory. Perhaps, too, we should remember how long it had taken to make prose acceptable in the theatre. Tynan, commenting in 1954 on this divorce between the colloquial and the poetic, described prose as 'the most flexible weapon the stage has ever had, and still shining new': 'If poetic playwrights did not exist, it might be an agreeable caprice to invent them: but it would no longer be a necessity. And in a theatre starved by the cinema and besieged by television, necessities must come first.'[17]

[16] George Steiner, *The Death of Tragedy* (1961), chapter IX.
[17] 'Prose and the Playwright' (1954), *Tynan on Theatre*, pp. 329–35.

# CHAPTER FOUR

# 1956
# Annus Mirabilis

The impression that theatre in Britain changed overnight with the performance of *Look Back in Anger* is, obviously, exaggerated. John Russell Taylor's description at the beginning of *Anger and After* (1962) is, however, extremely accurate: *Look Back in Anger* was the event which marked off 'then' from 'now' *decisively,* although not in itself a startlingly novel event. Before 1956, to quote Tynan, it was necessary—if one were to be eligible for dramatic treatment—to have an annual income of more than £3,000 net or be murdered in the house of someone who had.[1] It is a statement which is quite as true as any observation in civilised life should be. Events in 1956, of which *Look Back in Anger* was the most immediately striking, changed that. In fact, the change had been suggested by a piece of legislation in 1948. The Local Government Act of 1948 allowed local authorities to levy a rate of 6d. (3 New Pence) which laid the foundations for civic repertory theatres as an alternative to commercial touring. The effects of this legislation were slow but even the cynical could observe them by about 1970. The Arts Council had also set aside bursaries for young playwrights who were beginning to write plays about the life of a new generation which suddenly seemed to have appeared out of the post-war doldrums. This new generation found their spokesmen largely because of the

[1] *Tynan on Theatre,* p. 84.

foundation of the English Stage Company in its new home at the Royal Court. The suddenness of this appearance and the remarkable nature of the change were emphasised by the absence of any warning signs. *Theatre World* (January 1956) lamented the uninspiring nature of plays produced in the theatre in 1955 as far as plays by new writers were concerned. The same issue, however, contained an article by the designer James Bailey which defended escapism and suggested that the charm of the theatre lay precisely in its being a refuge from humdrum realities. Certainly the theatre looked like Harrods at Christmas. The fiftieth anniversary of the death of Ibsen passed without any new production of his work and the death of naturalism seemed inevitable.[2] Shakespeare was being performed in elaborate and curious settings, while Peter Hall was producing Anouilh. The verse dramatists had at least attempted something serious in the theatre, drawing attention to the possibilities available and emphasising the position of the writer. Their themes of restlessness and loss of direction were now to be taken up by dramatists who seemed to speak with more ordinary voices, and were angry in working-class accents. In retrospect 1956 was clearly a watershed between middle-aged theatre and young theatre. In Europe this new energy was largely harnessed to the cinema, particularly in France where cinema is both a fashion and a passion. Theories were explored in the magazine *Cahiers du Cinéma* and put into practice in films like *L'Année dernière à Marienbad* where the film itself was the end and reality is equated with possibility. In England, however, the creative drive was mainly channelled into the theatre, and, from the writer's point of view, the Royal Court.

The Court remained open from 2 April 1956 until October 1965, except for a few months when the theatre was closed for alterations, under its first director, George Devine[3] and since 1965 it has operated under William Gaskill, and others, who

[2] The ITA opened in September 1955, thus strengthening the challenge to naturalism from that source.

[3] George Devine, sadly, died at the age of 55 in February 1966.

have had the difficult task of carrying on the exciting history of discovery at the Court. The intention of the Royal Court was to provide a theatre for writers in opposition to the theatre of commerce. The first production, mounted in April 1956, was Angus Wilson's *The Mulberry Bush*. This had already been performed at the Bristol Old Vic and, if hardly a provocative play, at least clearly belonged to 'writers' theatre'. Devine's original idea had been that there must be many writers in their forties willing and wanting to write for the stage but the response to an advertisement in *The Stage* was meagre. One new play of interest, although hardly by a writer of forty, did arrive: *Look Back in Anger,* a play that provided much of the revenue to keep the Royal Court going.[4] After *The Mulberry Bush* the Court put on a production of Arthur Miller's *The Crucible,* and then *Look Back in Anger* which was revived in the autumn and allowed to run for ten weeks until the Court's first star attraction, Peggy Ashcroft, in Brecht's *The Good Woman of Setzuan.* By the time the Company had ended its run it was £13,000 in the red and was saved by its Christmas attraction, *The Country Wife* with Joan Plowright and Laurence Harvey. But the critics had been impressed by Osborne's play which had become a *cause célèbre.*

1956 was the year of Hungary and Suez, and anger, or petulance, was in the air. The Royal Court has been accused of left-wing bias but the range of their productions shows both catholicity and, from a financial point of view, impracticality. Apart from plays by Osborne, up to the end of 1962 only eight productions made a profit, with three others just covering their costs. Devine claimed the right to fail, and did not always get audiences. When he retired from the Court he summed up his tenure by saying that he had fought the commercial theatre and won. Certainly the box office was his least concern. Yet when Tom Milne took stock in 1958 for *Encore* he produced some disturbing statistics.[5] Only seven of the nineteen plays were premieres, three others had been produced in the provinces, there were seven foreign plays and two classics. The

[4] See Atticus, 29 April 1962.     [5] *The Encore Reader,* pp. 62–7.     47

premieres involved only four dramatists: Osborne, Nigel Dennis (a successful novelist), Ann Jellicoe (discovered through *The Observer* competition) and O. M. Wilkinson. The Court employed 139 actors, 86 in one rôle only, 21 in two which suggests that the aim of a repertory company in new plays was frequently abandoned in favour of specially engaged casts. And if five readers were looking why were the talents of so many dramatists not discovered? Nevertheless, under Devine, the Court supported three dramatists of stature, Osborne, Arden and Wesker as well as giving a home to other writers, and, surprisingly, Ann Jellicoe. We say surprisingly because Jellicoe came to the Court as a producer, and her first two plays are clearly the work of producer's theatre rather than writer's theatre.

The work at the Royal Court, then, can be summed up as primarily directed to producing plays written by dramatists who might not otherwise have been accepted in the commercial theatre, plays which had the appearance of contemporary relevance and which appealed to audiences who were unwilling to use the theatre as an escape from the problems of the time. But it was and remains primarily a writers' theatre. Its influence in 1956 was complemented by what was happening at the two Stratfords: Stratford East and Stratford-upon-Avon.

Two weeks after *Look Back in Anger* Joan Littlewood and her Theatre Workshop produced *The Quare Fellow* and, in 1958, *The Hostage* (also by Behan) and Shelagh Delaney's *A Taste of Honey*. Littlewood (b. 1924) had started her work in the theatre in Manchester and, before World War II, had formed (with Ewen MacColl) Theatre Union, a group dedicated to bringing the theatre back to the people. This group had been dispersed by the war but, in 1945, some of them regathered to form Theatre Workshop. For eight years this group toured Britain, Germany, Scandinavia, and Czechoslovakia until they settled in 1953 at Stratford East 15. While the Workshop's contribution to the International Theatre Festival in Paris was widely acclaimed in 1955 it was

48

not until *The Quare Fellow* in 1956 that its quality began to be appreciated here. Littlewood had premiered *Mother Courage* in 1955 in England, taking the leading rôle herself, but, not having a singing voice, she had cut the songs out which, as Tynan tartly remarked, was like performing *The Messiah* without the Hallelujah Chorus! After *The Quare Fellow* Theatre Workshop's subsidy from the Arts Council rose but the group was still forced to transfer to make ends meet and when economics forced productions into the West End to success and critical praise Littlewood felt that the artistic cohesion of the group was lost. In 1961 she decided to transfer herself to foreign theatres less troubled by financial difficulties. In her farewell note she said she was leaving because she could not do the work for which she was qualified. She did not believe, she said, in the supremacy of either director, designer, actor or even writer. Her knockabout theatre survived through collaboration but the West End had plundered and diluted her ideas, and she called upon the actors to take over the theatres. After two years abroad she returned to England and with a reassembled company put these principles of collaboration into practice once more with her production of *Oh, What a Lovely War* (1963). The idea for this production came to Charles Chilton when he was looking for his father's grave forty years after World War I and found only a name inscribed on a wall with 35,941 others of officers and men who fell in the Battle of Arras. The words were taken from actual documents and the music was originally inspired by the Black and White Minstrel Show singing songs from the war. Littlewood avoided dogmatism and too much social preaching (faults of a play like Hochhuth's *The Representative*) producing a picture of folly, greed, heroism and stupidity which stressed the insanity of war and the need for brotherhood. A high point in contemporary theatre, *Oh, What a Lovely War* was the end product of a long career which went back to the time when Littlewood began incorporating Pierrot, Music Hall, Piscator and Brecht into her productions in Manchester. She has said that she has found difficulty in

49

getting finished texts but she clearly prefers to improvise round a text with, or without, the author's aid. Behan, Delaney and Frank Norman seem not to have minded but Wolf Mankowitz, for example, liked the method less. Its dangers can be illustrated by the unhappy *Twang!* in 1964.

The idea for *Twang!* was Lionel Bart's and Littlewood offered her services, hoping to make money for her East End Fun Palace. The combination of Bart, Littlewood and Messel ought to have guaranteed success. Bart was established as a successful writer of musicals who had made his name when he collaborated with Littlewood and Frank Norman in *Fings Ain't Wot They Used T'Be*. He was very successful with *Oliver* (1960). *Blitz* (1962) had not repeated this success although the sets were even more of a triumph for Sean Kenny who then went on to design the sets for *Maggie May* (1964) with script by Alun Owen. When Bart had decided on *Twang!* and accepted Littlewood's offer he got Paddy Stone, the choreographer for *Maggie May* and Oliver Messel, the Establishment designer *par excellence*. It was a curious choice but Littlewood assured Bart that they would adapt the play to the sets. The actors, unused to her method of switching rôles during rehearsals, were soon confused, and she then rewrote the whole script rendering work already done useless. The Birmingham opening was cancelled, the costumes arrived (and pleased no one) and Bart and Littlewood began exchanging memos. The first night was disastrous and the reviews accurately reported on the disaster. Bart described the audience as only guinea-pigs a fact well known to provincial audiences but never before openly admitted; Littlewood delivered her usual speech about the wickedness of the English theatre and walked out to sit incommunicado (except to the Press) in the Piccadilly Hotel. Manchester paid for three weeks of dress rehearsals until the cast left for London, another rewrite and more damning reviews. Littlewood left for Hammamet and the cultural centre set up by President Bourgiba where she put on a multiracial entertainment called *Who is Pepito*. Since this time she has returned from Fun

Palaces and the emergent nations to stage occasional productions at Stratford. In 1967 she produced her own version of *Macbird* turning the original satire into something fairly innocuous, and *Mrs. Wilson's Diary,* an affectionate lampoon suggesting that difficulties arise when the Left tries to satirise the Left. In 1970 she put on *The Projector,* ostensibly a play about the Ronan Point disaster but generally accepted as a restoration romp with modern permissiveness. Not only does Littlewood appear to have dissipated her political and theatrical energy but her rebellion has now become orthodoxy. In 1971 she went to Paris to direct Conor Cruise O'Brien's *Murderous Angels* at the Théâtre National Populaire returning to Stratford in March 1972 with a revival of *Sparrers Can't Sing.* Ironically the Theatre Royal has been saved for another season by an Arts Council Grant!

Joan Littlewood is a perfect example of the virtues, and weaknesses, of producer's theatre. She dreads the finished product so rehearsals never stop, not even during performance. She hates finished scripts. She believed that theatre and scripts were dead, that it was clowning and improvisation in Fun Palaces which would bring the theatre back to the people. But, as John Bowen observes, the notion that improvisation is more true than written dialogue seems to come from turning practice into principle.[6] An author frequently finds changes useful or necessary during rehearsal. Actors using the Method principles are advised to look for specifics[7] so why not a whole play of specifics run by Littlewood? Stanislavski clearly distracts attention from the writer but only by teaching actors to live on the stage rather than act on it, and Littlewood's list of specifics is, after all, *her* script. Arden, a most careful writer, wishes to belong in a theatre as much as the players or stagehands and while he has no desire to direct he feels his presence is useful at rehearsals. He points out that his name on a

[6] John Bowen, 'Accepting the Illusion', *Twentieth Century,* February 1961, pp. 153–165.
[7] An incident from experience which can be recalled to produce the emotion an actor seeks to recreate.

playbill is not enough. If he as the writer cannot be integrated then we are back to the old days of actor-managers 'who could buy up a script, devour it, excrete most of it, and then toss the assorted ordure in a highly artistic manner before the multitudes'. Which could be an unkind description of what Littlewood does with her writers. It is, of course, extremely difficult to judge how far such an influence is detrimental or not. The second plays by Delaney and Behan do suggest that they wrote according to Littlewood rather than from themselves. On the other hand it is arguable whether, without her, they would have written them at all.

Brendan Behan (1923-64) sent the script of *The Quare Fellow* to Joan Littlewood who accepted it, characteristically, as source material for a new play. Behan's script contained the two major factors in Behan's life: prison and the IRA. Prison, which produced the novel *Borstal Boy* (1958) provided the background and the execution of a prisoner the catalyst. But Littlewood altered the central character, Warder Regan, who had been Behan's mouthpiece on capital punishment and Behan's willingness to accept changes, even radical changes, made him an ideal writer for Theatre Workshop. After this success he was asked to write a play by Robert McGoran, an executive of Gael Linn, an organisation for the revival of Irish culture and language. The result, *An Giall,* written it is said in twelve days, opened in 1958 and Littlewood offered to do it at Stratford if Behan would translate it. He was, apparently, slow in providing the script and for her version, called *The Hostage,* Littlewood added characters more appropriate to Chelsea than Dublin. Behan seems not to have cared, but the result was a play far less disciplined, with the tragic element submerged in farcical business that is not always relevant. However, this version got Behan an international audience while removing the strength of the original, the contrast between the innocence of the two main characters, Leslie and Teresa and the lust and violence in which they have become involved. John Russell Taylor has suggested that whereas *The Quare Fellow* needed compression *The Hostage* needed expansion and Littlewood's technique is too successful. The minor characters are too colourful and too successful in entertaining us. During its run new jokes were constantly being added to the play, as Behan's biographer acidly remarks, 'like stamps in an album'.[8]

Behan produced no further plays. Apart from radio sketches there was a one-act play in Irish which he hoped to expand into English but he never finished it and Littlewood was not interested in it. This rejection hurt Behan who offered the Irish draft to Gael Linn but they rejected it too, and the play was unfinished at his death.[9]

It is equally difficult to decide whether Littlewood was good for Shelagh Delaney. Delaney (b. 1939) wrote a play because she thought a fine actress like Margaret Leighton was wasting her time acting in a play like *Variations on a Theme*. The conflict between Theatre Workshop and the Lord Chamberlain caught her eye and she sent the manuscript of *A Taste of Honey* to Stratford East. John Russell Taylor has compared the manuscript with the final text and concludes that the quite considerable modifications remain true to the spirit of the play and help to show its author accurately and in the best possible light. Delaney did not object to the Workshop treatment and is said not to have noticed the changes in rehearsal until they were pointed out. In spite of her initial success—Lindsay Anderson hailed the play as a real escape from the 'middle-brow, middle-class vacuum of the West End'—she only produced one more play which was certainly a commercial flop and probably a critical one too.

Joan Littlewood's importance can now be seen as greater than even the Royal Court not so much because of her successes as her principles. Her belief in getting the theatre back to the people, however vague that phrase is, by the rejection of scripts and the use of improvisation techniques and strongly directed ensemble work turns out to be more

---

[8] Ulick O'Connor, *Brendan Behan* (1970), p. 205.
[9] Parts of *Richard's Cork Leg,* found by his widow, were performed at the Dublin Theatre Festival in 1972 and listed for production at the Royal Court in September of the same year.

significant than *Look Back in Anger*. She suggests a kind of theatre in which the producer is more important than the text, action than the word. She insisted on the spontaneous and the topical thus preventing any possibility that her kind of theatre could become a museum.

Curiously her principles can also be seen in precisely that theatre which could hardly escape being a museum, Stratford-upon-Avon. In 1960 Peter Hall was appointed director of the Shakespeare Memorial Theatre[10] at the age of 30 and by 1964 had extended the season to nine or ten months where Charles E. Flower had planned a modest fortnight in his Victorian Gothic theatre in 1879. The RSC also opened at a second theatre, in London, the Aldwych, with a performance of *The Duchess of Malfi* (with Ashcroft and Porter) and a new play by John Whiting, *The Devils* (1961). In 1963 Peter Brook and Charles Marowitz formed a subsidised minor company from the RSC to explore Theatre of Cruelty, resulting in the *Marat-Sade* and later *US* while by 1964 the tradition of a World Theatre Season, organised by Peter Daubeney in conjunction with the *Sunday Telegraph* had been established. In the spring of 1965 plans were drawn up for a new theatre on the Barbican site as part of an arts centre (which, in turn, was part of a plan to bring people back to live in the City): a non-proscenium, one-room relationship theatre for an audience of 1,250–1,500 at a cost of £1,300,000 to open in 1971. In 1971 the fate of this Arts Centre is still in the balance.

Peter Hall also ran an experimental season at the Arts Theatre Club in 1962. The work of the RSC in all three places—*The Wars of the Roses, The Marat-Sade,* Middleton, Rudkin, Scofield's *Lear*—all suggest a view of the world as an existential nightmare, a world bereft of hope, gentleness, compassion. Even at Stratford where there is a resident dramatist we see a shift from actor to collaboration and finally to Shakespeare dominated by the producer. Plays have, for some time, been done in sequence to suggest Shakespeare our contemporary in the narrow Kott sense.

54            [10] Royal since 1961.

After ten years at Stratford and the Aldwych the company's achievements are considerable. The RSC has staged 113 productions, won 48 national and international awards and been seen in 15 foreign countries. They have used producers like Peter Brook and John Barton and developed the talents of actors like Peter O'Toole, Vanessa Redgrave, Eileen Atkins, Alec McCowen, Geraldine McEwan, Glenda Jackson, David Warner, Judi Dench, Ian Holm, Janet Suzman—to name only a few. Peter Hall has now gone to Covent Garden[11] and been replaced by another young man, Trevor Nunn. Nunn's policy at Stratford still seems to lack firm direction and shows a tendency, very much in evidence in the 1970 season, to fall back on tricks and novelties that have already grown into clichés.

The experimental season at the Arts produced some new writers but, on the whole, by 1963, the possibilities of 1956 seemed to have faded and achievement was mainly in the realm of acting and production. In 1963 John Osborne's *Plays for England* was disappointing, Simpson had stopped writing, Jellicoe was adapting Ibsen, Wesker had gone to Centre 42, Delaney and Behan seemed to have been halted and Pinter's work was outside the theatre. Arden continued to write, and there were a few new writers—like Livings, Rudkin and Charles Wood—but the main impression was of decline. What, John Russell Taylor asked, in *Plays and Players* August 1964, had happened to the new dramatists? And by 1964 Whiting and Behan were dead, and even Bolt had turned to scriptwriting. One says even Bolt for the remarkable thing about this perfectly traditional playwright was that he had gone straight to the West End supported by none of the centres of achievement, and with plays that could have been written if the Royal Court, Theatre Workshop and the RSC had never existed. Theatrical prophets in 1956 would probably have decided that after the Court, Workshop and RSC the locus of

---

[11] He announced his departure in 1971; and will succeed Lord Olivier at the National Theatre when they occupy their new home on the South Bank in 1974 (?).

significant activity—the place for new dramatists—would be the theatre clubs. By 1962 the Arts was the only important theatre club left. The idea of a theatre club was current between the wars. Its registered membership provided audience potential for plays a little out of the ordinary that could be appealed to and that was willing to accept more in the ways of plays and less in the way of theatre décor. Such performances were held, erroneously, to be free from the ruling of the Lord Chamberlain. The Arts Theatre produced Fry's *The Lady's Not For Burning* and Whiting's *Saint's Day*. Before the arrival of the English Stage Company Campbell Williams, running the Arts from December 1953, had shown plays by Lorca, Pirandello, Siobhan McKenna in *St. Joan,* O'Neill, Betti, Anouilh, the first London performance of a play by Ionesco (*The Lesson* in a double bill with Obey's *Sacrifice to the Wind*) and in 1955 *Waiting for Godot*. In 1957 the Arts put on a production of Genet's *The Balcony*.[12] The English Stage Company proved a serious rival. The Court was a full-scale theatre which is, after all, preferable to club performances, and commercial managements, alive to many successful transfers were beginning to take chances. The double challenge of the English Stage Company and Theatre Workshop was a serious one but worse was to follow. The Arts lost three plays to the New Watergate revived, with a purely nominal fee, to evade the Lord Chamberlain who had also begun to relax his rulings on such matters as homosexuality in drama. From 1960 the Arts went on hire to any manager or author with sufficient money until 1962 when the RSC took it over for an experimental season of Middleton, Gorki, Giles Cooper, Livings and Rudkin. But they were forced to withdraw and the theatre was then taken over by Michael Codron and Oscar Lewenstein for a season which included James Saunders's *Next Time I'll Sing to You*. It then

[12] But this production was most curious. It was not sanctioned by Genet and the editors of *Encore* remarked that it was odd that the Arts Theatre, which existed to put on plays the censor would not permit, was here acting as its own censor.

declined steadily, with no fixed policy, until 1967 when Caryl Jenner took it over for children's theatre. Although her contract stipulates some adult productions these have hardly been significant. Some dramatists—such as Rudkin, Saunders and Livings—made their debut at the Arts and of these Livings in particular is important because of his structural device worked out when he was acting with Joan Littlewood. His plays are laid out in ten-minute units which, he believes, is the longest time the mind can hold a new situation totally and clearly. Each of these units is laid against what went before and what follows and this shape appears to be very much the basis of recent drama, particularly of the improvisatory kind. It is no accident that Livings excelled in the farcical kind of play where what was *done* counted more than anything else.

But a theatre club like the Arts was obviously not capable of sustained support of a dramatist such as the Court offered, say, to Osborne who has a straight line of eleven plays from *Look Back in Anger* (1956) to *West of Suez* (1971) all of which appeared first at the Court. Theatre Workshop was not exactly congenial to a writer and even Stratford, which had a resident dramatist, showed in its production of Shakespeare (and choice of other plays) a definite shift away from writer to production techniques. The Royal Court, founded as a writers' theatre, remains the most important single institution for the encouragement of the dramatist. It is hardly surprising, therefore, that it fostered three out of five of the major dramatists in the English renaissance: Osborne, Arden and Wesker.

# CHAPTER FIVE

# Three at the Court

Shaw once remarked that he could not cure follies without 'plenty of laughing gas'. Shaw's belief that he could cure is more important than his method, for it implies a conviction as to what is right for society. John Osborne (b. 1929) has no such conviction though he shares with Shaw a gift for language. He cannot have a programme of reforms but we should not think less of him as a dramatist because of this. The topical satire for which Osborne received the title 'Angry Young Man' was his laughing gas. Significantly it was the middle aged in 1956 who were angered by it, but by 1968 it is the young. To say that in the meantime Osborne had grown old and High Tory is too simple an explanation. He wanted, he said, to make people feel, to give people 'lessons in feeling'; they could think afterwards.[1] Hence Jimmy's outburst:

Did you read Priestley's piece this week? Why on earth I ask I don't know. I know damned well you haven't. Why do I spend ninepence on that damned paper every week? Nobody reads it except me. Nobody can be bothered. No one can raise themselves out of their delicious sloth. You two will drive me round the bend soon—I know it, as sure as I'm sitting here. I know you're going to drive me mad. Oh heavens, how I long for a little ordinary enthusiasm. Just enthusiasm—that's all. I want to hear a warm thrilling voice cry out Hallelujah! *(He bangs his breast theatrically.)* Hallelujah! I'm alive!

[1] 'They Call It Cricket', *Declaration* (1957), ed. T. Maschler, P. 65.

I've an idea. Why don't we have a little game? Let's pretend we're human beings, and that we're actually alive. Just for a while. What do you say? Let's pretend we're human. *(He looks from one to the other.)* Oh, brother, it's such a long time since I was with anyone who got enthusiastic about anything.[2]

The key to this passage is the adverb: 'theatrically'. Like Shaw, Osborne requires an operatic-style actor; even if his hero is working class he will still have to manage rhetoric—hence the list of actors who have played Osborne heroes includes Olivier and Paul Scofield and Richard Burton as well as Albert Finney. The adverb also alerts us to the way a thing is being said as much as what is said. Pamela, in *Time Present,* is constantly reminding the people around her of the importance of tone. The importance of tone here is that it makes clear what is happening, and, with the wisdom of hindsight, we can see Osborne's work as one long development: a series of personal tragedies. Such tragedies are related to contemporary social and political problems, of course, but the education Osborne proposes is sensual rather than political. Thus, if the reasons for his anger are never very clear in *Look Back in Anger* the anger is unmistakable as is the ambivalence from which the tensions stem. The emphasis shifts as play succeeds play but the ambivalence remains and it is this, rather than topical satire or technical devices, which makes Osborne a compelling dramatist.

He himself has described *Look Back in Anger* (apparently his sixth play) as 'a formal, rather-old-fashioned play' and it is difficult to recapture the sense of breakthrough, what it is about the play which brought in a new era and gave a label to it. Jimmy Porter has a superficial affinity with Lucky Jim, the hero of Iris Murdoch's *Under the Net,* Colin Wilson's Outsider and John Braine's Joe Lampton, but the affinity is superficial because he does not have Osborne's total support. Jimmy Porter insists that 'emotional' is no longer a term of abuse, and that the tyranny of good manners must be broken, and he spoke for a minority which Tynan rightly estimated would

[2] *Look Back in Anger* (Faber), p. 15.

include everyone between the ages of 20 and 30.[3] The play, therefore, suggested the idea of a generation gap and hinted at the mood ~of post-war Britain. Its hero went to a white-tile university where he was trained to be useful and then, according to him, denied any effective rôle. Its hero had married a girl who, he felt, was a constant reproach to him. The play at the time, seemed to be about commitment and protest. Its form seemed remarkably different though in fact its difference consisted in its being monologue rather than a play with characters. The monologue is interrupted, or when Jimmy is off-stage continued as the other characters talk about Jimmy; and, from a plot point of view, Alison even follows the lines laid down by Jimmy's fantasy.

The handling of social themes, by comparison with Shaw, is haphazard. But the lament about causes is not supposed to set us thinking up a list of causes Jimmy could support, it should focus our attention on Jimmy as the hero who suffers. The action is designed to illuminate that suffering not lead to conflict.[4] It is a mistake, therefore, to look at the play as a working-class drama reflecting a particular stage of social change. Youth and poverty are factors but what matters is that the life of these people is drifting and disorganised: it represents a general state of feeling rather than any particular social problem. This leaves us with an intensely personal cry from Jimmy and the only character allowed to stand apart from Jimmy is Alison's father, the Colonel. Jimmy is never allowed to shout *him* down and this suggests two things. Firstly the Colonel really has more to be angry about than Jimmy and his response compares with Jimmy, and secondly, in that comparison, the dignity of the Colonel produces a resonance in the play which is mildly disturbing.

Jimmy's failure, of course, reflects a national failure. But if the solution for national failure is political (*i.e.* socialist) the

---

[3] *Tynan on Theatre,* p. 42.

[4] Katharine J. Worth, 'The Angry Young Man', *Experimental Drama* (1963), pp. 147–68. This is a most useful essay on which I have drawn considerably.

personal failure is more important. *Look Back in Anger* as many have felt and observed examines a failed marriage in the manner of Lawrence or Strindberg, and from it emerges a kind of hatred for women (the only real tenderness in the play is between two men) and a sexual disturbance that leads, finally, to the refusal of an adult relationship. This expands, whether successfully or not, into a general criticism of the world, of what Raymond Williams has called 'a stupid Establishment, of a lack of causes, of a general emotional incapacity'. But Williams has, rightly, put Lawrence and Strindberg, the sexual matter *before* this social list.[5] It is possible that this expansion cannot work because of the indecision on a personal level. The sympathetic portrayal of the Colonel is only part of this indecision or ambivalence. Osborne seems unable to make up his mind about Jimmy and the ending. Some critics, with an appeal to the stage directions, support the hopeful ending produced by Tony Richardson at the Royal Court. But the hope in the ending is controversial; it is possible, and for some inescapable, to see the withdrawal to the idyllic world of squirrels and bears as a refusal of life. It is also possible to feel that the failure might only be a personal failure and in no way connected with the society which, it is suggested, might be responsible. When John Russell Taylor says that the muddle of this play is 'only a very minor consideration',[6] he is both right and wrong. In the theatre it is feeling that counts; but Osborne obliges us to think afterwards and we then recognise that Jimmy is not just a warmhearted idealist raging against perfidy and deadness, he is also a morbid misfit who is extremely cruel to a group of normal, reasonably well-disposed people. A. E. Dyson points out that if Osborne intended a self-portrait it is far from uncritical, and if Jimmy is offered as a typical hero he must be one of a minority in any generation, and with personality traits which most people generously suppress. Dyson calls Jimmy Hamlet, in domestic surround-

[5] Raymond Williams, *Drama from Ibsen to Brecht* (1968), pp. 318–22.
[6] *Anger and After*, p. 45.

ings, and our response must be suitably complex.[7] That the ending is ambivalent rather than muddled can mean richness but if it is only muddle then the signs for the future of Osborne as a dramatist are debatable.

*Look Back in Anger* may have dated as quickly as *The Vortex* but it seemed to capture the resentment of the times; it seemed relevant in the way that *The Chalk Garden* was not. Even unfavourable critics recognised the vigour of its expression. But it is surely ironic that so articulate a man should be so helpless in human relationships? This is the basic irony which Osborne sees in our time: the difficulty of being honest, feeling honestly and communicating that honesty.

The success of *Look Back in Anger* made the writing of Osborne's next play more difficult: he had expectations to live up to. Fortunately he had Olivier to portray the hero Archie Rice in *The Entertainer* (1957). Osborne continues the theme of failure in this character, an entertainer who has ceased to entertain, who bitterly recognises his own deadness:

Oh, you think I'm just a tatty old music hall actor who should be told the truth, like Old Billy, that people don't wear sovereign cases and patent leather shoes any more. You know when you're up there you think you love all those people around you out there, but you don't. You don't love them, you're not going to stand up and make a beautiful fuss. If you learn it properly you'll get yourself a technique. You can smile, darn you, smile, and look the friendliest jolliest thing in the world, but you'll be just as dead and smug and used up, and sitting on your hands just like everybody else. You see this face, you see this face, this face can split open with warmth and humanity. It can sing, and tell the worst, unfunniest stories in the world to a great mob of dead, drab erks and it doesn't matter, it doesn't matter. It doesn't matter because—look at my eyes. I'm dead behind these eyes. I'm dead, just like the whole inert, shoddy lot out there. It doesn't matter because I don't feel a thing, and neither do they. We're just as dead as each other.[8]

[7] A. E. Dyson, 'Look Back in Anger', *Critical Quarterly*, I (1959), pp. 318–26.

[8] *The Entertainer* (Faber), pp. 71–2.

His failure as an artist is reflected in the failure of relationships within the family, and the play works better than *Look Back in Anger* because the context of music hall allows Archie to talk without being answered back—both on and off stage. Even when Osborne uses a monologue like the one above in the family circle where it would be more appropriate elsewhere this is yet another indication of Archie's failure to know his audience. The minor characters, too, show an improvement; particularly Archie's father Billy Rice. Billy is a character reminiscent of Osborne's portrayal of Alison's father, the Colonel, but here the nostalgia which contrasts with the contemporary is less puzzling. Osborne looks back towards the Edwardian era when the mistakes were made which have resulted in the problems of today. Osborne recognises this but he also recognises that those people made their mistakes confidently, with assurance and that confidence and assurance showed in Billy's performances. For Billy was great in his time and represented the popular culture of the music hall whose death Osborne the artist as much as Osborne the romantic laments.[9] It is the music hall not Brecht which provides the form for this play and makes Archie's long speeches plausible. It is the state of the music hall (It's a very old building) which is symptomatic of the modern age, a symbol of modern decadence. Again the expansion from the personal to the national is not entirely successful. Once more the hero is so strong a character that the play becomes another solo performance. The social themes drop away and we are left with the impression of personal failure, personal anguish. When Archie is packed off to Canada by his successful barrister brother his farewell is both vicious and blatantly *theatrical*: it reminds us that we have been watching a performance the quality of which makes us ask whether Archie is the victim of society or just a mediocre person.

In 1958 the Royal Court staged *Epitaph for George Dillon*

[9] He follows Auden, who, in 1926, found the only remaining traces of theatrical art in the music hall.

63

a play written before *Look Back in Anger* in collaboration with Anthony Creighton. It is, therefore, difficult to decide what part Osborne played in the writing of this play and particularly how far the opposition which the hero faces is due to the collaborator. The hero is, however, a typical if less energetically portrayed Osborne figure. Dillon is an out-of-work artist who is willing to end up as the son-in-law of a surburban family and we do not know whether we are supposed to admire or condemn him. Is Dillon a victim of society or a mediocre talent in the first place? Certainly Ruth, the most intelligent character in the play, does say he may be a genius but the general impression is that he would be negligible in any context. Osborne's next work was a musical directed by himself and described as a Comedy of Manners with Music: *The World of Paul Slickey* (1959). This, too, was apparently based on a script written before *Look Back in Anger*. Remembering the song and dance routines in *Look Back in Anger* and *The Entertainer* Osborne's writing a musical is not surprising. Its total failure was. As Charles Marowitz commented it was not so much a bad musical as an opportunity for the bourgeoisie to hit back at Osborne.[10] There is a failure to provide a strong central character which would unify the play as Jimmy and Archie had. This is possibly because a musical requires a singer (Dennis Lotis) and songs rather than monologues. But also in *The World of Paul Slickey* it is the social questions which are in the foreground so that the musical looks like an anthology of the scattered dislikes of Jimmy Porter and Archie Rice. Although Jack is the central character (and, in his aspirations, looks forward to Luther) he seems to be only a hinge for two parts: the evasion of death duties at Mortlake Hall and the obsessional theme of Osborne, the journalist's invasion of privacy. The characters and the topics attacked include everything and touch nothing; even the attack on the central theme—the socialite gossip columnist—gets lost as Osborne once more vacillates about his hero as victim/villain and finally turns him into a frustrated

[10] *The Encore Reader*, pp. 103–5.

idealist. The final impression from this rag-bag of bad lyrics, satire and sentiment was that Osborne had turned feeling into self-indulgence.

Possibly Osborne recognised this, or possibly he recognised that he had created no new material since *The Entertainer* or possibly he felt the strain of creating new material which would live up to the energy of his two successful plays was too great; at any rate he turned to historical subjects. His first attempt was *A Subject of Scandal and Concern* (1960) a television play that is mainly interesting for its anticipations of his next play *Luther* (1961) produced at Nottingham Playhouse with Albert Finney in the title rôle. The subject of scandal and concern was George Holyoake, the last man to be imprisoned for blasphemy in this country. Osborne makes little attempt—in a series of short scenes linked by a pompous narrator—to enquire into the forces which were lined up against his hero and what the social background was. Once more it is a personal play about an honest man imprisoned for his honesty and unable to make his wife or captors see the logic of his actions. Once more Osborne is ambivalent about his hero. The real villain is not society but a newspaper, *The Cheltenham Chronicle,* which allows him to continue his vendetta with the Press; and Holyoake's honesty is excessive. When the Assize Judge offers a way out, a small compromise by which much suffering would be avoided, he refuses the offer. As a character he has too few of the moments of passion which would help us to overlook the inhumanity of his honesty.

Luther, like Holyoake, cannot compromise. For him, as Banham observes, the commandments are not something to be worked at but a direct command for obedience, which leads towards belief in salvation by Faith alone, and not through good works, penance and the forgiveness of sins.[11] Like *A Subject of Scandal and Concern* the play is a series of short scenes which look Brechtian. Osborne drew heavily for this play on documentary sources, using not merely themes and ideas but also key quotations from Erik H. Erikson's psycho-

[11] Martin Banham, *Osborne* (1969), p. 52.

analytical interpretation, *Young Man Luther* (1959).[12] This use of source material may explain why the parts dealing with the private life seem more vital than those sections which deal with the public world. Osborne has shown a disinclination in all his plays to explore the social forces at work on his hero and a tendency to concentrate on the private man and hope that national implications will emerge. Luther is convincing as a private rebel but he hardly emerges as the man who divided Christendom forever, and when Staupitz sums up Luther's achievements at the end of the play they hardly match what the play has shown us. Tetzel's speech, for example, may be vintage Osborne and excellent theatre but it does suggest that the Reformation took place over the matter of indulgences alone, while the Council of Worms fails to emerge as a crucial meeting in Church history. The private neurosis—with the usual nostalgia for childhood and a strong protective father—is well drawn but the sense that this rebel is a product of the period is hardly there. Thus, if *Luther* appears to copy the structure of *Galileo* and borrow Brechtian tricks, after the Council of Worms that structure collapses and Osborne introduces a Knight to tell us, in modern language, what has happened. Luther's motivations are ultimately seen to have little to to with exterior reality, and his opponents are thinly drawn or not allowed to oppose: there are no debates only interlocking monologues. Sympathetic critics have suggested that Osborne shows us a Luther forced to the division by the inability of the Church to respond to his pleas for reform; they also suggest that he only seems to betray the peasants. But it is doubtful if the peasants would agree. The result is Osborne's usual nostalgia and ambivalence. The Papal Legate warns Luther of the future he will cause in Europe:

You know, a time will come when a man will no longer be able to say 'I speak Latin and am a Christian' and go his way in peace.

[12] Erikson lays stress on constipation, epilepsy and father conflict, but some historians doubt the epilepsy, and constipation appears to have attacked Luther *after* he left the monastery.

There will come frontiers, frontiers of all kinds—between men—and there'll be no end to them.[13]

And, at the end of the play, Staupitz quietly continues this doubt:

I'm not leaving you, Martin. I love you. I love you as much as any man has ever loved most women. But we're not two protected monks chattering under a pear tree in a garden any longer. The world's changed. For one thing, you've made a thing called Germany; you've unlaced a language and taught it to the Germans, and the rest of the world will just have to get used to the sound of it. As we once made the body of Christ from bread, you've made the body of Europe, and whatever our pains turn out to be, they'll attack the rest of the world too. You've taken Christ away from the low mumblings and soft voices and jewelled gowns and the tiaras and put Him back where He belongs. In each man's soul. We owe so much to you. All I beg of you is not to be too violent. In spite of everything, of everything you've said and shown us, there *were* men, *some* men who did live holy lives here once. Don't—don't believe you, only you are right.[14]

Luther's only reply is to clutch his abdomen and ask what he can do. Luther, like Osborne's other heroes, may just be self-indulgent rather than a victim.

The sense that Osborne was losing momentum was not qualified by his next two plays—*For England*—produced in 1962: two slight comic interludes of which the second, *Under Plain Cover,* at least had a promising start. Here we have a couple who keep their marriage alive by playing games, as if, John Russell Taylor remarks, Jimmy and Alison having tired of bears and squirrels have 'gone on to a few more sophisticated party games'.[15] But the discovery that they are (albeit innocently) incestuously married allows a snooping reporter to take over the play which then lapses into the sensationalism it is supposedly criticising. Fortunately doubts about Osborne's staying power were resolved in 1964 with the appearance of *Inadmissable Evidence.* The rôle of Maitland was played by Nicol Williamson and whatever we think of the

[13] *Luther* (Faber), p. 74.   [14] *Ibid.,* pp. 99–100.   [15] *Anger and After,* p. 58.

play his performance was one of the great performances of the modern British stage. Many critics saw this play as Osborne's most successful, pointing out that the problem of dialogue (*i.e.* fondness for monologue) was solved here because the failure to communicate was as much the theme as technique. It should be remembered that all Osborne's heroes have been articulate: graduate, music-hall entertainer, teacher, preacher and now solicitor. *Inadmissable Evidence* begins with a dream sequence staged in Maitland's office in which he is accused of publishing 'a wicked, bawdy and scandalous object'. Maitland's defence is mediocrity and a recognition of failure:

I never hoped or wished for anything more than to have the good fortune of friendship and the excitement and comfort of love and the love of women in particular. I made a set at both of them in my own way. With the first with friendship, I hardly succeeded at all. Not really. No. Not at all. With the second with love, I succeeded, I succeeded in inflicting, quite certainly inflicting, more pain than pleasure. I am not equal to any of it. But I can't escape it, I can't forget it. And I can't begin again. You see?[16]

Maitland, at 40, is well off, a solicitor with a slightly unsavoury business, possibly in trouble with the Law Society, losing his wife, daughter and mistress, on the verge of a nervous breakdown and possibly, even on the telephone, only talking to himself. The fantasy at the beginning in which his office masquerades as a court-room and his staff as judge and officials provides the context in which he asks to be judged. The same actress plays the various clients, who obviously reflect aspects of Maitland and his unseen wife, but the homosexual episode is not characteristic of Maitland or his work (usually divorces) and the doubling of the rôle by the young solicitor Jones does not help us to understand why this case alone arouses in Maitland some involvement. He actually appears to listen to Jones-Maple. His daughter, in a brief appearance at the end of the play, is speechless which may be interpreted as many things: she is not there, Osborne cannot risk opposition or achieve dialogue. The technique may mirror

[16] *Inadmissable Evidence* (Faber), p. 20.

or coincide with the theme, or cover self-indulgence once more. Perhaps Maitland, as Walter Kerr suggests, is just an English puritan at heart.[17] He has totally liberated himself, sexually and socially, furthering his career with other men's work. He should be in harmony with his desires having found a complaisant wife and mistress. Yet he feels obliged to teach others to detest and abandon him, and feels himself so loathsome that he cannot even form effective relationships when they are part of his working life. It is possible to describe Maitland as a hero in tune with existentialism, casting doubt on meaningful continuity in the outside world and left at the end facing what is called the obscenity of his existence. But this does not chime in with Osborne or the play. Moreover Martin Esslin has raised serious objections.[18] We are told that Maitland is a solicitor yet it is difficult, on the evidence, to believe that he could pursue that profession for one year let alone twenty. He does not listen to his clients and even if he is on the edge of a nervous breakdown he would surely by now have acquired a routine and act like a solicitor: as Archie Rice says in *The Entertainer*: If you learn it properly you'll get yourself a technique.

Moreover a man in the process of breaking down is best understood by some sense of what he was previously like and we are made to understand that Maitland has always been mediocre. Finally, because he has always been like that the relationships which have existed were formed with that knowledge, yet nothing happens in the play, beyond the need of the play to strip Maitland of everything, to precipitate the crisis. The sense of disgust is certainly very strong, and the usual tirades against contemporary social phenomena are, as always, outward signs of inward disgrace. The only compassion occurs in the homosexual episode the relevance of which is doubtful. The play seems, therefore, to be a muddle about another hero who refuses to be devious.

In fact the muddle seems to pervade the three plays written

---

[17] Walter Kerr, *Tragedy and Comedy* (1967), p. 294.
[18] *Plays and Players,* November 1964, pp. 32–3.

about this time. *A Patriot for Me* was not produced until 1965 because of its subject matter (and then only as a club performance at the Royal Court). It is certainly a play that does something more than provide work for homosexual actors[19] or an opportunity for a long battle with the Lord Chamberlain. In it Osborne returned to a play based on fact: the career of Alfred Redl in the service of the Austro-Hungarian empire who, in spite of his social background (it is not stressed, but he is Jewish) rises through hard work to the rank of full colonel in the Intelligence service but is blackmailed by the Russians for his homosexuality and finally ordered to commit suicide by his superiors to preserve the honour of the Empire. Like all Osborne's plays, *A Patriot for Me* works on two levels: the private and, by extension, the public. We are shown the decline of a great society and the injustices perpetrated by that society and the private anguish of an individual who finds himself in that society and comes to learn that although the society knows and condones the practise of homosexuality it will persecute the individual honest enough to acknowledge his inclinations. A parallel was clearly intended with the England of the 1960s and, as in *Luther,* the method and the writing suggest a movement towards the objective, possibly to counterbalance the personal obsessiveness of *Inadmissable Evidence.* But Redl does not dominate the play; nor do we get satisfactorily inside or outside of him. The historical material points up the fact that times do not change and the private scenes suggest the loneliness of an honest man who happens to be homosexual. But Redl takes a very long time to discover what he is although it is obvious to the audience very early in the play. In Act 2 Osborne replaces short scenes with three—one of which is devoted to the Drag Ball which by its length is disproportionate to the relevance it has. In the third act the public and private scenes are still not blended. Redl is far from being a big enough, or colourful enough character for a one-

[19] In fairness, Miss McCarthy modified this foolish view, under pressure from Tynan.

man play and he is not presented fully either in the documentary or psychological sense. We are left asking what the play can be about? If society is to blame for anything Osborne does not examine how and why, yet since most of the characters in the play turn out to be homosexuals it cannot be supporting the argument that homosexuals do not make good patriots. As in *Luther* the centre is personal but insubstantial, and the final scene—in which the Russians are taking the same interest in the psycho-analyst that they took in Redl—is baffling.

The same sort of bafflement continues in Osborne's next work *A Bond Honoured* (1966). This play, an adaptation of Lope de Vega's *La Fianza Satisfecha,* was commissioned by Tynan for the National Theatre. The subject was very much in Osborne's own territory: a hero rebelling against the values of his time in long speeches. Many critics felt that the subject was *too* congenial and that this interlude was unfortunate. Put into a double bill with Peter Shaffer's *Black Comedy* it got audiences but was not popular. It was not popular with the critics either. Yet the play was impressive to watch and made a more than usually visual use of the theatre. Osborne insisted on a production resembling a religious rite and the audience were confronted with a semicircle of actors on stage all the time but sitting, dimly lit, on the periphery and advancing into full light to play their parts. The acting was to be primitive, violent and the whole thing had a Japanese quality about it. The hero, Leonido, challenges the world and God. He thus manages to draw a great deal of attention to himself, and at the end asks, like Meursault, for a 'harsh tribunal and the full exercise of justice'. But once more, without opposition, Leonido is in danger of becoming a bore, his victims are inadequate and unconvincing and the result looks very much like a parody of an Osborne play.

The adaptation has been rightly described by Dr. Esslin as an 'unholy mess'. The programme notes suggested that at the end Leonido had found his identity and was an existential hero at peace with himself, whereas the play showed him as far from having either identity or peace. The original play can be found in the *Comedias de vidas de santos* which, as Dr. Esslin remarks, leads us to infer, correctly, that Leonido is to become a saint and that the play is about the conversion of a wicked man. Leonido meets Christ after his father has preferred death rather than allow his daughter to be raped incestuously. In Osborne's version brother and sister have been having sex happily together since adolescence. Christ appears to Leonido as a shepherd carrying a sack of martyr's emblems which, in Osborne's version, Leonido assumes when he announces his surrender to the Moors. The act of redemption takes place in the original when the Shepherd is revealed as Redeemer carrying the Cross and Leonido finds his identity the moment he realises his guilt. Osborne, trying to write an atheistic play appears to have left in most of the religious plot, and his hero rather than finding identity appears to go temporarily insane. From all points of view the play remains a theatrical curiosity, and it is a relief to turn to Osborne's plays 'for the mean time'.

*Time Present* is, so far in Osborne' work, unique, because the central character is a woman, and the fact that she was played by Osborne's wife, Jill Bennett, and that there were rumours of hidden references lent the play interest. Many critics felt that the play itself was not very interesting. There was, of course, a great deal of unease at finding the Angry Young Man of 1956 in the rôle of Tory in 1968 and they immediately concluded that the tirades must be only half-hearted. They are exactly as meaningful as anything Jimmy Porter says, and, like Jimmy Porter's outbursts, they cover up a private anguish. But Pamela is an actress and she is constantly warning other characters, and us, to listen to the way a thing is said rather than what is said. Pamela is no more likeable than Jimmy ever was and she is only more unlikeable (to some people) because she is firmly on the side of nostalgia—the era of her father, Sir Gideon Orme, and a liberal consumption of champagne. Also, Pamela couples her love of the past and champagne with one or two harsh remarks about Vietnam, modern youth, modern drama and modern economics. All of which is not the stuff to please audiences at the Royal Court. This material—the topical asides Osborne has never been able to resist—and a complicated, not to say conventional plot, should not distract us from recognising the skill with which relationships occur in this play. It is true that Pamela is the only character but she is not allowed *long* speeches, she is put carefully in the context of an actress (*i.e.* an artificial person) who recognises the meaningfulness of tone and inflection as well as what the words mean, and who is allowed relationships in some detail. Pamela is related to her father, her flat mate Constance, her lover and, of course, as an actress playing an actress, her audience. This last makes her behaviour more plausible; we are expected to expect that she will cover up her true self with a series of acts, set speeches and so forth and the experience of the play is detecting the anguish beneath. For too many people anger in a woman is bitchiness and this coupled with an unfashionable view of the young, hippies and happenings was sufficient to damn the play. Many were relieved when Osborne returned to the male hero in *Hotel in Amsterdam,* nominated by *Plays and Players* as the Best Play of 1968.

Here, too, the characters are wealthy, successful people who are not particular happy. Three men and their wives plot a weekend away from their despotic boss, a film producer, K.L. This device permits their relationships to unfold both personally and collectively *vis-à-vis* K.L. who has committed suicide by the end of the play. The main impression of the play is listening to Laurie, played by Paul Scofield, who, like Pamela, talks to cover a loneliness and sense of failure only momentarily revealed when he tells Annie, Gus's wife, of his love for her. The play is about feeling and works through the dialogue. There is very little action except for the occasional waiter who brings the drinks, and finally Gillian, Laurie's sister-in-law, who shatters the precarious holiday atmosphere and prepared for the final news about K.L.'s death. Osborne is making an effort here to create a pattern of emotional and social relationships and sustain

73

those relationships through the dialogue. The set pieces are still there, and a great deal of slick chatter, but at no time do they shatter the care with which the play written. In both these plays disgust for the mean time is matched with compassion—which the audience is invited to share—particularly for the central character. There is little visually to distract from the conversation and there is a sense of discipline not previously seen in Osborne's work. It is as if these two drawing-room comedies reflect his distaste for contemporary experimental theatre:

sort of about leaving nude girls in plastic bags at railway stations. Non verbal, you understand, no old words, just the maximum in participation.[20]

It is clear that Osborne shares Pamela's distaste. Apart from a few film-scripts, including the enormously enjoyable *Tom Jones* directed by Tony Richardson, and a couple of recent television plays, Osborne has remained faithful to the old-fashioned verbal theatre. His latest play, *West of Suez,* opened at the Royal Court in 1971.[21]

The word 'old-fashioned' sounds derogatory. Osborne has always been conventional in his stage-craft showing little desire to abandon the proscenium arch. He has said he would like to write something for a circus, and he has incorporated Brechtian devices but without any sense of Brechtian method. He may use short scenes, film clips, placards, historical sources but he does so without any profound sense of social implications. His plays fail when their tragic hero is not strong enough to *be* the play and the audience has to fall back on history, society and ideas. Osborne has never maintained a consistent style, nor used his wide variety of techniques judiciously, and he has frequently sacrificed coherence for topical laughter. As a lively figure he has often been confused

[20] *Time Present* (Faber), pp. 46–7.

[21] In 1972 Osborne adapted *Hedda Gabler* for the Royal Court; the title rôle was played by Jill Bennett. The Court will also produce his next play, *A Sense of Detachment;* Osborne has also written another play called *A Place Calling Itself Rome.*

with his heroes and like them been in danger of becoming shrill and indulgent. Osborne has never been able to reconcile his concern with social issues and his obsession with the private individual even when that individual should represent the many. We say 'should represent' for, clearly, Osborne's success is in presenting the unusual person whose personality is such that it overshadows any basic representational traits. This failure, however, ensures that Osborne is never restricted to private grievance or simple didacticism. His plays have always been essays in feeling and, as one critic puts it, 'more instinctive than calculated and more passionate than coherent'.

Unlike Shaw it is not the argument which counts in the theatre but the words and the character. This explains why a large number of actors and producers have been drawn to his plays. Yet, like Shaw, Osborne sees the theatre as a weapon. His targets are often irrelevant, muddled or assiduously topical but his observation is nice, and his work consistent. The targets are always aspects of society which deny feeling or, more lately, insist on mindless feeling. Osborne has always attacked the British way of feeling: 'I offer no explanation. . . . All art is organised evasion. You respond to Lear or Max Miller—or you don't. I can't teach the paralysed to move their limbs.' He has done this through specific characters drawn, obviously, from his own experience. But he faces the difficulty, which he recognises, that he has no common audience with a store of general reference to draw on. The English renaissance was tenuous and the new audience was not working class but lower middle-class intelligentsia who found their frustrations given voice in *Look Back in Anger*. If Osborne has never achieved a stable form he did bring back into the theatre controversy, vivid language and the tirade so appropriate to the new breed of heroes who never listen to the opposition and who are not well-bred enough to conceal their feelings. If necessary we can defend his use of monologue as thematic: in these days no communication seems possible between characters. Like Beckett he relies on two things: strong situation and strong language. In 1970 when the use of language is being abandoned in the theatre in favour of gesture Osborne's work remains as something more than—to quote Ionesco—'onedimensional bourgeois triviality'. Osborne aims at tragedy; he succeeds in giving us personal documents but that perhaps is all our fragmentary time can expect. The personal voice is always refreshing.

It contrasts with the more sombre public voice of John Arden. Not that Arden is lacking in personal anger but he is the dramatist *par excellence* who translates that anger into situations of a strictly impersonal nature. Arden's characters are primarily used as representatives, and his plots bring about conflicts between social groups. His characters, of course, exist as very colourful individuals, but their personality is shaped at all times to suggest what they stand for (Arden has a tendency to name in the Jonsonian manner) and add to the picture of the community as a whole. Thus, the isolated town or national politics reflected in local government is observed with an accurate social eye and a strong historical sense which combine to 'translate the concrete life of today into terms of poetry that shall at the one time illustrate that life and set it within the historical and legendary tradition of our culture'.

Arden (b. 1930) began writing plays when he was sixteen but was trained as an architect. He was first recognised through a radio play *The Life of Man* (influenced, *inter alia,* by *Moby Dick* and 'The Rime of the Ancient Mariner') which attracted the attention of the Royal Court. The Court, after rejecting his first play, based on Arthurian legend, accepted *The Waters of Babylon* for the first of their low-budget Sunday night ventures. Since then the Royal Court has supported Arden faithfully in spite of general dislike for him shown by audiences and critics alike. It is easy to understand this dislike. Though we can guess at Arden's beliefs we cannot find them directly in the plays which consistently suggest that 'hero' and 'villain' are no longer meaningful terms. As John Russell Taylor remarks an audience is prepared to stand a certain amount of uncertainty but seldom the idea that there are as many causes and as many moral standards as there are

76

individuals.[22] An audience that is not allowed to participate and is not then guided into either agreement or disagreement becomes truly alienated, and probably bored. It is the theories of Brecht which seem to be at work here. Yet Arden's plays would surely have been written even if Brecht had never existed. Like Brecht, Arden is a political playwright but only in the sense that he feels it is impossible to avoid being political since man is a political animal. Everything that man does is a political act. For Arden politics means the art of living together and if the actual technical aspects are the province of the politician everyone should be concerned and recognise that any play about people is political. But where Brecht, as a practising communist, is didactic, Arden sees the Marxist analysis as only one of many sources and solutions. It can be used, as in *Sjt. Musgrave's Dance,* but not to the extent of making the play Marxist. Arden discovered Brecht the theatre technician only after writing plays and believes that both Brecht and himself had been inspired by the same things: the Middle Ages, the Elizabethans and various styles, such as the Chinese and Japanese theatres. Arden does invite us to watch and judge the action of the play (like Brecht) but like his contemporary dramatists on a human rather than an ideological level. He achieves alienation through the use of blatantly theatrical devices, like song and dance, but for Arden such devices must be integral rather than interrupt the performance.

*The Waters of Babylon* (1957) showed the Arden method albeit in confused shape. Starting as a satire on Macmillan's Premium Bond scheme it deals with the career of Sigismanfred Krankiewiecz—a pimp, an unscrupulous landlord and at work during the day in an architect's office. The play shows a use of plot, a large amount of incident and a large number of characters—all three necessary to exhibit the triple life of the central character. The plot proceeds with Jonsonian complexity until Krank is accidentally shot (an early example of accidental violence) and possibly this complexity is self-

[22] *Anger and After*, p. 84.

defeating. The dialogue is written in too many styles, and the private lives of the characters are too lively for them to be submerged in the public events which are Arden's main interest. But the play is always interesting and presents, if one looks at it closely, the embryonic shape of that opposition between vitality and order which is the basis of most of Arden's work.

This opposition emerged in his next play *Soldier, Soldier* (1960) which was produced on television. Here most of the characters speak in prose but the central character uses a rough type of blank verse. Arden intended this to suggest values: the strident, disorderly soldier (verse) and the respectable, quiet townsfolk (prose). The soldier enjoys the kind of life which invites trouble while the townsfolk sacrifice everything, including pleasure, to avoid trouble. The soldier cheats them, lies and takes money from a family by pretending that he can help their son who is missing. He seduces the wife of that son and leaves, taking with him what he can. Arden intends this soldier to be seen as representative of every soldier and likeable: as the poetry in life. But he also insists that we do not think of the victims as contemptible, a balance explored dramatically in the second play staged at the Royal Court, *Live Like Pigs*. Directed by George Devine in 1958 this play remains Arden's most naturalistic. It is written almost entirely in prose and looks at the results of putting a gypsy family on a housing estate somewhere in the West Riding of Yorkshire. Many critics felt that it could well do without the interspersed ballads sung before the curtain by Mr. A. L. Lloyd[23] and that it needed pruning; but they also noted the racy, turbulent vitality of the play. Most critics also seem to feel that our sympathy was intended for the intruders and that at the end, as with the town in *Soldier, Soldier,* order may be restored but life is non the better for that. If sympathy on Arden's part is limited for restored order his dispassionate presentation scarcely makes the gypsies likeable as neighbours. In fact Arden

[23] Arden's stated intention is that if the songs cannot be integrated they should be cut.

sees them as an anachronism and the Jacksons as 'undistinguished but not contemptible'. Both, he suggests, lose 'their own particular virtues' under the stress of the confrontation.[24]

Arden broke with naturalism fairly decisively in *Sjt. Musgrave's Dance* (1959) and has since been moving towards simplicity, extreme formalism and a bold use of primary colours. Some of the preoccupations of *Sjt. Musgrave's Dance* had already appeared in *Soldier, Soldier* and the two plays deal with the same basic action: the arrival of a soldier in a colliery town and the bringing of violence into an enclosed community. The action of *Sjt. Musgrave's Dance* concerns the arrival of a recruiting team under Sjt. Musgrave in a northern town isolated by winter and fighting its own war between the miners on strike and the town authorities. Both sides take advantage, after initial mistrust, of the campaign as a diversion but Sjt. Musgrave and his team are, in fact, deserters and Musgrave's mission is to return the bones of a local lad to his home town and urge the punishment of those who sent him off to war. This discovery throws the town into confusion during which the dragoons break through to the town and restore law and order. The play ends with the dance which celebrates this restoration and anticipates Musgrave's own dance on the gallows. The defeat of Musgrave seems to begin in the differing aims of his fellow deserters one of whom is accidentally killed and the complex plot is hardly susceptible to précis and confusing in the theatre. Is Arden supporting pacifism in his play, as he certainly does in life, or is he pointing out the complex roots of violence with a pessimistic conclusion? Arden himself confesses that he had problems; he started with the climax of the play and was then left with the task of making that climax credible in a number of scenes which would allow both the soldiers and the townsfolk to reveal their attitudes. He later felt that three acts would have been more usual and useful to do this and also confessed that he had not entirely solved the problem of how to release information without losing tension. The play owes something to Brecht's

[24] Introductory Note to *Live Like Pigs*.

version of *The Recruiting Officer*—*Drums and Trumpets*—
and took hints from an American film called *The Raid*.
It is Arden's first excursion into a historical setting. But
where dramatists like Osborne and Bolt concentrate on an
individual, isolated and therefore modern, and using language
in a heroic manner, Arden is interested in groups and his
historical setting deliberately suggests no particular period
while evoking many. The central character, Musgrave, is
surrounded by soldiers who only gradually took on names as
they moved from numbers to arbitrarily assigned tem-
peraments (*e.g.* the Surly Soldier). Some of the characters
are still far from convincing even as representatives (*e.g.* the
mayor and the parson) but Arden has described them as
caricatures by omission rather than exaggeration. Some of the
situations are clearly decided by the plot rather than by
character—for example the reaction of the soldiers to Annie
in the stable. The colliers, who are to look like figures in a
Lowry painting, do not need to stand out but when one has to
speak as an individual the dialogue is not strong enough. Possibly this weakness stems from the ballad tradition espoused
by Arden.

Arden admits that Fry had a very strong influence on him
and although he has outgrown the influence he retains a sort of
'literary first love' feeling for him. The trouble, Arden felt, was
that Fry, in spite of a great gift for language, did not marry
that language to a strong situation. As in Wesker, Arden's
constant preoccupation with verse and/or prose is closely
related to politics. When America gained political power,
American pop culture began to dominate the cultural scene
and part of this culture was the ballad which, Arden believed,
had been better preserved in America than in England. Arden
sees the ballad as the bedrock of English poetry and the
method by which he could become a poet of the theatre. He
recognised that he must not become too private or his plays
would be valuable only for reading, or, like Yeats's, actable
only in a drawing-room theatre before an inevitably élitist
audience. The ballad, with its sense of season, the passing of

time, strong primary colours and strong narrative line was suitable for a theatre where costumes, movement, verbal patterns and music must all be strong and hard. If verse is to be used it must be obviously verse as opposed to the surrounding prose and never allowed to droop into what Arden calls 'casual flaccidities'. Arden, therefore, sought simple but basic situations and themes to express social criticism and a framework of traditional poetic truths to give weight to what might otherwise be only contemporary documentary facility. Such a technique can be misunderstood since audiences find it difficult to give a simple response to the story. In the ballad, as in the fable, we draw our own conclusions. Arden chose verse[25] though he recognised that other forms are available and has remarked, for example, on the effects gained by Pinter whose dialogue *becomes* poetic. His choice of the ballad is political. It reaches back into history and works in a moral atmosphere of multiple standards which he prefers and demonstrates in *Sjt. Musgrave's Dance*. There we meet the dilemma of war and violence in which pacifism (his own instinctive choice) is shown to be not self-sufficiently right. The accidental death of Sparky suggests, as much as Musgrave's attitude, that violence cannot be met either with violence or non-violence; and the industrial context (another form of violence) reinforces the dilemma and the irony of the ending:

Officer: Law and order is established?
Parson: Wiser counsels have prevailed, Captain.
Bargee: *I* caught him, *I* caught him, *I* used me strategy!
Officer: My congratulations, all.
Walsh (*with great bitterness*): The community's been saved. Peace and prosperity rules. We're all friends and neighbours for the rest of today. We're all sorted out. We're back where we were. So what do we do?
Bargee: Free beer. It's still here.
No more thinking. Easy drinking.
End of a bad bad dream. Gush forth the foaming stream.

[25] In all his plays the images, verbal or visual, are organised as if in a poem.

81

The issue of war and violence, of order versus anarchy, has now shifted into terms of good government and the clash between principle and expediency.

During 1959–60 Arden was playwrighting Fellow at Bristol University where he produced *The Happy Haven,* a play that does not deal with this conflict in either a realistic or political sense. *The Happy Haven* was clearly influenced by the conditions which produced it. And possibly these special circumstances allowed, encouraged or even compelled Arden to experiment. He uses the masks he has already met with during improvisations at the Court with the Writers' Group. The commedia dell'arte mask obviously appealed to Arden for this play. He wanted a style of theatre which used types and was using young people to play old characters. The masks were appropriate, for age is seen as a mask which has hardened over the years and can be ripped off by rejuvenation. Possibly, too, the circumstances of the play led Arden to award the victory to anarchy in this play as the old people refuse to be made young (albeit for very childish reasons) and turn the doctor into a child.

Arden returned to the subject of good government in 1960 with his nativity play written for performance in the village church at Brent Knoll, Somerset. *The Business of Good Government* is an odd title for a Nativity play but Arden's version is scarcely orthodox. Its central character is really Herod, a man pushed into a corner from which the only escape is by massacring the innocents. Arden admits that his Herod is blatantly unhistorical. Critics have complained that the end of the play is inconclusive and that Arden should have kept his initial focus on Herod. However fascinating that exercise would have been the play is restored to its proper direction and ends with the miracle of the field of corn that shields the Holy Family on its flight into Egypt. Arden is noticeably trying to simplify the dramatic action aware that people have no time to watch *and* listen. But he still uses language contrasts. The Angel speaks with Biblical grandeur:

Angel (*addressing the audience with sadness*): Not one stone shall be
    left upon another.... Ye shall hear of wars and rumours of
    wars. And nation shall rise against nation, and kingdom against
    kingdom: and there shall be famines and pestilences and earth-
    quakes in divers places. (*His voice rises in a torrent.*) And
    there shall be signs in the sun and in the moon and in the
    stars, and upon the earth distress of nations, with perplexity; the
    sea and the waves roaring; men's hearts failing them for fear
    and for looking after those things which are coming on earth:
    for the powers of heaven shall be shaken! (*He seems for a
    moment afraid of his own vision: then his voice quietens and
    he delivers his next lines with sober stillness.*) And then they
    shall see the Son of Man coming in a cloud with power and
    great glory. Verily I say unto you: this generation shall not pass
    away till all be fulfilled.

Herod on the other hand uses colloquial prose although at the
end of the play when he discusses the business of good
government this rises to something nearer the poetic.

This development was momentarily interrupted by a brief
excursion into naturalism with a television play *Wet Fish*
(BBC TV 1961) which revived Krank from an earlier play and
introduced Sir Harold Sweetman who is to appear more
substantially in *The Workhouse Donkey*. Arden, meanwhile,
was working on a translation of Goethe's *Goetz von
Berlichingen* under the title *Ironhand*.[26] Translation is possibly
not the right word. Using Sir Walter Scott's version Arden
attempted to rewrite the play much as Osborne rewrote Lope
de Vega, and in both cases the original served to stimulate the
themes and theories of the translator. What attracted Arden
here was obviously the conflict between free-will and
statesmanship, between anarchy and order. Goetz, like the
gypsies, is an attractive anachronism; a robber baron chosen
by rebellious peasants as their leader, a good man who ends up
outside the law while the less scrupulous Weislingen enjoys the
favour of the Emperor. Weislingen is given more scope to
declare his case in Arden, naturally. One of the more

---

[26] Peter Hall was interested in it but it was not produced until 1963, and
then at the Bristol Old Vic.

important consequences of this translation was that it gave Arden epic scope with which to treat themes he had previously explored, and Goethe sent him back to Shakespeare since when he has not returned to the domestic level. He did, however, write an apparently domestic play, a comedy or as he called it a 'vulgar melodrama' in an idiom close to that of 'low music-hall and seaside picture postcards'. In this he revived a favourite character Alderman Charlie Butterthwaite (seen *after* his northern disgrace in the early play *The Waters of Babylon*). *The Workhouse Donkey* was commissioned by the Royal Court but produced at Chicester in 1963. It is a full picture of the local borough as a modern city state (and hence not domestic in scope) derived from Arden's observation of how councils still ran the boroughs of the West Riding in the grand nineteenth-century manner. Its subject is the business of good government dealt with through groups which cover all the social elements (except, curiously, the working class) attached to a story which centres, as in *Ironhand,* on two men, Butterthwaite and Feng. The 'story' is about the appointment of a new police chief called Feng and based on an episode at Nottingham. Various groups attempt to get him either on their side or dismissed. Feng is austere, fanatical (like Musgrave) but moral in outlook while Butterthwaite, if more likeable, is quite unscrupulous. Another energetic anachronism, in short. In the end both men lose their positions and Arden pointed out that if his personal preference was for Butterthwaite he does not want to convert anyone. There are many people who would have integrity at any price rather than corruption. But the only conclusion, as in *Ironhand,* is that the ones who survive are the compromisers, the little men.

Apart from a short play written for Peter Brook's Theatre of Cruelty and produced in 1964 (and in which Arden moved even nearer to the techniques of the Theatre of the Absurd than in *The Happy Haven*),[27] Arden reaches his clearest statement of the basic theme in his work with *Armstrong's Last Goodnight* (1964). This was first produced at the Glasgow

84

[27] Both these plays were written for particular circumstances.

Citizen's Theatre and then included in the repertory at Chichester in 1965. The Ballad of Johnny Armstrong was first envisaged as a film but the difficulties of film-making made Arden think of it in theatrical terms. After reading Conor Cruise O'Brien's *To Katanga and Back* he fused the desire to write a play about the Congo with this incident in Scottish history making O'Brien into Lindsay and Tshombe/Lumumba into Armstrong. Through these characters he shows the inadequacy of political expediency and yet deliberately avoids suggesting whether there is an alternative. As before, the characters fall into groups and the plot resolves itself into the familiar conflict between two principles: anarchy (the robber baron Armstrong) and order (the mature, but devious, Lindsay). Arden is on record as saying that Lindsay was wrong but the play does not support this. By showing Lindsay as a politician who is also an intellectual the dilemma is made all the more poignant. For, if Armstrong is out of date so, too, is Lindsay who is in advance of his times in seeking a rational solution to a crude political situation. In the end Lindsay, stung by the senseless wounding of McGlass, has to stoop to a trick below the high standards he has set himself and thus puts himself in the same situation as the Armstrong who betrayed Wamphrey at the beginning of the play. As in previous plays violence cannot be cured with non-violence and it is the little king who survives at the end.

Arden's next play *Left-Handed Liberty* was commissioned by the Corporation of the City of London to commemmorate the 750th anniversary of the sealing of Magna Carta and was staged at the Mermaid Theatre in 1965. As in his Nativity play Arden shifts the centre to the character usually thought to be the villain of the piece: King John. The conflict here lacks epic scope but it also lacks the linguistic difficulties encountered in *Armstrong's Last Goodnight* where Arden had deliberately invented his own version of Middle Scottish. The themes are liberty, the value of treaties and the irony of history. There is clarity of argument but also the sense that texture and individuality are lost beneath historical research. At the

85

suggestion of his wife, Margaretta D'Arcy, Arden streng-thened the character of the Papal Legate, Pandulph, to gain his usual opposition. Characteristically it is John, with his sense of humour and fondness for dandelions, who is the most appealing figure in a play which is not so much about the signing of Magna Carta as its failure. The play sustains the idea that 'an agreement on paper is worth nothing to nobody unless it has taken place in their minds as well'.

Since this play Arden has been completely, and apparently happily, involved in collaboration with his wife on a variety of projects all linked together by the general idea of community drama, as seen in the Kirbymoorside experiment. This was modelled on Wesker's work at Centre 42. Arden had of course followed Eliot and Fry in writing plays for performance in church and a play for the City of London, but he sees modern society as too large and too divided for a return to simple dramaturgy or, for that matter, simple democracy. He believes that community drama can only exist on a modest scale and for anything more he would have to use the professional theatre even though it is remote, irrelevant and unable to attract popular audiences. Mere literature will not do, although he welcomes the various ways in which a Wesker or a Littlewood tackle the disease. Until the political problem is solved, however, for Arden, there cannot be more than a modest progress with the artistic problem.

This sense of community drama and the use of the ballad form as the best medium for popular theatre combined with his relative unpopularity in the theatre leaves us with Arden as very much of a paradox. He has always been interested in experiment. He finds the idea that a play must be in either prose or verse limiting, although he himself has always held that the two should fulfil different rôles—prose being more useful to convey plot and character relationships while poetry offers a sort of comment on them. Even this is not rigid, for when characters speak under emotional pressures Arden finds that they lapse into verse or, where that is not appropriate, heightened prose. Arden has no sympathy with Eliot's attempts to make verse sound like a Noel Coward play nor with the infiltration of seriousness through such a device. He recognises, too, the dangers of easy sentimentality and predictability which generally accompany the portrayal of a hero. He aims at a social play written so that we can understand the person's problems without necessarily approving of the reactions to those problems; and cites the plays of Ibsen as an example.

If the central attitudes to naturalism have not been seriously challenged, Arden has added ambiguity to identification and illusion as a theatrical method. This is more than lip service to Brecht whom Arden places with dramatists like Euripides, Jonson and Ibsen as makers of a new idiom in the theatre. Since Brecht is closest in time he is probably the strongest influence. But Arden's dramatised attitudes are seldom absolutes—right or wrong—and his personal preferences never obtrude and are, as he continues to insist, irrelevant. These attitudes he tries to strengthen and make universal by the use of historical parallels which challenge an easy judgement and require, as it seems to him, that mixture of prose and verse he has worked at with such earnestness. As far as staging is concerned, Arden seems to prefer the open stage. Often described as a cold writer the proscenium arch is not a good context for him. He personally dislikes theatre in the round because he likes to relate his characters to an architectural point and he feels that theatre in the round has an amorphous quality.

It is the plays themselves that create a sense of strangeness—by incident and language—revealing a vision of the world which is essentially pessimistic, and shows life as senseless, absurd. But it is more than Brechtian devices that separates Arden from the theatre of the Absurd. His plays are acted out in the real world not dream or fantasy, and the vision is not subjective. Absurd Drama reaches social problems through individuals whereas for Arden individuals are representative, and however vigorous and lively as individuals, their failure or success is first and foremost a tragic comment    87 on the state of society. It is always the *social* predicament that faces us at the end of the play. Moreover, Arden needs plot to create the network of social inter-relationships from which this judgement proceeds, whereas the theatre of the Absurd must positively discourage plot to convey its sense of futility.

Arden appears to be sitting on a fence; and he pleases few. As he ruefully recognises, from *Live Like Pigs* onwards, his plays have resisted the propagandist and the poetic: not programmatic enough for the former and too documentary for the latter. The only absolute to emerge from Arden's work is that absolutes—even in good causes and for better reasons—only drive their followers into a simplistic attitude. This attitude overlooks the complex nature of human beings and society and finally serves only itself rather than human ends and desires. By *Armstrong's Last Goodnight* Arden can show sympathy towards both Lindsay and Armstrong but he curtails warmth towards either; the audience probably expects warmth. More than any other contemporary dramatist Arden seems to find the lack of forms and conventions frustrating. He continues to be worried by the fact that people find his plays incomprehensible. Theatre, after all, is a public art and a dramatist who is out of touch is failing to practise his art properly. On the other hand, if theatre is not to atrophy, a dramatist must get out of touch to step forward. Perhaps a lapse of time is needed to show whether Arden took one step too many and resolve the paradox of this twentieth-century poetic dramatist.

No such ambiguity faces us with Arnold Wesker, although it would be too easy to describe him as a writer of politically committed plays. Yet, as John Russell Taylor observes, more than any other writer—even Osborne—it is difficult to separate the plays from the man, to look at the plays as works of art rather than as sermons preached by Wesker's mouthpieces.[28] He is the dramatist with the clearest political point of view which is expressed in his plays but they are plays not exercises in ventriloquism. He is the dramatist who

[28] *Anger and After*, p. 147.

became director of Centre 42, who was noted for naturalistic detail and frequently attacked for failing to make those details convincing. He is also the dramatist who wants to write a play which begins: Once upon a time. . . . Wesker was born in a Jewish, East End, working-class family[29] and he is constantly and terribly aware of the quality of brutishness in the world and a feeling that something ought to be done about it. How can the underprivileged mass become more fully human? Wesker's answer is socialism, not because he believes that socialism would solve problems but because it ought at least to remove the economic problems and leave people to face up to the real battle: the problem of being alive. His solution in terms of socialism is that of an artist rather than a propagandist or moralist. And this is significant because it suggests the personal level of Wesker's commitment, that, as usual in British theatre, he is a dramatist who believes it is possible to write a private work and still feel part of a movement.

He began writing poetry at the age of twelve and, apart from a short period in the RAF has had a number of jobs—furniture maker, bookshop assistant, plumber's mate, kitchen porter and, after a short stay with his sister in Norfolk, trainee pastry cook. Much of which figures in his plays in one way or another. He went to Paris where he saved enough money to attend a short course at the new London School of Film Technique. His first play *The Kitchen* was sent to *The Observer* competition and was rejected as being too short but Wesker was confident enough to ask Lindsay Anderson to read a short story 'Pools'[30] which was submitted to the Committee of the British Film Institute of Experimental Film Fund who approved of it in principle but found their resources insufficient to film it. In any case seeing *Look Back in Anger* had convinced Wesker that important things could now be said in the theatre and he went on to write his first full-length

---

[29] His consciousness of being Jewish has nothing to do with religion. He describes it as a sense of family and lack of privilege.

[30] Published in *Six Sundays in January* (1971).

play *Chicken Soup With Barley. The Kitchen*[31] was a play aimed at television performance and turned down by every company to which it was sent. Wesker's concern about enjoying the possibilities of life and art leads him to be didactic frequently to the extent of allowing social concern to distract him from character and the art which he wants to do the job. Yet no one had put quite so much of the working class into his plays which have not been easy to stage even with the support of the Royal Court. *The Kitchen* was produced there by John Dexter in 1959 after *Chicken Soup With Barley* and *I'm Talking About Jerusalem* using no food, only mime, and handling the large cast with skill. At Dexter's request Wesker provided an interlude between the two working scenes. Many critics still feel that it is one of his best plays and that the image of the kitchen is an excellent metaphor for the working world. Wesker manages to balance argument and action here which is not something he does easily. Although he sees the theatre as something to watch he obviously has to use words to get his message across. He is impatient with two people who do nothing more than talk to each other on the stage and yet conversation is necessary to convey the points he wishes to make, and more so since he affects a surface naturalism. We can find in most plays embarrassing stage directions to explain the play!

His revision of *The Kitchen* took place after *I'm Talking About Jerusalem* and reflects disenchantment with modern life. In the bustle of the kitchen we see a knife fight, a miscarriage and finally a cook who runs amok and breaks the kitchen up—all of which illustrates what could happen when people are cooped up. But when the proprietor reflects at the end that a man works, eats and is paid his wages and what more could be done we have to sympathise. According to Wesker, in a stage direction, the play shows what more there is but if in fact the characters have no more to their lives than what the play shows then the proprietor can do no more. The much-

---

[31] Written in 1956, revised for stage production 1958, produced 1959 and filmed in 1961. The film has been released only in the USA.

praised naturalism has been attacked. That Wesker had worked in a kitchen might be no guarantee that the details were plausible. If the kitchen were like this life would be hell but in dramatic terms the image is melodramatic; or larger than life.[32] Trussler uses the adjective Jonsonian and points to the circular and ritual quality of the play (like *Waiting for Godot)*, concluding that the naturalism is modified.[33]

*Chicken Soup With Barley*, originally called *When the Wind Blows*, was started in 1957, produced at the Belgrade, Coventry, in 1958 and subsequently at the Royal Court. The Arts Council had decided to encourage repertory theatre up and down the country and had offered a special grant to mark the fiftieth anniversary of the opening of the Gaiety, Manchester, by Miss A. E. F. Horniman. The Court had offered its stage to any provincial rep with a promising new play but the standard had been so poor that the Court, wanting at least one new play out of the scheme, sent *Chicken Soup* to Coventry with a producer and the promise of a week's showing in London. Critical reception was respectful although hardly compatible with the showing of one of the first serious political plays in the post-war theatre. Even for Wesker the idea of a triology on the working class looking back as far as 1936 for the causes of present-day effects was bold and getting it produced no mean achievement. As John Russell Taylor has pointed out, the two levels on which the play works do not exactly help one another.[34] On the personal level we see recurrent patterns of personality behaviour (circular) and on the social level the loss of purpose in a working-class family with the arrival of the Welfare State (linear). Furthermore most of Wesker's ideas—social and political—seem to have been pushed into this first play as if the possibility of another two plays had not yet occurred. *Chicken Soup* covers the history of the Kahn family from 1936–56 and we see how disillusion sets in, and revolution turns sour—themes still

---

[32] John Russell Taylor, *Anger and After*, pp. 161–2.
[33] Simon Trussler, *The Plays of Arnold Wesker* (1971), chapter 1.
[34] *Anger and After*, pp. 149 ff.

being discussed in *The Friends* in 1971. On the personal level the family falls apart. The mother Sarah is strong, her husband weak and the children seem to follow their father and fall away. Dave and Ada are disillusioned to discover that they have nearly destroyed themselves by living for others when those others are neither heroic, deserving nor grateful. Ada, looking at her mother, sees her own personal life threatened and she and Dave withdraw to the Cotswolds to preserve their relationship and their ideals. Ronnie[35] loses his faith after Hungary, but Sarah, who grew up in revolutionary times, is able to keep hers:

> You think it doesn't hurt me—the news about Hungary? You think I know what happened and what didn't happen? Do any of us know? Who do I know who to trust now—God, who are our friends now? But all my life I've fought. With your father and the rotten system that couldn't help him. All my life I worked with a Party that meant glory and freedom and brotherhood. You want me to give it up now? You want me to move to Hendon and forget who I am? If the electrician who comes to mend my fuse blows it instead so I should stop having electricity? I should cut off my light? Socialism is my light, can you understand that? A way of life.[36]

Here Wesker touches on the dilemma that runs through his work: to preserve the ideal (against the facts and even when it is seen to be sterile) or to compromise and be effective but betray or at least get dirty by doing so. Ronnie's is perhaps a less subtle adjustment to Hungary than Sarah's and illustrates the difficulty of being a young socialist. Ronnie (like his generation?) has to have things black and white. Ironically Monty accuses Sarah of wanting things black and white but she sees that most things are grey and thus her response to the dilemma, although apparently simple, is in fact complex. Unfortunately we are not directed strongly in our attitude to Ronnie. His character is clearly weak, like his father's, and yet we have to concede the truth of his attack on Sarah. Her family and her ideal have collapsed, and complex as her

[35] Ronald is, of course, an anagram of Arnold.
[36] *Chicken Soup With Barley*, *New English Dramatists*, I, p. 236.

response may be in political terms in dramatic terms it comes down to a warning against apathy which at best can only be a personal response. The conclusion of the second play *Roots* is also highly personal. Wesker saw his trilogy as showing three aspects of Socialism: communist, personal and William Morris. *Roots,* started in 1958 and produced at the Belgrade in 1958 (before it transferred to the Court) is more directly about the brutalisation of man by mass culture. The most striking thing about the play is that Wesker keeps his antagonist, Ronnie, off-stage throughout the whole action. *Roots* was well received possibly because of the acting of Joan Plowright. George Devine seems to have had his doubts but Ashcroft showed it to Plowright who said she would play Beatie anywhere.[37] It is on the effectiveness of Beatie Bryant that the play stands or falls. She is shocked by Ronnie's defection into awareness and articulacy. She sees that his view of the country labourer is false, and that their condition is their own fault: they want the third-rate:

Oh yes, we turn on a radio or a TV set maybe, or we go to the pictures—if them's love stories or gangsters—but isn't that the easiest way out? Anything so long as we don't have to make an effort. Well, am I right? You know I'm right. Education ent only books and music—it's asking questions, all the time. There are millions of us, all over the country and no one, not one of us is asking questions, we're all taking the easiest way out. Everyone I ever worked with took the easiest way out. We don't fight for anything, we're so mentally lazy we might as well de dead. Blust, we are dead! And you know what Ronnie say sometimes? He say it serves us right! That's what he say—it's our own bloody fault.[38]

Like Sarah, Beatie achieves her own salvation—suggesting that indirectly Ronnie can do some good; which may be comforting to Wesker. The naturalism of the play has been called in question and clearly Norfolk is not honestly represented. The Bryants are exceptional just as the Kahns could hardly be seen as typical. The Kahns were first-

[37] But not in America; where critics felt the play lacked power.
[38] *Roots,* Penguin Plays (1959), pp. 75–6.

93

generation Jewish immigrants and it is possible that Wesker was trying, with the Bryants, to shape an English rural family by the standards of his own background. *Roots* also suggests a one-act play inflated to meet the demands of theatre: Act 2 adds little to Act 1 for example. The Bryants may be intended to be boring (though Ribalov insists that their fullness is a cover and their behaviour is paradoxical enough to suggest unrealised potential) but they tend to bore the audience. However, we must see them as Jonsonian; drawn to make an ideological point summed up in the bridge image, suggesting communication—of which making love is the crucial form—which in Beatie's parable becomes a ferry, emphasising difficulty.

With his third play *I'm Talking About Jerusalem* Wesker is no longer insisting on naturalism. In retrospect, perhaps it was only his critics and audiences who insisted on it anyway. Wesker accepts that realistic art is a contradiction in terms since art must be the recreation of experience not a copy of it. His title suggests parable. Again the details have been objected to but they are based on the experiences of Wesker's sister and her husband in their rebellion against mechanized man in urban squalor. If, however, we can produce a real Jewish couple withdrawing into the country they are still exceptional. Started in 1958 and produced at the Belgrade in 1960, *I'm Talking About Jerusalem* marks a return to the time span of *Chicken Soup*. Where *Roots* covered a short period (just over two weeks) *Jerusalem* covers about ten years and continues with the theme of disillusionment in the wider political sense expressed in the failure of a personal experiment. Dave and Ada go to Norfolk (and not, after all, the Cotswolds) to learn how difficult it is to build a new Jerusalem, which can be seen as an early version of the Golden City. The play ends in 1959 with the election of a Conservative Government and Ronnie's bitter cry about caring:

Cry? We must be bloody mad to cry, Mother.

(Sarah *goes off leaving* Ronnie *to linger and glance once more*

*around. Suddenly his eye catches a stone, which he picks up and throws high into the air. He watches, and waits till it falls. Then he cups his hands to his mouth and yells to the sky with bitterness and some venom—)*
RONNIE: We—must—be—bloody—mad—to—cry!

Many critics have objected to what they consider the weakness of this ending but in fact the whimper is exactly right.

Again the play shows problems of structure. Act 1 says very little and the play really begins in Act 2 with Dave's dismissal for stealing linoleum.[39] This theft seems more necessary to the plot than important for character or theme. Colonel Dewhurst reminds us of Colonel Redfern in *Look Back in Anger* but what Wesker stresses here is his non-human relationship with Dave. Although he is neither brutal nor unkind the dismissal is what counts. Like the officers in *Chips with Everything* actions count, not personality. Dave, like all Wesker Males, recognises defeat (a comparison with Jesus in the wilderness is left without comment) and Ada begins to resemble her mother. There is also doubt as to whether we should accept the naturalistic details or concentrate on the games played by characters at crucial moments. In an interview in 1961 Wesker confessed that he was moving towards a reduction of scenery and dialogue and becoming more conscious of style. He was also aware of the theatre as a place 'where one wants to *see* things happening'. This is particularly clear in the next play, *Chips with Everything,* begun in 1960 and produced at the Royal Court in 1962. Language is used in this play with an economy that is new to Wesker, and the play works through a sequence of actions—possibly in the fashionable Brechtian manner—which are not used as excuses for political discussions so much as replacements for discussion. The life and language of the RAF is stylised.[40] Also, as one critic suggested, the audience knew so clearly which side would win that it could give itself wholeheartedly to the perennial

[39] John Russell Taylor, *Anger and After*, p. 158.
[40] For a 'real' view of life in the RAF see Henry Livings's *Nil Carborundum.*

enjoyment of square-bashing and barrack-room life as in *Worm's Eye View*. This service life is offered, as in *The Kitchen,* as a microcosm of the social and economic system that says: Conform, or life will be made hell for you. But where cooks are free to go, servicemen are not. Moreover Wesker resorts to stock figures causing the immediate reaction that officers on the whole are not like that, nor are the men. The NAAFI rebellion is not really convincing, although it is useful to demonstrate the leadership of Pip. And it is Pip who represents the central problem of the play. He is an outsider who has thought about the working classes and decided that they must stop having chips; although, as John Russell Taylor tartly remarks, they appear to be replaced by *sautée* potatoes. Pip organises the rebellion substituting Burns for a pop song.[41] Pip organises a splendid raid on the coke yard but is finally broken at bayonet practise and emerges as faithful to a talent for leadership rather than to the masses who need leading. Here Pip as vehicle becomes Pip as character, and as character he is confusing. Presumably we are intended to admire the ideas not the character; and presumably we should not ask whether *sautée* potatoes are all that different from chips. Is Burns, a notorious trimmer to audience expectations, necessarily better than a pop song (*e.g.* the Beatles, Dylan or the Rolling Stones)? Beatie's introduction to culture in *Roots* was after all, modestly, Bizet's tuneful *L'Arlésienne* not Stockhausen. Could not, the doubt occurs, Wesker be playing the game he affects to despise. More probably he is reflecting honest anguish and doubt. Ronnie accuses Sarah of wanting everyone to have strawberries and cream whether they like them or not. It is not absolutely certain that chips with everything is wrong but Wesker would hope for a working class educated into a state where they *chose* chips with everything. His play, he said, was an attack on a state of mind not a show of hostility to any specific group or individual.

While in prison in 1961 for anti-nuclear activities Wesker assumed responsibility for Centre 42. His interest in this

[41] Wesker says Burns; in fact, an anonymous seventeenth-century dirge.

experiment begins in a talk delivered to the NUS Festival at Oxford in 1959 which was turned into a pamphlet, published in *Gemini* and finally sent to the secretary of every trade union in the country. A second pamphlet followed, pointing to the civic theatre in Coventry as an example of theatre subsidised by elected representatives of the people and citing Trade Union support for the theatre in the USA, Norway, Israel and Japan. Wesker suggested that shorter hours and more pay were only part of the work of a trade union. The Centre took its name from resolution 42 put down at the Trades Union Congress in the Isle of Man in 1960 by the Association of Cine and Television Technicians and calling for greater participation by the Trade Union movement in cultural activities. Wesker joined up with Doris Lessing and a group of writers who wanted to make contact with a larger and more popular audience. He had not intended to become Director but, while in prison, decided that his commitment must be total. Centre 42 was a limited company incorporated on 4 September 1961 and having charitable status since October of that year. It was based on the idea that just as society accepts responsibility for health, welfare and education it should support the Arts. Various Festivals were mounted and the project was welcomed by Jennie Lee; but Joan Littlewood had a point when she shrewdly observed that it took ten or eleven years to make a good playwright, which was Arnold's job and he should stick to it. Wesker wrote a libretto called *The Nottingham Captain* about the Luddite Riots of 1817 for the festival at Wellingborough in 1962 and apart from the television play *Menace* (1963)[42] devoted his time and energy to the Centre which finally took shape in 1966 at the Round House, Chalk Farm. Since the original intention had been to decentralise theatre, nourish the provinces and backwaters of England its final resting place in London is ironic if inevitable. In 1965 Wesker was still speaking of it as a great cry of joy at being alive and asking the architect René Allio to draw up

---

[42] Both *The Nottingham Captain* and *Menace* have been published in *Six Sundays in January* (1971).

designs for converting the Roundhouse. For some time now, however, it has been on hire to anyone who cared to pay for it. Wesker's own play *The Friends* was produced there, followed closely by *Oh! Calcutta!* Where Wesker fitted in to the new pattern was far from clear. His resignation as artistic director of both Roundhouse and Centre 42 was announced in 1971 and was followed by a rather bitter correspondence in the pages of the *Sunday Times*.

The original idea was that an enthusiasm to take part in the cultural life lay dormant in the majority of workers, an enthusiasm that only needed awakening. The location of the Centre in London and its transformation into another theatre for hire will ensure that this sleep continues. Wesker must certainly have been very disappointed, but, as Macey remarks in *The Friends,* one has to learn not to elevate personal disappointments to the level of a universal philosophy. Nevertheless some of this disappointment is surely present in the next full-length play, *Their Very Own and Golden City*.[43] Begun in 1963 and finished—after nine drafts—in 1965 it was performed in its final version at the Royal Court. Trussler is sensible when he points out that the parallels between Andrew Cobham and Wesker are 'critically irrelevant, often actually misleading and best ignored'.[44] Wesker is not declining into bad-tempered old age! *Golden City* carries on the theme of *Chips with Everything*: the relationship of the rebel and an Establishment that tries to win him over. Andrew is not corrupted as completely as Pip and he does get one city built although to do this he has to accept the help of a Conservative Minister when he gets no more than token support from the Trades Union movement.

Wesker had just visited Durham Cathedral and was left 'breathless' by it; his architect-hero takes that cathedral as his inspiration. The action of the play covers 65 years and if the city is not convincing the struggle is. It must be remembered

---

[43] The original title, *Congress,* had to be dropped when a popular edition of *The Kama Sutra* was published.

[44] Simon Trussler, *The Plays of Arnold Wesker* (1971), p. 111.

that the vision of the cities is itself only a patchwork in an unchanged society, and the rebels seem to know that the dream is impossible, rather than a dream to be fulfilled. This suggests a great deal about the state of the Left in contemporary England. Wesker also recognises that special skills contradict democracy: people turn to a poet for words, the Church for guidance and Andy for homes. To convey this complex Wesker uses a time span of 65 years, setting the present of the play in 1926 and moving forward to 1990 in a series of flash-forwards which, since they go not merely into the future of the play but the real future as well, can enjoy a less factual basis than the usual flashback technique. Wesker is emphasising here the failure of love, which is closely linked to political failure—a theme present in the trilogy—but the strands do not co-exist happily. The image of the cathedral, the main relationships (between Andrew, Jake and Kate) and the main theme (the new socialist society and the necessity of compromising with the Establishment) seem to pull in different directions which are almost contained in the final image where the young characters are accidentally locked in the cathedral and have to look for a door to let them out: the empty, unused building has now become a prison rather than a vision. The result is an ambitious play which tries to justify the ideas and demonstrate their practical failure simultaneously. And its chagrin seems to stem from the naive assumption that the TUC would ever implement the resolution whose number was conferred upon the Centre.

The theme of love, so crucial in political existence, is continued in Wesker's next play, begun in 1964 and finished in 1965 when it was produced at the Belgrade. Written after *Golden City* Wesker has described it as a year's sabbatical for Andrew and Kate from building their golden city, a year spent in a deserted house. Wesker himself insists that the play is not a break in his work and points to the continuing list of male–female relationships all of which are based on the rows between his parents; both of whom he loved. The immediate sequence is *Menace,* Kate/Andy and now Adam/Beatrice.

THREE AT THE COURT

Wesker believes it is an essential part of art to remind people that they are not alone but part of humanity and that even in private pain they share an experience common to us all. This is, for Wesker, as much a part of socialism as his more obviously political writing. And this is very much a play of private aches. Wesker has said that not all the great, good causes in the world can stop him crying for a passing love. *The Four Seasons* was generally regarded as a failure, but if so, it is an interesting failure. Although clearly a verbal play the most memorable things in it are wordless—for example the baking of strudel—and it is clearly a non-political play about love. Two characters pass through the four seasons of love. There is no explanation as to how they exist or where, though we do learn that each has had one marriage (and at least one infidelity). The characters are called Adam and Beatrice and however much Wesker insists that he wants the play simple and straightforward these names must carry with them certain connotations. With equal ingenuousness he points out that actors ought to learn how to bake strudel just as they learn how to fence. The theme is probably jealousy, particularly since all the relationships appear to have been destroyed by the jealousy of woman and critics divide as to whether the pattern saddens by its inevitability or bores. The most successful parts occur when A and B relate through action, yet there is a conspicuous absence of the physical presence of love. What Wesker seems to be aiming at is poetic drama and he too often relies on beautiful language—at times on bombast, at those times, that is, when the language does not grow out of heightened situations. He has not solved the problem of doing away with words and still getting over his ideas. Indeed he seems suddenly to return to the use of words and a need for poetry. This need is confirmed in his last play *The Friends* a combination of the themes, moods and manners of both *Golden City* and *The Four Seasons*. Begun in 1966, rewritten in 1968, produced in Stockholm in 1969 and finally at the Roundhouse in 1970 it continues, as its title implies, to explore the political situation through personal relationships.

Possibly the difficulty in getting a production stemmed from Wesker's desire to produce the play himself. Both Terry Hands and William Gaskill offered to produce it in 1968. The insistence may also help to account for the behaviour of the actors during this production. Certainly they seem to have fought Wesker every inch of the way resenting, perhaps, his firm view of their function:

The artist is the human being chosen, by the order of things, to articulate for the rest of us our understanding, and both despair and joy, at the human condition. The actor in the theatre is the interpreter ... however great ... his rôle is an ephemeral and secondary one.

The critics, too, were strangely unfavourable and Wesker has replied, in some detail, to their charges very convincingly.[45] *The Friends* reminds us of Osborne's *Hotel in Amsterdam* as a play about a group of people facing a crisis although in Osborne's play the friends are united by an off-stage monster and here the friends are disunited by the removal of Esther's strong personality. Meditative and elegiac, the play discusses why revolution turned sour, and the strength offered by the dead. It is in fact an anthology of Wesker's themes, doubts, preoccupations and faith. What is important is that Wesker was intensely aware of the internal rhythms of speech in his dialogue. He said he wanted to write it like a symphony but chamber music would be nearer the truth, and it was hardly appropriate for the Roundhouse.[46] The play is a Shavian discussion brought about by the death, from leukemia, of one of the friends at an early age. As the play opens Esther is working on a collage of old family photographs helped by her lover Roland while her brother Manfred reads about science and their partner Crispin constructs a new toy. Esther asks the first question of the play:

Who do I hate, who do I love; what do I value, what do I despise; what pleases, what offends me?

[45] For a full account, and casebook on rehearsals, see *Theatre Quarterly* (1971), no. 2.
[46] Wesker makes considerable use of contrapuntal dialogue and litany.

Two more of the friends arrive, Tessa and Simone, with their manager Macey who announces that their boutiques have gone bankrupt through their indifference. Of the friends Simone is an outsider; her class credentials are not acceptable to the other five who have all come from the same northern working-class background. It is Simone, therefore, who challenges their attitudes and their beliefs. For it turns out that the friends are not really bankrupt; they have large private accounts of which they are ashamed, the bills will be paid and the staff given adequate notice.[47] Macey begins the argument, for Simone at this stage is trying to belong. When Manfred refers to McLuhan and the idea of civilisation being crippled by the printed word, Macey points out that two-thirds of the world are still illiterate and even those who can read seldom do so, so how can we be crippled by something we have never engaged in? Words, for Macey, are gates not dams, magnificent, precious, lovely. Macey is prepared to concede that the younger generation have a 'sweet-natured grubbiness' but he also points out that they are susceptible to loud-mouthed culture and political fraudulence. The friends themselves indulge in extreme gestures—little gestures for big angers. What can we make of Crispin's cruelty to Simone but that they treat her desire to communicate as wrong and ugly?

By the second Act Esther is dead and Simone drunk. Unlike the others Simone is not afraid of death. She finds that she talks but the friends won't listen, she offers but the friends won't take, she is full but not needed; used, but not needed. She is now drunk enough to tell Roland that Yoga will not help him come to terms with death. The friends are in a muddle, they are sterile and all they have created is the habit of discontent. They were young terrorists who never thought they might grow old and die. Macey admits that he has failed. He does not love the woman he married fifteen years ago but he practises discipline:

It was to avoid building up those little heavyweight philosophies

[47] When one has become unemployed through the whim of the employer, what *is* adequate compensation or notice?

about man and the world out of my own personal disappointments; to avoid confusing self-hatred with hatred of all men; to face the fact that though I had failed others hadn't.

Simone is attacked for her class but as she points out if her father was a company director rather than a railwayman Tessa herself is now a company director. Simone's terror at speaking out at the friends makes her inaudible and she has to speak through Macey (an echo of Beatie's situation?). But Simone does not mind being fed words by Crispin. She appeals for order, a liberating order, not sameness or conformity. Tessa replies that this is irrelevant. Esther is dead and the room into which they have put so much of themselves (unlike their ruthlessly twentieth-century interiors) is now hateful. But Simone insists that a room that is full of memory, the past, signs of human activity, should be loved and challenges the slogan: Property is theft. Wanting an eighteenth-century chair is, after all, responding to beauty. Crispin remarks that she has returned to her class, and Tessa uses the same phrase as Mrs. Bryant in *Roots*: the apple doesn't fall far from the tree. This moves the argument into the whole business of class. If only working-class values were beautiful what, Macey asks, were they complaining about in the first place. To which Simone adds:

you can't come to people and claim that the things you like are superior to the things they like because that will then place you in a class you are asking them to overthrow.

Simone points out that she has only spoken about the working man in terms of what he could be and felt anger that he is abused for what he is. She will not dress down to share his cause nor pretend to have his tastes and values. Esther was a revolutionary not a rebel because she was not obsessed with responsibility to the twentieth century but rather to twenty centuries of sensibility. It is with her dead body that the friends come together at the end of the play overcoming their personal fears, pretensions and disappointments. The friends were opting out, concluding that they must love one another or die

103

and this does make them sound like another Bloomsbury group. If such relationships are felt as standing for something wider, the general tenor is one of defeat, a generation who have conquered the world only to discover that their standards are now those of a world they deplored. So Wesker has moved from the Kahns (unusual in the sense that everything they do is an act of commitment or betrayal and for whom human feelings are part of the ideological crisis) to the Bryants who have neither passion nor ideology and whose existence is death. From the beginning the insistence is on caring, feeling, loving. Until Beatie is abandoned she does not feel and cannot, therefore, think and ask her own questions. She will have no effect on society but she echoes Sarah and later Ronnie: caring is foolish but.... In *Chips* Wesker muddled the personal and the political, and then withdrew to Centre 42 from which came *Golden City* a more than usually autobiographical play. But where previously it was personal weakness or dishonesty which had threatened ideals and the vision, now it is the vision itself which undermines and *isolates*. This is truly pessimistic. Wesker is remarkable for a stubborn honesty. He constantly recognises that people are only people. For him optimism in art is not happy endings but the recognition of truths whether sad or not. He has said that if fame is important he will not compromise himself for it. Throughout his plays he has shown what ought to be, while admitting that what ought to be, seldom is. He has also recognised that what is, might democratically have its own validity. This ambivalence, with his insistence on personal feeling, with its wider implications of social political issues brings him, in spite of the overtly political and frequently didactic nature of his work, very close to Osborne and Arden.[48]

[48] Wesker's latest play, *The Old Ones,* announced for production at the National Theatre, opened at the Royal Court in August 1972.

# CHAPTER SIX

# The Theatre of the Absurd

If the Royal Court is conventionally associated with committed drama the Arts Theatre, because of its early productions of Ionesco, Beckett and Genet gained the reputation of being the home of the theatre of the Absurd. This label, as we have seen, was applied by Martin Esslin to a certain group of dramatists.[1] The suggestion that European man was dominated by an 'essential Absurdity' was first made in 1925 by Malraux and later expanded by Camus in his essays on *The Myth of Sisyphus* (1942) and Sartre. Both Camus and Sartre were, in a sense, committed dramatists who used old-fashioned methods in their plays. Their successors, Ionesco and his contemporaries, sought a more appropriate form, rejecting language, plot, character and meaningfulness—thus entering a dramatic cul-de-sac whose essential limitations would finally triumph over the desire to write plays. John Russell Taylor defines this theatre neatly in *The Penguin Dictionary of Theatre* (1966) as a group of dramatists who share attitudes to man's predicament, an awareness of the purposelessness of everything that we do, producing a metaphysical anguish which is the central theme

[1] The connection had been made, briefly, in an essay by Walter Stein called 'Tragedy and the Absurd', *The Dublin Review*, no. 482, winter 1959–60, pp. 363–82.

of such writers. He concludes that the movement seemed to have spent its force by 1962 although its liberating effects continue in the theatre. Charles Marowitz, also writing in 1966, agrees on the date of 1962 but describes Absurd Theatre as a 'brief vogue' and defines 'absurd' as a synonym for potty and screwed-up. The brevity of its life in the difficult world of theatre should not diminish its importance nor alarm us. It is largely compensated for by the impact of its two distinguished dramatists who cannot influence but do invite imitation. If Absurd Theatre passed quickly, it raged like Artaud's plague and was seized upon as the final stage in the 'theatre of great insurgent dramatists'—Ibsen, Strindberg, Shaw, Brecht, Genet and Beckett—where myths of rebellion were enacted before a dwindling audience, where the word 'hero' had lost its meaning and the central character—usually a tramp, old man, prisoner or criminal—lives out a nightmare and becomes the most potent Icon of the modern stage![2]

Adamov, Beckett, Genet and Ionesco work in French by accident and presented their plays in Paris because it was convenient rather than belonging to a school of dramatists. The place, Paris, is not surprising for they wrote at a time when the theatre in France had, over the years, recaptured the prestige it had enjoyed in the time of Louis XIV. And, if it revealed no Molière or Racine, it produced many brilliant directors and actors and a great deal of enthusiasm and energy. Indeed most, if not all, of the tricks beloved of English producers' theatre in the 1960s had been used in the years 1918–39 by producers like Copeau, Dullin, Jouvet, Baty, Artaud, Barrault and Rocher.[3]

Certain events seem to presage Absurd Theatre and one of the first was when Fermin Gemier said a certain word on the stage of the Théâtre Nouveau on 10 December 1896. Alfred Jarry appropriated the *mot de Cambronne* by adding a single

---

[2] The baroque prose is culled from Robert Brustein, *The Theatre of Revolt* (1965), chapter 1.

[3] Or earlier: see J. A. Henderson, *The First Avant-Garde: 1887–1894* (1971).

letter[4] but he made little impression on the theatrical scene until interest was awakened by two volumes (one edited by Malraux) and, more importantly, the book by Charles Chasse which challenged Jarry's authorship of *Ubu*. By 1924 the Surrealists had named him their patron saint, three biographies had appeared and Gide was to use him in the banquet scene in *Les Faux-Monnayeurs* (1925). In 1927 Artaud and Vitrac named their theatre after him and in 1949 the College d'Pataphysique was founded to spread the new science. Jarry's rebellion was applied by Artaud to theatrical matters and drama was seen as a means of expressing rebellion against the human condition—that helplessness and despair that we feel living, as we do, in a universe that is implacably hostile. This despair was formulated in non-dramatic terms by Malraux, Camus and Sartre. In the theatre Ubu is the prototype of elemental man, stripped of his inhibitions, of the veneer of culture and civilization. Artaud sought to arouse just such an Instinctive Man, dispensing with speech, which is literary not theatrical, and creating a theatre which matched the universe and must, therefore, be cruel, ecstatic and spontaneous.

But it must be remembered that Artaud was—apart from the years 1927–9 when he ran his theatre with Vitrac—a theorist. We should also remember that the Absurd still preserved its comic innocence and provoked laughter—qualities that begin to fade. *Ubu Roi,* the paintings of Rousseau, the writings of Apollinaire and Satie still have this innocence but by 1918 art has become more calculating.

The year 1917 saw two significant events: *Parade* and *Les Mamelles de Tiresias.* Diaghilev's Russian Ballet visited Paris for the first time in 1909 (the year of Marinetti's first Futurist Manifesto) and *Parade* was one of the first modern ballets to arise from that intimate collaboration of writer, musician, painter and dancer. In spite of being dogged with ill luck and not much seen, *Parade* announced the New Spirit and used the talents of Diaghilev, Cocteau, Satie, Massine and Picasso. It

[4] Ubu says 'Merdre' not 'Merde'.

made Satie's reputation and led to the formation of Les Six although, again, that group worked together on only one work *Les Mariés de la Tour Eiffel* where Cocteau sought to make poetry of the theatre.[5] Satie's last work *Relâche* (1924) sums up the movement. His music was intended as a background for a film by René Clair and was in fact used for the Picabia-Satie ballet *Entracte*. It anticipated all the nightmares of surrealism and had as its climax a hearse drawn round the Eiffel Tower by a camel. The occasion, November 1924, was scandalous. Relâche means no performance and the first-night audience found the title accurate. A week later the ballet was performed: the dancers smoked incessantly, a fireman wandered through the set (made out of rows of metal disks), costume changes took place on stage and film was incorporated for the first time into a ballet. The Gesamtkunstwerk celebrated so religiously at Bayreuth had become a farce in Paris where, as Cocteau put it, to be taken seriously was the beginning of death.

*Parade* was followed by *Les Mamelles de Tiresias*. Apollinaire's desire to establish the date of composition as 1903 may well stem from the fact that *Parade* was performed first. This play-opera-ballet, too, caused uproar at its performance and showed a deliberate cultivation of frivolity although Apollinaire defended the play as an appeal for an increased birth rate—on which, in those days, the prosperity of a nation depended. Probably Cocteau was more accurate when he claimed that the experiment liberated through anarchy. Cocteau himself believed that drama should consist of the commonplace transfigured by poetry and produced *Les Mariés de la Tour Eiffel* with the Swedish Ballet at the Théâtre des Champs-Elysées in 1921. He took as his subject a wedding party at the photographers on the Eiffel Tower on the fourteenth of July.

On the whole such drama stemmed from breaking forms

[5] Cocteau's slogan is, of course, anti-literary. It aims at the fullest exploitation of theatrical resources, using dialogue as only one element of the end-product: performance. But, by 1943, he had changed his mind and wrote *Renaud et Armide*, a Racinian tragedy in classical alexandrines—to save the French theatre once more!

rather than making them and ultimately came to mean, as Eric Bentley puts it, the 'merely brilliant, the technically clever, the assiduously heterodox, the forever incomplete'.[6] Nevertheless, although at times such events appear to anticipate Happenings rather than Absurd Theatre, they were attempts to revitalise a theatre that had been dominated for many years by realism, naturalism and the thesis play, to get back to primitive sources and discover new techniques. The fourth (and last) production of the Jarry Company under Artaud and Vitrac was Vitrac's *Victor ou les enfants au pouvoir* (1928) and it epitomises the seriousness and the dangers of such intentions and methods. The play shows a sustained revolt against bourgeois morality. Three or four hours before his ninth birthday Victor, a model child, suddenly sees how ugly and hypocritical the world around him is and spends the rest of the play smashing everything he can until his death at the end of the play. Vitrac follows Artaud's dicta on language, often ignoring sense to concentrate on sound alone, but the play is mainly remembered for the entrance of a stunningly beautiful lady who breaks wind (in Anouilh's production of 1962, to Beethoven).

Artaud is spokesman for this theatre and prophet of the more recent producers' theatre. Artaud's acting career began in the 1920s with Lugné-Poe but he found Dullin more to his taste, particularly the improvisation and the use of Japanese-style acting. Artaud fought Sire Le Mot. He reminded us that theatre makes use of everything—gestures, sounds, words, screams, lights, darkness and that to limit drama to one medium, language, is its ruin. Artaud had been entranced by the Balinese Theatre he saw at the Colonial Exhibition of 1931 (though he had already seen a group of Cambodian dancers in Marseilles in 1922) and he sought to recreate this effect, to restore the theatre to its original destiny by eliminating the author in favour of the director. But the director was to become a manager of magic, of sacred ceremonies. The stage was a space to be filled, where something happens. Literary

---

[6] *The Playwright as Thinker* (1955), pp. 194-5.

masterpieces were rejected because they were fixed in forms no longer relevant to the needs of the time. Artaud compares theatre to the plague which induces delirium and is contagious: the true theatre should disturb the senses' repose and incite a kind of virtual revolt. Artaud was careful to insist, however, that the full effect could only be achieved if the revolt was virtual. In responding to the contemporary situation the new theatre would have to be a Theatre of Cruelty which reminds us that we live in a Universe where the sky can fall on our heads at any time. His frequent attempts to define cruelty suggest that he recognised how irresistible the obvious definition would be; particularly as his own examples are both cruel and violent. He wished to teach actors to scream when now they could only talk, and the audience was to be placed in the centre and surrounded by lights, colours and actions which would induce a trance. The sole production in this theatre was Artaud's version of *The Cenci* which looks forward to such events as the Peter Weiss-Peter Brook *Marat-Sade* of 1964.

We should not be surprised that, until recently, dramatists have continued to write plays criticising language but not excluding it. As Sartre pointed out, if words are useless they are the only tools that we have. Artaud should be seen as a special case. It is possible that his failure as a poet led him to seek a physical theatre where he could reject language. He saw theatre as the double of life, not imitating reality but *being* it, and the pure kind of theatre he wanted existed only once, since Artaud had to be subject, actor and spectator. It is difficult to find out what actually happened during the two hours when Artaud gave a lecture about himself at the Vieux Colombier in 1947. Gide, in a letter to Henry Thomas found it 'atrocious, painful, almost sublime at times, but revolting too and almost unbearable'. Artaud was beguiled by the Balinese theatre but overlooked the fact that it had its roots in Balinese village life and tradition and could not easily be grafted on to Western life.[7] His absolute claims for the *mise en scène* are too vague.

[7] Cf. Gide's reaction after attending a rehearsal of Nō drama by Copeau. He noted in his journal: A play without any relation to our traditions, our customs, our beliefs. . . .

What happens in the theatre is not that a space is filled with things and sounds but that persons behave in their places, actors act on us. Possibly he was misled by his experience of the cinema where the man who makes the montage is paramount since what we experience is a flow of pictures. The theatre, however, requires the traditional collaboration of three: dramatist, director and actor.

Artaud's influence can be seen immediately in the career of a producer like Barrault (although Artaud would not enter into collaboration with Barrault). After four years with Dullin Barrault emerged with *Autour d'une Mère* (1935) a spectacle based on Faulkner's *As I Lay Dying* which concentrated on the power of physical gesture. Artaud approved of it because it was 'organised in relation to the stage and *on* the stage and had no existence apart from the stage'. It was the Renaud-Barrault Company which, in 1959, worked on Ionesco's *Rhinoceros*.

In our present-day world many claim that the unstable world of dream and 'game' appears more valid than other forms of illusion. The drama that does not reflect but merely presents will be less literary than other theatrical forms for the language of dreams is often wordless and uses objects. Such a theatre is, however, parasitic: it needs another theatre to protest against. Moreover it can be seriously objected to. Moravia has called it the theatre of chatting—using Heidegger's word Gerede. A way of life passed in idle talk rather than in communication. He admits that it works in Chekhov, but suggests that in *Waiting for Godot* you can feel you are being profound for the price of a theatre ticket. Ironically, Moravia believed that the theatre of dialectics would restore words to their privileged position whereas the opposite has proved to be true. It is dialectical theatre, theatre with a message, that has reduced language to headline and slogan. Absurd Drama was not an answer to the ills of modern life nor the only description of those ills but it was an adventure; and Beckett's Godot was as much a landmark as a tombstone.

Properly, it was Ionesco's *The Bald Prima-Donna* (1950)          111 which ushered in the decade and Absurd Drama but it was *En Attendant Godot* (1953) which broadcast the methods and themes and showed that, in spite of the fundamental pessimism, success was possible. It was Ionesco, properly speaking, who made us aware of the 'mixed' play, who thought he had written a tragedy and found audiences laughing at it. Henceforth he demonstrated the arbitrary nature of our critical labels calling his plays anti-plays and by suggesting that the comic is tragic while the tragedy of man is derisory. The definition of comedy and tragedy has never been easy, and certainly in our time tragedy seems difficult if not impossible. Contemporary dramatists, lacking conventions and forms on which they and their audiences could agree, have taken the liberty and blurred the conventional ideas more than ever before. J. L. Stylan, in his study of what he has called 'Dark Comedy', presents us with a long list of distinguished antecedents—including Shakespeare and Molière—but reminds us that the mixture of laughter and pain must be more acute in our time because it operates within no accepted nor acceptable convention. The audience at a dark comedy nowadays is tricked into laughing, muddled in its response, compelled to reassess values it had thought solved and then abandoned without the benefit of a couplet which can restore order. The solution is to call the play a tragicomedy!

For most of us, Beckett's tragicomedy *Waiting for Godot* is Beckett and it comes as a surprise to find that critics treat the plays almost as a footnote to his major work, the novels. Samuel Beckett, appropriately born on Good Friday, 13 April 1906 and rightly called a 'polyglot punster', has explored the themes and forms of discontinuity in all his work. In *Whoroscope* (1930) he attacked the Descartes of progress and achievement just as he attacks the Voltaire of progress and achievement in *En Attendant Godot* (1953). Man's stature is not increasing it is diminishing and his work reflects this as it proceeds. All Beckett's people are men and women who have dwindled as a result of what they did or what was done to them and all that is left for them to do is play. In this sense the plays are all epilogues.

Beckett's first hero is Belacqua, who takes his name from the lutemaker of Florence and friend of Dante found on that lonely plain where souls wait, lost to this world but not yet ready to enter purgatory: a space of blankness and indolence and indecision. *More Pricks Than Kicks* (1934) traces the career of this hero through three marriages to his accidental death and solemn burial. This is a continuation of the central experience of the early poems: a deep painful consciousness of loss, absence and exile. In the story 'Assumption' Beckett suggests that as a lover loses something of himself when he makes love so, too, an artist dies a little whenever he writes or speaks. All Beckett's heroes, therefore, subscribe to the basic maxim taught by the Sicilian rhetorician that nothing has any real existence and if anything real did exist it could not be known and if anything were to exist and be known it could not be expressed. And yet all Beckett's heroes are concerned with knowing and expressing and use the most careful, rational language to do so. Beckett himself turned to writing in French about 1937 to check his own fondness for verbal and imaginative play and the temptations of a language that was too rich and varied. He sought for the economy which has long been the French ideal. Like Joyce, Beckett believed in the need for exile and isolation but he did not share Joyce's faith in language. Joyce believed in words; all you had to do was rearrange them and they would express what you want, but Beckett could not believe this, feeling that painting and music stood a better chance of expressing the inexpressible. Yet Beckett, at least initially, continued to use language (bilingually) with such success that his plays have been rightly called poetic dramas. For want of a better tool words have been turned into instruments for naming the unnameable.

In his essays on the painter Bram Van Velde, dated 1948 and 1949, Beckett made one of his rare utterances on art—rare because, unlike Ionesco, Beckett has consistently refused to explain or talk about his work. In these essays he suggests that his task is to create a new form of art: the          113 expression that there is nothing to express, nothing with which to express, no power to express, no desire to express, *together with the obligation to express*. The two enemies of art, as he sees it, are social existence, which is blindness opposed to the solitary nature of art that strives to see, and the intellect, which includes language, which opposes the unique and elemental quality of art by trying to 'raisonner sur l'unique' and 'mettre de l'ordre dans l'élémentaire'. The artist, for Beckett, is caught in the paradox of needing privation, needing fulfilment and needing to make and this third term mediates between the two opposites: the thing made testifies to the need for fulfilment (it exists) but by its lack of motive demonstrates the need for privation. Art, therefore, in itself futile and meaningless, can point to man's deepest needs. This paradox is illustrated by his heroes who reject learning and philosophy and yet are perpetually concerned with the basic philosophic questions: the nature of Self, the World and God. And since Beckett has divorced his heroes from social situations he can force them to a moment of decision which is totally uncluttered.

The one undeniable influence on Beckett is, of course, Proust, beginning with the publication of the essay in 1931 where Beckett faces the themes of both writers: the tyrannies of time and language. But Beckett—and it is curious in an Absurdist writer—insists on answering the questions through rationality. When Arsene in *Watt* is handing over the job of looking after Mr. Knott he gives the hero the benefit of his experience and the Change in a paragraph that runs for some 28 pages. The Change is an awareness that man is imprisoned in his rationality involving him in the logical contradiction expressed by Beckett in a joke shifted from Ireland to Wales: Do not come down the ladder, Ifor, I haf taken it away. What Beckett points out is that if you say that meaning does not exist you use terms which imply that it does. The ladder of affirmation cannot exist and yet one has to climb down it. Beckett's solution is in mathematics. Even his blind and dumb heroes can usually count. In mathematics numbers exist because they function in relation to others, but we have no way of proving their existence or even of defining them precisely. As Hugh Kenner points out, somewhere between $1\frac{169}{408}$ and $1\frac{70}{169}$ we may expect $\sqrt{2}$ to exist, though we should not expect to find it; although impossible, we can name it and know it is there.[8]

Given that the novels search for the instantaneous present and that the spoken word approximates this more than the written a move into the theatre seems natural, though putting his heroes into a play means that they will have physical presences and since his work is about immobility, this, in itself, represents a challenge. Beckett, working for the Resistance in Paris during 1942, had to be smuggled out of the city to Vichy, then Avignon and, finally, to Roussillon, near Apt, where he worked and wrote *Watt*. At that time permission to glean the potato fields was a great privilege and much of the starved quality of *Godot* may very well be more naturalistic than is realised. Also the use of art to fill the vacant hours. Proust's solution had been art, too, but art as a remedy for the disease of life. But, whereas Proust sought through art to recover a lost past in sensuous totality, Beckett is the poet of absence and want, of an old man whose words and silences force on us an awareness of the nothingness to which we must all come. Around 1944-5 a host of new ideas came to Beckett which he tried to work into a new novel called *Mercier and Camier*: the story of the journey of these two men was used in the trilogy but the idea of the two halves of a man, suggested by the reference to them as a 'pseudo-couple', took on independent life in the play *En Attendant Godot* which also incorporated the cross-talk begun there. But whereas Mercier and Camier part company at the end the two tramps stay together.

Beckett's first play *Eleutheria* (1947) has been neither published nor performed; *En Attendant Godot*—a tragicomedy in two acts was written 1948–9 and produced in 1953 (at the Arts Theatre in 1955): it is a play in which nothing happens twice. The setting is a country road with a

[8] Hugh Kenner, *Samuel Beckett: A Critical Study* (1961), p. 107.

single tree; the time evening. Two tramps, Vladimir and Estragon (Didi and Gogo) are waiting for Godot, or night to fall; presently two men appear. Pozzo the master is leading his servant Lucky and, to amuse them, Lucky is made to dance and then to 'think'—a long incoherent tirade which is forcibly ended and Pozzo and Lucky leave for the market where Pozzo hopes to get a good price for Lucky. A boy arrives to say that Mr. Godot will not keep his appointment that night and Didi and Gogo, after some conversation and a discussion about hanging themselves, decide to move. They remain motionless as the curtain falls. In Beckett there should be a proscenium arch and a curtain. The second Act repeats this basic pattern with slight differences. The tree has acquired four (or five?) leaves and when Pozzo and Lucky reappear Pozzo is blind and Lucky, apparently, dumb. The boy who appears as Godot's messenger is the same boy and he delivers the same message but he insists that it is his first visit. Again Didi and Gogo talk, discuss hanging themselves, decide to go and remain motionless as the curtain falls.

More than any other Absurd dramatist Beckett dispenses with plot. As Martin Esslin remarks, *En Attendant Godot* does not tell a story it explores a static situation where even the differences between Acts 1 and 2 only serve to emphasise the essential sameness.[9] But the play is rich in echoes.[10] The set, for example, harks back to Copeau's production of *L'Échange* by Paul Claudel just before World War I where a back-cloth of sky and a single tree focused attention on the movement and gestures of the actors. The dialogue is strong reminiscent of music-hall patter and mine:

> *Long silence.*

Vladimir:
Estragon: *(turning simultaneously)*: Do you—
Vladimir: Oh, pardon!

---

[9] *The Theatre of the Absurd* (revised 1968), pp. 45 ff.
[10] Thus Act 2 opens with a round poem which is a variant of one used by Brecht as a practice exercise: see *Schriften zum Theater,* p. 208, quoted Wulbern, *op. cit.,* p. 58.

Estragon: Carry on.
Vladimir: No no, after you.
Estragon: No no, you first.
Vladimir: I interrupted you.
Estragon: I interrupted you.
Estragon: On the contrary.
*They glare at each other angrily.*
Vladimir: Ceremonious ape!
Estragon: Punctilious pig!
Vladimir *(Violently)*: Finish your phrase, I tell you!
Estragon: Finish your own!
*Silence. They draw closer, halt.*
Vladimir: Moron!
Estragon: That's the idea, let's abuse each other.
*They turn, increase the space between them, turn again and face each other.*
Vladimir: Moron!
Estragon: Vermin!
Vladimir: Abortion!
Estragon: Morpion!
Vladimir: Sewer-rat!
Estragon: Curate!
Vladimir: Cretin!
Estragon *(with finality)*: CRRITIC!
Vladimir: Oh!
*He wilts, vanquished, and turns away.*
Estragon: Now let's make it up.
Vladimir: Gogo!
Estragon: Didi!
Vladimir: Your hand!
Estragon: Take it!
Vladimir: Come to my arms!
Estragon: Your arms?
Vladimir: My breast!
Estragon: Off we go!
*They embrace. They separate. Silence.*
Vladimir: How time flies when one has fun!
*Silence.*
Estragon: What do we do now.
Vladimir: While waiting?

117

Estragon: While waiting.[11]

Finally the title in English introduces implications which cannot be dismissed as accidental. Knowing Beckett's care for language he must have allowed the word Godot to stand knowing what it would stand for. In French Godot is a nonsense word but in English it suggests God-ot (little God) as well as referring to Godeau, the racing cyclist, recalling Simone Weil's *Attente de Dieu* and possibly Balzac's comedy *Le Faiseur*. This play is generally known as *Mercadet* after the speculator who explains all his financial difficulties by blaming his former partner Godeau. Godeau absconded with their joint capital but returns at the end of the play with a huge fortune to save the situation. The play obviously has religious content. The story of the two thieves appears early in the discussion:

> Vladimir: And yet ... (*pause*) ... how is it—this is not boring you I hope—how is it that of the four evangelists only one speaks of a thief being saved? The four of them were there—or thereabouts, and only one speaks of a thief being saved. (*Pause.*) Come on, Gogo, return the ball, can't you, once in a way?
> Estragon (*with exaggerated enthusiasm*): I find this most extraordinarily interesting.[12]

Apart from the problem of reliability of sources, the implication of the story would seem to be that these two malefactors happened to be present at a unique moment in time. One of them happened to make a hostile remark and was damned while the other happened to contradict him and was saved. Chance remarks damn or save; assuming that anything really happened or that there is anything to happen.[13] Godot, as reported by the boy or boys, if he exists, is just as unpredictable. Hope of salvation, then, may certainly be a subject of the play but in accepting that hope ourselves we may be guilty not of Faith but of what Sartre would call Bad Faith: a refusal, with the tramps, to face up to reality. The

[11] *Waiting for Godot* (Faber), pp. 75–6.
[12] *Ibid.,* p. 12.
[13] Martin Esslin, *The Theatre of the Absurd* (1968), p. 53.

reality being that there is no Godot and that by believing that there is we can avoid responsibility for our lives and actions by simply waiting. The act of waiting can, of course, be a symbol of faith, witness T. S. Eliot's 'Burnt Norton' and 'East Coker' but in Beckett it looks suspiciously like a reflection of the efforts of Sisyphus. Waiting may be heroic (at least it implies that a personality has been maintained for a period of time which in an Absurd universe is heroic) or it may be a linguistic delusion. Like the play, the argument would be circular: we are, therefore we wait, therefore we wait for something, therefore we are. Godot may be nothing more than our name for a life which misinterprets itself and part of the language that aids and abets the falsification. Merely because Beckett's characters are, they wait and commentators have borrowed Heidegger's term 'Geworfenheit' to describe this. But Beckett's heroes, thrown into life as they have been (see *Acte Sans Paroles I*) do not see this as a beginning of decision or action, rather they champion the theory that even in a meaningless situation life must have meaning. Beckett portrays not nihilism but the inability to be nihilist which frustrates man. Whether Bad Faith or not, *En Attendant Godot* contains warmth and comedy as well as a possibility of hope and has been his most popular play. It is also his longest.

After a silence of about six years Beckett wrote *Fin de Partie* (1956) which no French producer would touch and it was, therefore, given its premiere at the Royal Court in a double bill with *Acte Sans Paroles I*. The Royal Court has produced a great deal of Beckett after the first production of *Godot* at the Arts. In *En Attendant Godot* two characters pass the time waiting on the open road by playing games; in *Fin de Partie* the final game has been played in a closed room and where, previously, we wondered whether Godot would come, here we wonder whether Clov will leave.

In a bare interior Hamm is seated, wearing a dressing gown and dark glasses. Clov his servant cannot sit down just as Hamm cannot walk. Near by, in two dustbins, Hamm keeps his parents Nell and Nagg, legless as a result of a bicycling accident. The world outside is dead or at least these four characters understand they are the last survivors of the race after some great catastrophe. Although Clov hates Hamm he must obey him, and the 'plot' is whether Glov will leave or not: although if he does he will die but, then, if he stays he will also die since the supplies, including painkillers, have run out. Like *Godot* this play has been the subject of wide interpretation including the suggestion that it is an autobiographical account of Beckett's relationship with Joyce.[14] It could be said that the four characters of *Godot* have been compressed here into two: Hamm combining the tyrant Pozzo and the poet Estragon while Clov combines the practical Vladimir and the slave Lucky; certainly the pattern of mutual dependence is repeated as is the final immobility. Clov changes into his travelling clothes but stands with his umbrella and bag motionless as the curtain falls. The sense of deadness is unrelieved except for the reported vision of a small boy who contemplates his navel (*i.e.* Nirvana) and is a potential creator.

*Fin de Partie* was followed in the same programme by *Acte Sans Paroles* written for the dancer Derek Mendel in 1956 with music by Beckett's cousin John. This is a mime for a single actor who is flung on to an empty and brilliantly lit stage (Beckett's image of birth) where he meets various situations which sum up the life we lead. From the flies descend a tree, scissors and a carafe of water (though this is kept out of reach). Three cubes of assorted sizes are pushed on but when he climbs on them the carafe is raised so that he cannot grasp it; a rope is lowered but when he starts to climb it this too rises and he is forced to cut it to regain the stage. He now tries to hang himself but the bough of the tree folds up against the trunk and when he turns for the scissors to cut his throat they and the cubes are pulled off the stage. He gives up the struggle, lying motionless on the ground even when tempted by the lowering of the carafe. Comic clowning, but his final gesture is to look at his hands—tools given him to be useless.

120

[14] See Lionel Abel, *Metatheatre* (1963), pp. 134-40.

In 1957 Beckett's radio play *All that Fall* was broadcast by the BBC Third Programme. Although a radio play it was apparently more conventional: the setting was not symbolic but the Irish countryside and a railway station and the characters seemed to be ordinary people in a commonsense world, but the use of sound effects modified this impression. Mrs. Rooney, fat, ailing and in her seventies is struggling to meet her blind husband Dan at the railway station and grieving over the death of her daughter as a child. It is Dan's birthday (though he has forgotten it) and she wants to meet him at the station as a surprise. Curiously the train is late but when it arrives Dan gives no hint as to why and it is only the arrival of the boy who usually guides Dan home which gives us the news, as they trudge home through wind and rain. The journey was delayed because a child fell out of the carriage and was crushed under the wheels of the train. There are pointers to suggest that Dan pushed her but this is not a murder mystery. Whether the child fell or was pushed it was an arbitrary, irrational act which illustrates the nature of the universe we live in. In 1958 Beckett wrote *Krapp's Last Tape* for the actor Patrick Magee; it is the study of a disillusioned old man, a writer, staged at the Royal Court, who has recorded the past and thus meets it in the present. A familiar Beckett solitary, he passes time by playing back this diary of over forty years, looking at his discarded selves and particularly that moment when fearful of being invaded by someone else he rejected love and thus ensured his present loneliness. This play has been described as Beckett's *Peer Gynt* but there is, of course, no Solveig waiting faithfully to redeem him; Krapp will die as he has lived, alone. The use of tapes as voices of the past suggests radio rather than stage, and Beckett composed three short pieces for the radio which are essentially sound poems exploring ambiguity and abstraction: *Embers* (1959)—the monologue of a lonely old man talking to himself, his dead father and his dead wife by the sea where his father was drowned; *Words and Music* (1962) and *Cascando* (1963) a play about a character called Woburn who never appears. In 1960 *Acte Sans Paroles II* was performed in New York (performed at the Aldwych in *Expeditions I*, 1964) and, as might be expected, was a mime for two actors, with sacks. It was also in New York in 1961 that Beckett had a new play produced, *Happy Days* (Royal Court, 1962) which carries on where *Fin de Partie* seems to have left off. The setting is a low mound with scorched grass. In Act 1 Winnie is immobilised, like Hamm, but this time she is buried to her waist in the exact centre of the mound (as Hamm had to be in the exact centre of his room) and like Hamm she has her possessions around her to handle which include a revolver. At the back of the mound lives her husband Willie who can only move on all fours and spends the day reading a newspaper. In Act 2 Winnie is buried to the neck and though her possessions remain they are now only objects to talk about. She, too, invents stories to pass the time. But Willie, now 'dressed to kill', makes a great effort to crawl up to Winnie. She can no longer give him a hand and he falls back twice, but this visit which she assumes was to her rather than to obtain possession of her revolver makes her feel it has been one more happy day and she sings the waltz from *The Merry Widow* as the curtain falls. It was a sign of things to come and in his next play, called simply *Play*, written in 1963 and produced at the National Theatre in 1964, he produced three characters in urns, nameless, all action, movement—even facial gesture—having been abolished. They were not even permitted to use inflections in the voice. All this was to suggest that they were in Hell. George Devine compared the text to a musical score although the effects are gained as much by lighting as by the method of delivery (frequently rapid and polyphonic) and the ultimate in stage directions: *Repeat the play exactly*. This repetition at least helps in hearing the play as well as insisting on the repetitive nature of this *post-mortem* existence. For many, this was a difficult but poetic experience in the theatre; for most it was just difficult. But it was not quite the end. *In Come and Go* (1966) dedicated to John Calder, three spinsters re-live that brief part of their lives when they were vitally alive, when as schoolgirls they sat on a log holding hands and dreaming of the love that has never come to them. This piece, with 121 words, 23 speeches and 12 silences lasts for three minutes and looks forward to recent non-verbal brevities such as the non-prologue for Tynan's *Oh! Calcutta!* (1969) in which a lighting scheme plays over a pile of miscellaneous rubbish, including naked people, to the sound of amplified breathing for about 15 seconds.

Yet, curiously, Beckett wrote *Eh, Joe* in 1965 (BBC Television, 1966) which is less abstract and more concerned with human suffering. Joe, like many Beckett characters, is haunted by voices of the dead which he has managed to exclude thus ensuring that he is completely alone. A voice of a woman disturbs him, however, reminding him that (like young Krapp) he could never return love, of a woman who managed to break away and find love elsewhere. And also of a girl whom he rejected, who committed suicide, successfully at the third attempt, whose love is seen as comparable with the love of God. This warm interlude is unusual (and, even so, is about a suicide remembered by a lonely old man!). The previous year (1964) Beckett had written a film script which was called, characteristically, *Film* and was intended to show, without the use of words, the principle: *esse est percipi*. It emphasises that when all outside perceivers have been abolished, including God, there is still no escape from the perception of ones-self. The protagonist here is split, not into two tramps, or Hamm and Clov, or man and wife, or man and memory but into E (eye played by the camera) and O (object, that is the person perceived). In the film O tries to avoid being perceived: in the street, at home where he puts out the cat and the dog, covers the parrot and the goldfish, takes down the picture of God the Father and smashes the mirror. In vain—since this is a film he is being filmed by E. He then settles down to abolish other witnesses: seven photographs of himself at previous stages of development which he tears up and tries to sleep, to fall into the oblivion of a nonperceiving being. But E, of course, is still filming, a disturbing gaze, and O wakes up. We see him for the

123

first time full face, with a patch over his left eye and wearing an expression of agony. The part of O was played by Buster Keaton and the film won the Prix Filmcritica in Venice in 1965.

Beckett's plays, then, have shown a lack of plot and character: for character presumes personality and plot assumes that events in time have significance and neither of these assumptions is thematically appropriate. Beckett's plays and novels examine the difficulty of finding meaning in a world subject to incessant change, and with only language to arrive at or express this meaning. Originally in his plays Beckett uses devices like stichomythia to suggest not the expected interchange of classical French drama but how completely each man follows his own thoughts. But mainly Beckett has developed the use of silence and pause to isolate words, just as repetition suggests the monotony and bafflingly circular nature of living. There had been a Theatre of Silence in France previously. Lugné-Poe, impressed by the effect gained by silences in the work of Maeterlinck and the mimed plays at the Théâtre Funambulesque had tried to produce *Pelléas et Melisande* in 1893 and shortly after World War I Baty and Les Compagnons de la Chimère had attempted to render the unexpressed by indirect language. But it was the use of indirect expression rather than intercalated silences. Beckett has moved more and more into illuminated silence, with sound effects to emphasise that it is only the silence from words that he seeks. His novels are not likely to reach as wide an audience as his plays, which is a pity, for they represent his major achievement and the exclusion of movement and exterior action, if still a limiting exclusion, is less felt there than it must be in drama. It may have been inevitable that, given his preoccupations, Beckett turned to drama but given those preoccupations it is also inevitable that his plays have got less and less theatrical, and dwindled to the point of non-existence; total disappearance is presumably only prevented by the need for fulfilment of the artist. What is surprising, to echo Ronald Hayman, is that his achievement under such auspices is so substantial in the theatre.[15]

In looking for British Dramatists of the Absurd we come up against the same problem as when looking for Committed Dramatists: the English temperament. British (and American) dramatists tend to put more stress on historical, social or national aspects of a problem rather than exploring a general metaphysical condition. Beckett himself is inimitable, but his dustbins, after the first shock, soon became a cliché and were easily imitated. What was lacking in the imitators was both originality and the philosophical rigour Beckett so doggedly displays. Martin Esslin, therefore, can only find two English representatives: N. F. Simpson and Harold Pinter. Curiously he omits David Campton and we could add, more recently, Tom Stoppard.

The omission of Campton (b. 1924) is at first strange. He started at Scarborough in 1955 with Stephen Joseph's Theatre in the Round and the subtitle of *The Lunatic View* (1957) was 'A Comedy of Menace' a phrase subsequently applied to Pinter and Simpson. Comparison with Pinter is chronologically impossible and *The Lunatic View* was written before Campton admits to having seen Ionesco, although when he read Ionesco he recognised that that was what he had been waiting for. When John Russell Taylor tells the 'story' of Campton's four sketches it shows how odd they must have been to an England which had not got used to Ionesco and could not accept either Simpson or Pinter.[16] Unlike Absurd dramatists, however, Campton has a prominent social conscience. His comedies can be reduced to brief statements like: The Bomb is coming, or, politicians are dangerous fools. If Campton is an Absurd dramatist he sees the theatre as a weapon against complacency, although he anticipated, correctly, that once Absurd became a label it would lose its force. In 1957 the menace for Campton was clearly the Bomb and it is no accident that three playlets were performed before marchers to Aldermaston in 1960. They are quite explicitly

[15] Conclusion to Ronald Hayman, *Samuel Beckett* (1968).
[16] *Anger and After*, pp. 180–8.

125

about nuclear war and prophetic about future conditions. Thus *Mutatis Mutandis* requires a father to break the news to his wife that their baby son has green hair, a tail, three eyes and so on. A great deal of Campton's writing is one-act, and done to order. As he points out in the introduction to *On Stage* (1964) there is nothing wrong in this. He takes a simple situation and comments on it. He also insists that comedy is a serious business but if taken seriously it will be fun. His plays are brief, well constructed and do what they set out to do, but such qualities, in the wider prospect of theatre, can be limiting.

Simpson, too, seems limited. If he is an Absurd dramatist he is so in terms of the philosophical technique: *reductio ad absurdum*. N. F. Simpson (b. 1919) shared third prize for *A Resounding Tinkle* in *The Observer* competition for 1956 and the play was performed, in a shortened version, at the Royal Court in 1957. Simpson, a schoolmaster, may use logic in a way that reminds us of Beckett but it is used on social matters and if the results suggest comparison with the plays of Ionesco they show up, to borrow John Russell Taylor's adjective, as parochial. His world is unmistakably suburban England and he carries the English habit of understatement to a set of conclusions out of Alice's Wonderland. The final message of his plays would appear to be an attack on a way of life which makes humans machines, the deadliness of habit and social convention. Thus, Esslin claims for Simpson the rôle of a 'more powerful social critic than any of the social realists' and for Absurd Theatre the quality of producing effective social criticism.[17] But Simpson more properly belongs with the social realists, with Osborne and Wesker rather than Beckett and Pinter. He evokes menace by producing characters who nothing can surprise. The same point is repeated over and over again. Irving Wardle correctly points out that wit emerges when characters share a pattern of behaviour and are devoted to conversation rather than action: comedy of manners could be the better description for Simpson's work, done, with what Marowitz has described as 'civil service levity'. Simpson has a

126    [17] *The Theatre of the Absurd* (1968), p. 301.

splendid facility for reducing common human behaviour to absurdity but without any sense that such a condition springs from metaphysical doubt or anguish. He writes of a world that is admittedly crazy and hypocritical but he writes as a satirist and with a satirist's conventional morality.

It is with Harold Pinter that we come nearest to an English Absurd dramatist and if he is compared to Beckett (and frequently to Kafka as well) he, too, looks parochial. But it is a sturdy and prolific parochialism. In fact any system breaks down with Pinter who is properly described by John Russell Taylor as *sui generis*. Although born an East End Jew his work seems to have little in common with that of either Wesker or Kops. Indeed for a long time he specifically rejected political affiliations declaring that though he recognised that politics were responsible for a great deal of suffering they bored him and he mistrusted ideological statements of any kind. He has been less a-political of late, but given his upbringing in the East End as a Jew it is hardly surprising that his plays concern a fight for living space, the use and abuse of power—themes which Wesker would certainly recognise as political—but expressed in Pinter through characters in the process of finding out about themselves. For it is this existential adjustment which must come first, and then condition social, political and other general ideas. Pinter's orderly career begins there, with a long look at this crucial adjustment reminiscent, perhaps, of Heidegger but very much in his own terms. If, as Pinter freely admits, Kafka and Beckett 'rang a bell', his own plays are firmly based in everyday reality. The characters and settings are minutely observed, the dialogue is realistically full of faulty grammar, syntax, repetitions and contradictions all of which intensify the mystery. There is plenty of evidence but it only serves to contradict or confuse and behind the simple situations and uncannily ordinary dialogue mysterious terrors lurk and the plays are haunted by questions to which there can be no answer: whether we can ever know the truth, or whether there is a truth to be known or more finally who am I the knower.

127

Pinter would say that this mystery is itself realistic: we do not know the motives of others and our own are obscure. He rejects the idea that a dramatist can 'know' his characters more fully than people can be known in life and therefore contents himself with offering what life offers—the *status quo,* an intrusion and the changes that follow. His plays work, then, like poems, offering short lyrical insights rather than an argument and asking questions, not to answer them, but because life is a series of questions.

Pinter would also reject the purposeful dialogue of a dramatist. Just as the dramatist pretends he knows his characters so, even in the most naturalistic plays, dialogue only pretends to be natural but is in fact working a great deal harder than ordinary conversation has to. Even when characters should speak to purpose Pinter cannot make them: he is a shaper, he arranges and he listens. But the fact that we have the adjective 'Pinteresque' suggests that his style is a memorable thing, memorable enough, certainly, to invite imitation and, in Pinter himself, the temptations of parody and self-indulgence. He uses the two silences, defined in a lecture at the Sunday Times Student Drama Festival of 1962 as, first, when no words are used and, secondly, when a torrent of words is spoken. We can see the use of silences in Chekhov, for example, but where Chekov only pretends not to write purposeful dialogue Pinter seems to carry the pretence even further. He is not, however, demonstrating that cliché of recent times, the failure of communication. Pinter believes that communication is not merely possible, it is alarming and that where there is no difficulty, as there will be with naturally inarticulate people, there will be deliberate evasion for to let yourself be known through speaking is to admit someone to your room.[18] Words and silence, then, are both stratagems to cover nakedness and Pinter's dialogue is more controlled than much of what nowadays passed for verse. Indeed this

[18] Cf. R. D. Laing, *The Divided Self* (1960): If the self is not known it is safe. It is safe from penetrating remarks; it is safe from being smothered or engulfed by love as much as from destruction from hatred.

unexpected precision, economy and control in plays apparently full of irrelevance, repetition and gratuitous incident aligns Pinter not so much with Beckett and Kafka as with English high comedy, with Wilde and Coward.

Of course Pinter is still pretending not to write purposeful dialogue; the speech is relentlessly everyday but, in John Russell Taylor's adjective, 'orchestrated'. Life never shapes itself as well as in his plays nor speech as carefully. The choice of the right word is a poet's avoidance of redundancy but it is also part of the battle: to use the right word is a mark of the superiority of one character over another. Pinter has even developed a distinction between 'Pause' and 'Silence': when the former is asked for it suggests that thought is being attempted, when the latter, that a movement has finished and another will now begin.[19] However economic or mysterious his situations, character and dialogue, Pinter's grasp on the outside world never slackens: whatever terrors lurk, his buses run.

Pinter (b. 1930) spent two terms at RADA in 1948; he also (and it is scarcely the act of a non-political man?) risked imprisonment for refusing to be called up for National Service. He began to publish poems in 1950 and in 1951 toured with Anew McMaster's Company in Ireland and later with Wolfit in London where he first met his future wife Ada Thomson (*i.e.* Vivien Merchant). About this time he assumed the name David Baron, and after a period of repertory acting met Vivien Merchant again, in 1956 and they married. In 1957 he wrote his first play *The Room* (in four days) which was so successful when performed by the Drama Department at Bristol that the other Drama School there put it on for the *Sunday Times* Drama Competition where it impressed Michael Codron who asked to see any other plays and was offered *The Party* and *The Dumb Waiter*. He chose the former which was produced, as *The Birthday Party,* at the Arts Theatre, Cambridge and then at the Lyric, Hammersmith, where it ran for a week and was slaughtered by the critics although defended by Harold

[19] Martin Esslin, *The Peopled Wound* (1970), p. 219. See chapter 4.

Hobson who summed it up as a 'grand Guignol of the susceptibilities'. Codron has since confessed that he was offered a safe thriller and took *The Birthday Party* off before the *Sunday Times* notice, which he now thinks was his mistake. In 1959 *The Dumb Waiter* was first performed, in Germany. Pinter fortunately did not allow the disaster with *The Birthday Party* to discourage him and the BBC helpfully commissioned a play which he wrote, as well as revue sketches.

In retrospect the poems[20] seem to suggest the dramatist: dreams and obsessions firmly planted in a sordid reality, a grasp of strong situations, lonely characters and a love of words—and some fairly precise anticipations of the plays. Even so Pinter was remarkably successful in finding, in his first play, the basic image or situation: 'I went into a room one day and saw a couple of people in it.' His early plays were rightly called 'Comedies of Menace' by Irving Wardle in 1958 borrowing Campton's subtitle, and take as their central subject a room, warm and safe, if stuffy, surrounded by a cold, dark hostile world which threatens to intrude and dispossess. Pinter, also in his first play, established his second leitmotif: the male–female relationship—the man cold, silent and passive the woman motherly, nagging, fussy and talkative, an uncertain relationship complemented by the uncertainties of life in the room suggested by visits from the landlord, that equally uncertain young couple called the Sandses and finally by a blind Negro. If this too-allegorical Negro was a mistake, and the end, when Rose is struck blind, overinflated it is still a striking *coup de théâtre*. And as an ending it neatly ties together sexuality and racial hatred (the husband seems to derive equal satisfaction from driving his van hard or beating the negro to death), introduces the image of blindness as related to sexual inadequacy and/or death and asks a character to come home; posing the basic question: where is home?

Pinter's second play repeated this basic situation of a room, a dark outside and a door that will open and whoever enters

[20] Collected and published, with exceptions, in 1968.

will be killed. However, in this play there is a noticeably greater use of business as well as dialogue—business reminiscent of Beckett. But as we watch the door there is another entrance, a dumb waiter, down which come more and more outrageous demands which the killers try to fulfil. For so we learn these two men are; and because they are killers they do not wish to give their presence away and are accustomed to obeying orders without question. Or they have been. For this amusing business reveals a difference between Gus and Ben. Gus is beginning to ask questions about the organisation (the last killing was female and messy), is ceasing to be a dumb waiter. Ben, on the other hand, remains apparently unchanged, receives his orders via the speaking tube and at the end of the play presumably eliminates Gus. It is possibly that in doing so he, too, will begin to question the arbitrary nature of his orders. *The Dumb Waiter,* however, is a comedy and it ought not to be overloaded with implications. It should remind us before we meet the 'killers' in *The Birthday Party* that hired emissaries are human just like us and that the menace is already inside the room.

*The Birthday Party,* Pinter's first full-length play, continued this exploration of intruders from a mysterious organisation. They arrive at an out-of-season boarding house to collect Stanley whose offence is left vague, a catalogue of possibilities which allows Pinter to exploit the lyric potential of a litany which includes just about any kind of offence a man might have committed:

Goldberg: Where is your lechery leading you?
McCann: You'll pay for this.
Goldberg: You stuff yourself with dry toast.
McCann: You contaminate womankind.
Goldberg: Why don't you pay the rent?
McCann: Mother defiler!
Goldberg: Why do you pick your nose?
McCann: I demand justice!
Goldberg: What's your trade?
McCann: What about Ireland?

Goldberg: What's your trade?
Stanley:  I play the piano.
Goldberg: How many fingers do you use?
Stanley:  No hands!
Goldberg: No society would touch you. Not even a building society.
McCann:   You're a traitor to the cloth.
Goldberg: What do you use for pyjamas?
Stanley:  Nothing.
Goldberg: You verminate the sheet of your birth.
McCann:   What about the Albigensenist heresy?
Goldberg: Who watered the wicket at Melbourne?
McCann:   What about the blessed Oliver Plunkett?
Goldberg: Speak up Webber. Why did the chicken cross the road?
Stanley:  He wanted to—he wanted to—he wanted to. . . .
McCann:   He doesn't know!
Goldberg: Why did the chicken cross the road?
Stanley:  He wanted to—he wanted to. . . .
Goldberg: Why did the chicken cross the road?
Stanley:  He wanted . . . .
McCann:   He doesn't know. He doesn't know which came first!
Goldberg: Which came first?
McCann:   Chicken? Egg? Which came first?
Goldberg and McCann: Which came first? Which came first? Which came first? Stanley *screams*[21]

Meg, too, is terrified by just such vague suggestions on the day before the two men arrive. Goldberg and McCann are, of course, the traditional joke Irishman and Jew though here their familiar manner is connected to no very clear function. They, too, suffer from doubts and menaces (as Gus and Ben before them) before they carry away the respectably dressed, mute and possibly blind Stanley. It is not clear that they will kill him as do the two men who take away K (whose offence was also nameless) in *The Trial*. Perhaps Pinter's poem on the play which makes Goldberg and not Stanley the centre is a clue to our understanding of the play.

After the failure of *The Birthday Party* the BBC commissioned a play and got *A Slight Ache* (1960) which was novel in two ways. The action takes place in a higher social

132       [21] *The Birthday Party* (Methuen), pp. 54–5.

milieu and ushers in the theme of finding a tart in a lady. It also slightly relaxed the grip of the room by allowing the characters to go out in the garden. The initial episode between Edward and Flora at the breakfast table, when a wasp is drowned in the marmalade, suggests latent cruelty behind polite surfaces. It also, with its references to blindness, hints at the sexual inadequacy of their relationship which is then explored in terms of the silent matchseller. Even on radio he must surely exist, although on the stage and television he is an embarrassment. Edward, appalled by his silence, tries to make him speak but fails while Flora finds him a stimulus for her sexual fantasies, gives him a name and finally, when Edward has collapsed under a second failure to discover who or what the matchseller is, takes him as the baby-lover-husband she desires. There are hints that Edward has married into a higher social class which would account for some of his uneasiness but primarily his collapse is brought about by the activity which is fatal in Pinter's plays; asking questions and trying to find the answer to the question: who or what are you? Significantly, as in the short story 'The Examination' the intruder is invited in and, by doing nothing, awakens all the fears and menaces already inside.

Until 1959 Pinter had made little impact in the theatre. His revue sketches showed developments of his basic theme—*Applicant* explores menace while *Trouble in the Works* shows the fascination for technical language—but they are essentially social, not metaphysical, on content. They show people trying to live together without giving too much away about themselves. Pinter is interested in people, not in any moral that can be drawn from them. In *The Caretaker* he took a step forward in the direction of simplicity. It was this play which brought him recognition as well as into a maturity which rejects the more baroque trappings of the earlier plays, including violence. That this was deliberate can be seen from his rejection of a play called *The Hothouse* (1958), a heavily satirical study of a rest-home in the manner of Ionesco in which a character called Lamb is tortured by the use of

133

electrodes and which ends with practically all the staff being slaughtered. Pinter found he was unable to like any of the characters and the material was gathered and redefined in *The Caretaker* where the projected murder of the tramp is finally turned into the more poignant thrusting out at the end of the play. Here, too, the intruder is invited in but Davies cannot resist the temptation to use the knowledge about Aston which Aston—on the one occasion when he speaks at length—gives him. If Davies is the matchseller who speaks and Aston cousin to Stanley we have a third character, an original creation, Mick (who looks forward to Lenny in *The Homecoming*). And if the two brothers remind us of Didi and Gogo, two halves of the same person, they are also meticulously observed individuals whose intentions are clear. Indeed Davies is the only character in this play subject to ambiguity and that is entirely appropriate since he is covering up his tracks. Even so, his lies and evasions seem as much part of his character as a comment on the world in which he lives.

*The Caretaker,* if felt by some critics to be over-rated, brought Pinter welcome success. 1960 saw *A Night Out* (BBC Third Programme and Television), *Night School* on television and *The Dwarfs* on radio and in 1961 Pinter was earning high praise from no less a master than Noel Coward who in 1966 still thought of him as a genuine original. Clarity of motivations or their unimportance was part of this new directness and a sense of going out. Pinter had never, of course, said that his characters did not go out; someone has to fetch the cornflakes, but the sense had been that going out was difficult. In *A Night Out* Pinter used a large number of sets, good realistic dialogue on a large variety of topics, characters whose motives are clear (in the television production even the liberty-taker was clearly identified) and whose lies are known to be lies. This leaves us with the simple story of Albert, 28 years old and still dominated by his mother. Even as a paying customer Albert cannot escape the nagging gentility which reminds him of his mother and after a minor victory he returns to the room as if nothing had happened. *Night School* (rewritten 1966 and published in 1967) was even more of an anthology of Pinter's themes and methods: a struggle for a room, between a man and woman, with evasions and lies. But Wally's attempt to pin down Sally as a schoolteacher or Sally as a whore opened up the subject of woman which now runs through Stella, Sarah and Ruth. *Night School* was a slight comedy, successful enough, but Pinter, rightly, feared that he was slipping into a formula. *The Dwarfs,* originally a radio play, ensured that he was not. Based on a novel written between 1953–7 what is interesting is that just as Pinter begins his exploration of the multiple nature of woman he abandons it, deliberately cutting the female character out of the play. In the original novel the three men are joined by a woman called Virginia but in the play there are only three male characters: Len, who has a mental breakdown, and his friends Mark and Pete whose friendship Len destroys, leaving himself at the end alone in a prosaic ordered world. Pinter has described the play as being about betrayal and distrust. It is also about the gradual emergence from adolescence into adult respectability, the split-up of boyhood friends. The removal of a female (an obvious cause of such a break-up) leaves him at liberty to describe the natural, if painful, process. Possibly encouraged by the medium of radio, Pinter allows us inside the mind of one of his characters so that if the question 'who are the dwarfs?' leads to the usual 'who is anyone?' here a character shares our problem. The result is a more acute apprehension of Pinter's interest in understanding people 'at the extreme edge of their living, where they are living pretty much alone'. This play, baffling and enigmatic, contains much of Pinter's finest writing, at least until *Landscape* and *Silence.*

Pinter followed this play with two written for television which explored knowledge about people through the husband and wife relationship, since if anyone can know anyone else, surely husband and wife should? *The Collection* (1961), produced at the Aldwych in 1962, also began a full exploration of woman's rôle in a male-dominated society. The interest is more acute here than with any other character for

135

whereas a man is the sum of his reflections they do not raise moral problems: he is a heavy drinker, a gardener, a mechanic—and even if we add the rôle of adulterer the double standard qualifies our response. However a woman can be a wife and mother, mistress, prostitute and whore and each of these rôles raises a response which contradicts the other rôles. In *The Collection* Pinter also moved into a more elegant sophisticated milieu—the rag trade—with intelligent and articulate people. The problem of articulacy removed, we are left with the problem of whether or not Stella had sexual intercourse with Bill in a Leeds hotel. Both James and Harry would like to know: Harry because it might be a sign that Bill is leaving him (and anyway after James's intrusion Bill seems to be developing a relationship with him) and James because he finds Bill attractive and is disturbed to discover that the wife he thought he knew must be either a whore or a liar with a taste for sexual fantasies; which would suggest inadequacy on his part. The collection of 'truths', the abundance of motivations, much worse than no motivations at all, leads to the existentialist conclusion that any attempt to pin down the infinite sum of reflections as an absolute is doomed to failure and will cause pain. Stella, during the television production, was kept in focus, passive, playing with her kitten, excluded from the world of passionate action shared by the men.

The suspicion that a wife and mother might also be a whore is examined in his next play *The Lover* (1963). Here husband and wife play at being lover and mistress (or is it whore?) in the afternoon, or lover and whore play at husband and wife in the evening until the husband finally tries to bring the excitement of the afternoon into their respectable but dull evenings; forcing the two aspects of their relationship together to the alarm of the wife who prefers to separate her social self from her instinctive self to, possibly, the disadvantage of both. The economy and style of the play have been justly praised. The criticism that the milkman episode is superfluous and only there to give Richard time to change his clothes will not bear scrutiny. The milkman first appears to us as her lover (as traditionally he would be) but then turns out to be only the milkman. His offers of cream then suggests that he could still become her lover and this is confirmed by the wife in a later speech. *The Lover* has been aptly described as a contemporary version of *The Bacchae* in elegant miniature.[22]

Meanwhile Pinter had read his short story 'The Examination' on the BBC Third Programme, written the screenplay for *The Servant*, begun filming *The Caretaker* (which appeared in 1963 but was renamed as *The Guest* for the USA), written sketches for the BBC, produced *The Lover* (with *The Dwarfs*) at the Arts Theatre and *The Birthday Party* at the Aldwych. In 1965 Pinter was awarded the best screenplay of 1964 for *The Pumpkin Eater,* BBC television showed his play *Tea Party* (based on a short story read by Pinter on the Third Programme in 1964) and, after a short provincial tour, his full-length play *The Homecoming* opened at the Aldwych. In *Tea Party* the lady who is a whore is separated into upper-class wife and working-class secretary both acquired by Disson at the same time. Disson has come up in the world through the manufacture of sanitary equipment and there is both the clash of social classes and the blindness of *A Slight Ache*. The medium also allowed Pinter the interplay of objective and subjective vision simultaneously as the protagonist 'sees' so many exclusive possibilities co-existing in situations and characters that he cannot make sense of them and, like Edward, collapses under the strain. The social unease is stronger in this play than it was in *A Slight Ache* but the horror of what Disson 'sees' at the tea party is protected by the possibility that Disson cannot know the truth as he sinks into a catatonic trance, a very safe room.

No such protection exists in *The Homecoming* (1965) which puzzled many critics who registered their shock in terms of complaints about self-indulgence and mystification as an end rather than the means. Esslin has demonstrated that the play can be valid on a realistic level and contains a perfectly credible series of events; which is rather like insisting that

[22] *The Peopled Wound* (1970), p. 136.

miracles can be explained.[23] It is a simple play: six people in a room, two have come home and intensified conflicts already there. It is simple, as John Russell Taylor suggests, in the manner of a child's story which goes: and then ... and then ... [24] It is also economical. Critics who have complained about indulgence, for example, in Lenny's stories about women fail to see their function. But Ruth does not, she understands them, not whether they are true or not but as a challenge which she accepts when she calls Lenny by the name his mother gave him and declines to give up the glass from which she is sipping water. Is the story credible? Would a husband, a college professor with three children and a successful career, just walk out accepting the final proposals? The promise of the title is fulfilled, but not in any cosy fashion. It is, of course, Ruth who comes home, answering the invitation first issued in *The Room*. Critics who have added Biblical and Shakespearean sources (is Teddy scapegoat or fatted calf? and what is the difference between kith and kin?) merely support, if they are accurate, the sense that Ruth recognises and accepts the rules of the game. In another setting, Teddy's Ph.D and detachment would work, but not here, and while he modifies concepts Joey is upstairs with his wife. The theme—the secrecy and silence of woman is one Shaw would have approved of; Ruth, like Ann Whitfield, says no more than she must, but she accepts the Gods of the house, becoming mother and whore while Sam collapses and Teddy walks out with the disturbing injunction not to become a stranger.

In 1966 Pinter was awarded the CBE and worked on the screenplay for *The Quiller Memorandum*. BBC Television took up his film script *The Compartment (circa* 1963) intended for the Grove Press project with Ionesco and Beckett (his contribution was filmed as *Film*) and now retitled *The Basement*. This piece seems to be closely related to 'The Examination' (probably completed in 1958) where two men change places in a conflict over a room and its properties and

[23] *The Peopled Wound,* pp. 137–57.  [24] *Anger and After* (1969), p. 356.

the prose poem 'Kullus' (1949) where a girl is included and gains the room at the end. Here the two themes of sex and the room combine but the switches from winter to summer and the changing furniture in the room suggest a joy in images which filming, even more than television, would have conferred. Esslin sees the play as either fantasy in Law's mind (as his name implies he tries to play this game according to the rules and loses) or an abstract symphonic pattern. Rhapsodic would probably be the better word. The games are reminiscent of *The Lover* but also of various films. Apart from films of his own plays *The Caretaker* (1962), *The Birthday Party* (1968 and *The Homecoming* (projected 1969) Pinter has written screenplays for *The Servant* (1963), *The Pumpkin Eater* (1963), *The Quiller Memorandum* (1966) *Accident* (1966) and *The Go-Between* (1969) which clearly gave him more scope than television for using different and symbolic locations and they contain many Pinter motifs even if, as scriptwriter, he was subordinate in a film-making team. They also left him free, financially, to write as he wanted and what he wanted. In 1968 the Aldwych abandoned the stage project of *Landscape* after a clash with the Lord Chamberlain and it was broadcast on the BBC Third Programme. Pinter finished the companion piece *Silence* in 1969 and the two plays were then, at the end of the Lord Chamberlain's rule, produced at the Aldwych. Both are austere, very short plays, exchanges of recollections. There is no sense at all of menace but neither is there any sense of communication. The plays work through monologues. In *Landscape* Beth and Duff sit in a kitchen of a country house; Duff seems to want to talk to Beth though he does not appear to listen to her, but Beth neither listens nor looks at Duff. Her landscape is in the past, a lover on a beach (Duff, in fact) whereas Duff is concerned with more recent, practical, less idyllic matters: the weather, the house and so forth. How have they got like this? Possibly an infidelity or a too crude sexual demand on Duff's part. Certainly the opposition seemed to be between Duff, coarse but firmly planted in reality and Beth, delicate but given over to fantasy and nostalgia.

*Silence* continues the themes and method. The three characters are now in separate acting areas (or rooms?): Ellen and two men with whom she has had relations—Rumsey, tender, lyrical, with his own house and Bates, younger, coarser who had to find a place to have sex with Ellen. By the end of the play we gather that Rumsey lives alone but fairly contentedly in the country while Ellen and Bates are in the town, isolated, unhappy and longing for the country. *Silence* reminds us of *Play* particularly in its use of repeated fragments of dialogue out of which a story of a quite simple kind is built; but told from three points of view and two, if not three, points in time, simultaneously. In 1969 Pinter also contributed a short sketch *Night* to the production *Mixed Doubles*. This, too, if slight and comic, is a memory sketch as a man and woman recall the first meeting which led to their getting married and having a family; amusingly their memories contradict one another. A more elaborate and possibly more sinister version of this episode, in the poetic style of *Landscape* and *Silence,* appeared in 1971 under the title *Old Times*. This was Pinter's first full-length play since *The Homecoming.* [25] Recently Pinter has shown a preference for directing plays and, clearly, choices have to be made. In 1971 he directed Simon Gray's new play *Butley*.

In all his work Pinter has exhibited a dual nature: fantasy and realism. Real speech, real situations but questions about the nature of reality. Twentieth-century dialogue but nonsense poetry as well; the comic and the tragic—multivalent as life itself. He is the craftsman who shapes and the poet haunted by images of menace to which no amount of shaping can give purpose; in this sense he belongs to Absurd Drama. In that same sense he is also our most ruthless and uncompromising naturalist. He sees himself as a traditional playwright, insisting on a final curtain, seeking an over-all unity and suspicious of happenings and eight-hour

[25] Full-length, however, now means scarcely one and a half hours. The Pinter magic is there, but the sceptics may have more support than ever before in describing it as a conjuring trick.

movies. Unlike Kafka and Beckett, whose contexts strike us as unreal, his presentation of menace is intensified by his realism: the ordinariness of setting and situation emphasises the horror the intruder causes. His recent work has marked a new departure, a return of the poet. After *The Homecoming* he said that he could not stay in the room with these people any longer. He now writes short plays full of nostalgia for lost things like innocence and love—elegies comparable to those recently produced by Wesker and Osborne. But he is not trapped, like them, by the autobiographical nature of his material. His first play was neither autobiography nor obviously imitative and he has continued on his own way ever since. Many critics find his vision of the world limited even allowing for the development of his argument and that his work moves consistently forward. If Pinter is limited he is so in the sense of Jane Austen rather than Beckett, but his work in 1971 has suggested Beckett in themes and style and the tendency to shrink is ominous. It is the other side of Pinter's nature which will surely keep him from vanishing completely?

Although Pinter seems, like Beckett, to invite imitation his style would make imitation obvious. Probably the only recruit to the line of Beckett and Pinter, or, if preferred, to theatre of the Absurd, is Tom Stoppard. But whereas Pinter opposes craft with instinct and observation with obsession, Stoppard is an intellectual and his plays have, in spite of his denials, the air of being very thoroughly worked out. It was Stoppard who probably introduced National Theatre audiences to Absurd Drama—there can be no other explanation of their ecstatic reception of *Rosencrantz and Guildenstern Are Dead* (1967). Originally a one-act farce, as much of it as was finished was performed at the Edinburgh Festival in 1966 and the National Theatre asked him to write a last act. It opened in 1967 to great acclaim not merely by the public but also by critics. This is puzzling since as the play opens we recognise Theatre of the Absurd. What remains then, is, to what purpose and how well and the answer must be to little purpose and no more than competently. National Theatre audiences were familiar with

141

*Hamlet* and less so with Absurd Theatre, so the play could work well but this cannot explain the excitement of critics who should have known better. The idea basically is excellent but it is not endowed here with any great weight. What we see is a clever author manipulating rather than exploring, a parasite feeding off Shakespeare, Pirandello and Beckett and however ingenious the idea, the over-long execution is relentlessly familiar. It could be argued that the originality of Stoppard lies in grafting the philosophy of Beckett on to Shakespeare's image of the world as a stage; that Stoppard, a philosophy graduate, uses *Hamlet* as Sartre used the Orestes myth and the lack of freedom imposed by the original story represents the absence of choices in human lives. But like Sartre, Stoppard cannot play fair. He must turn his principal characters—cold, ambitious, political young men into garrulous and likeable heroes. Thus he has to omit the recorder scene. It is a great pity that the play does not have the economy of its sources. Too much of the play is gratuitously laboured and where *Waiting for Godot* works in a bare context Stoppard's baroque clutter merely suggests that there is a great deal of life happening outside if only you do not insist on staying in antechambers. And where Didi and Gogo still wait, Stoppard's pleasant young gentlemen disappear leaving behind the odour of University wit.[26]

The bloodless nature of Stoppard's work can be seen in his other plays. His latest, *After Magritte* (1970) has been described as a cross between John Le Carre and T. S. Eliot! His success can only be seen as a reflection of the state of the theatre rather than a just assessment of his work; if parochial describes Pinter it is difficult to think of the word for Stoppard.[27]

[26] Robert Brustein, *The Third Theatre* (1970), pp. 149–53.

[27] His career at the National Theatre continues with the production of *Jumpers* in 1972, described in *Plays and Players* as an 'ingenious and witty, if slightly over-indulgent attempt to bring literate comedy back into style' which 'almost works'. It was voted Best Play of 1972 by the critics in *Plays and Players* Annual awards.

# CHAPTER SEVEN

# Recent Dramatists

By 1963, the historian of British Theatre has a hard task in deciding what are the most significant features of a wider but less definable panorama. The New Wave was no longer confined to Sloane Square and Stratford East, and commercial managers found it profitable to book Osborne, Pinter and even Wesker, in response to a shift in public taste. In 1963 the National Theatre opened[1] but it cannot be said that its policy under Olivier and its dramaturg Kenneth Tynan, captured from *The Observer,* was to have any marked effect on the writing of new drama or, indeed, on the life of the theatre. Its productions, usually well received, seemed to aim at fulfilling the maxim: *épater les bourgeois.* George Devine retired from the Royal Court in 1965, proclaiming victory over the commercial theatre but asking, also, where the writers were to fill this victorious theatre, and, in 1966, Charles Marowitz was lamenting that there was no second wave of writers.[2]

One obvious source of drama was television.[3] The theatre

[1] See Appendix I.

[2] The indefatigable John Russell Taylor has discovered it; see *The Second Wave* (1971).

[3] Television began with experimental two-hour daily programmes in 1936 when there were 280 sets in the London region, and by 1939 interest was spreading. There was no fresh start until 1946 and even then the popularity of television was small. As late as 1953 (Coronation Year) people watched the ceremony in bars and hotels. By 1955, however, commercial television was added to the BBC and development was rapid and inescapable.

had resisted to some extent the threat of the talking pictures but now both cinema and theatre found themselves increasingly threatened by this latest cuckoo. Television could provide everything either of the other two could provide without the hardships which a visit to the cinema or theatre entails. In retrospect, the cinema appears to have suffered most, possibly because it was, itself, a mass media. The inter-relationship of the three media is too complex for any convincing generalisation but it would be generally admitted that television is not so much a substitute for art in the theatre or the cinema as a factor which changed the habits of much of the population. The audience for television is certainly much larger and more varied than any other audience, and though it is fashionably considered an uncritical audience and productions are controlled by programme ratings or the need for regular advertisement breaks, we cannot ignore the fact that, for example, in the case of Pinter, television seems to have been a great help. Television requires the eighteenth-century virtue of regular, competent writing and provides an outlet for decent, even distinguished, dramatists like Clive Exton, Alan Plater, John Hopkins, Alun Owen and John Mortimer. These writers have moved into live theatre at some time or other but the emergence of a truly important dramatist out of television seems more occasional than, logically, it should be. David Mercer springs to mind as a dramatist who started on television before he went to the West End (with Peter O'Toole) and he has returned to television. But it is difficult to justify his selection on more than personal grounds, or indicate in what way he is more important than, say, Plater, Owen or Mortimer. There is that in Mercer's work—in his striking treatment of contemporary themes—which marks him out from other dramatists. In 1965 Mercer (b. 1928) almost seemed dramatist of the year: he had produced an ambitious trilogy *The Generations, A Suitable Case for Treatment* (1962) and *Ride a Cock Horse*. In 1970 Mercer is still very much a name in the theatre with stage productions of *Flint and After Haggerty* and television productions of *The Cellar*

144

*and the Almond Tree* and *Emma's Time*. It was in 1970, too, that Mercer announced his swan-song to politics, confirming a basic trend in his work. *The Generations* was three plays based on working-class background in the collieries of Yorkshire. *Where the Difference Begins* (1961) showed how two sons grow away from their father because of their education and gradually move into the middle class, while *A Climate of Fear* (1962) tackled the important issue of the time, nuclear disarmament. But to these strands was added, in the third part, *The Birth of a Private Man* (1963), the personal theme of Mercer: alienation and the confusion that follows when a personality tries to escape the confines of ideologies and formulae. One of the main characters, Colin Waring, tries to withdraw into private life, to marry and have a family, but this movement from the public life is only a symptom of his total withdrawal from the horror of the world as he sees it, and leads to his suicide on the Berlin Wall. Balancing Colin is Jurek who, coming from a concentration camp, has seen the horror, but also sees that, as a private individual, he must go on fighting it.

All Mercer's important characters are trying to be born as private individuals and Mercer's way of describing the experience is to show them either going mad or turning into animals. His next group of plays was about alienation: *A Suitable Case for Treatment* (filmed as *Morgan), For Tea on Sunday* (1963) and *In Two Minds* (1967). The same theme runs through his first two stage plays, *The Governor's Lady* (1965) (originally a radio play) and *Ride a Cock Horse* (1965) a tragic play about a working-class man, his guilt and the women in his life, who ends up as a big baby in his father's arms rather than continue the fight for survival as an individual. Mercer's own life is in these plays—his first-hand experience of mental illness, his movement from old-fashioned liberal socialist to Marxist to, finally, a communist without a party. In an interview of 1965 Mercer spoke of himself as much less committed to narrow social and political causes. In writing his first play he felt strongly about things like CND

145

and that drama was the way to deal with such feelings. But, clearly, plays are plays not propaganda, and the ideas and feelings would occur in the context of people, whose personalities would colour them. Thus, by *The Birth of a Private Man,* he had become interested in the character of Colin, a disillusioned idealist who goes mad attempting to escape his social situation. The plays that followed were concerned with the idea of social alienation expressed in terms of psychological alienation. Much of Mercer's work, therefore, is sympathetically concerned with madness, loneliness, neurosis and the blurred frontier between what society calls sane and insane, with the balancing act that some individuals have to perform to preserve the appearances of sanity while inwardly confronting what we call insanity.

In this Mercer has been influenced by the work of the psychoanalyst, R. D. Laing, one of whose theses is that schizophrenia may be a response to the breakdown of personal relationships within the family; that a person (*e.g.* Morgan) struggles to act consistently with himself regardless of whether his actions are socially acceptable or not, and that neurosis may, therefore, simply be a creative way of revealing the personality. The judgement of society on such a struggle is as much a political as a medical act. Thus, Morgan is a failed revolutionary. Unable to give his allegiance to revolutionary social change, haunted by the deterioration of those ideals in a country where the revolution has taken place, he produces a new mythology out of the debris: a world where the innocence of animals is the counterpoint to the corruption of men, where the gorilla, which seldom uses its great strength aggressively, becomes the image of Morgan's *alter ego.* Mercer believes, like Wesker, that the logic of events has carried us beyond the time when it was possible to give ourselves simply and wholeheartedly to clear-cut causes like nuclear disarmament. The realities, now, are an affluent society and no brave causes. But it is useless to complain; we must learn to live in such a world. Wesker is elegiac in his response, Mercer sees the only possible revolution left in terms of an individual. Thus any expression of individuality is a revolutionary gesture and helps us to escape categories. He does not see such a man in romantic terms as a divine fool, indeed he makes no great claims for him, but he does wish to suggest that our dividing line between what is or is not sane may be too arbitrary, and designed to reassure us. The experiences of insanity may, even if they do not fit into our preconceptions, have some validity.

The companion piece, *The Governor's Lady,* was commissioned by Barbara Bray in 1960 for the BBC but she left before it was finished. It was actually written after *Where the Difference Begins,* during the writing of the rest of the trilogy when Mercer, like his compatriot, David Storey, was trying to find out whether the two halves, social-realist and comic-fantasist, could co-exist. By 1965 the theatre, for Mercer, was a place where ideas could be raised, questions posed and conclusions reached, but in a ritual form which would synthesis the disparate and contradictory elements; where, in some mysterious way, the play would bind together centripetal elements.

*Belcher's Luck* (1966) celebrates the maverick quality of an individual who escapes from the Establishment but, as in the later *Flint* (1970) is finally defeated. In the elegant television play *The Parachute* (1968) a young airman, played by John Osborne, had his present, and past, overshadowed by a masterful father, though the setting was no longer the West Riding, but Germany. Essentially a memory play it was followed by *The Cellar and the Almond Tree* and *After Haggerty*—plays about a past when, whether happily or not, things were manageable, suggesting that the past can be recreated as either a withdrawal or to serve our present needs. *After Haggerty* (1970) also showed a return to the ideas of *The Generations* and to the West Riding in the splendid creation of the protagonist's father. Bernard Link, a theatre critic about the same age as Mercer, has given up the struggle. He is successful but, after two broken marriages, with his political faith in ruins (he happened to be in both Hungary and Czechoslovakia when the Russians marched in), he is resigned

147

to getting through the day on whiskey. Link has moved into a new flat to escape from the past but becomes 'linked' with the lives of its previous occupants. Claire arrives looking for Haggerty (the previous owner) and bringing his baby son; and the flat is being decorated by two acquaintances of Haggerty, one of whom is queer. Into this ménage comes Link's West Riding father—an engine driver—flooded out of his Yorkshire home. It is the absent Haggerty who 'links' all these people together, sending enigmatic telegrams, a wreath and, finally, a coffin announcing his death on the African Freedom trail. Stirred by these things, Link and Claire relive the seminal moments of their lives, such as Budapest and Hungary, and everyone gets on everyone's nerves. For, in spite of the serious political, and sexual, questions, Mercer writes this play as a drawing-room comedy with great energy. The same energy and comedy can be seen in *Flint* (1970) but without any really serious questions beneath the surfaces. The protagonist, an Anglican minister whose life has been scandalous with no respect for the faith he is supposed to preach or the seventh commandment, is transformed by the arrival of a simple Irish girl, unmarried and pregnant. Critics have seen Flint as a kind of genteel Belcher (and life is kinder to Flint than it was to Belcher) and made much of the play as a study in truth and hypocrisy, old age and youth but Mercer seems to be simply enjoying the use of language, the creation of a large number of minor characters and frequent comic interludes. The result is amusing but somehow fails to melt into significance, particularly as no one can match the energy and optimism of Flint himself which makes the play very one-sided. 1970 also saw the completion of Mercer's second trilogy of television plays begun in 1968 with *On the Eve of Publication* and now completed with *The Cellar and the Almond Tree* and *Emma's Time*. In the first part Kelvin, a Left-Wing novelist and Nobel Prizewinner, is assailed by doubts at the end of his life, just before the publication of his last book; in part two, Mercer looks at the fate of Kelvin's friend. Sladek/Volubin who is tortured first by the Nazis and then by the post-war communist government, while the third part looks at the situation of Kelvin's mistress, Emma, who finds herself alone after his death and who meets Volubin. All three were distinguished pieces of television drama and even if Mercer is, as yet, not as impressive as the dramatists of the New Wave, his impact is greater than most of his contemporaries.[4]

In any less fertile period there would be place to discuss the work of dramatists like Marcus, Orton (whose death was a serious loss at a time when brilliant and entertaining theatre was rapidly vanishing beneath voguishness and pretentiousness) or Simon Gray. There would also be scope to explain why the Shaffer brothers were so successful in the West End when David Halliwell failed. And Halliwell's failure with a play like *Little Malcolm and His Struggle against the Eunuchs* (1965) and its pioneer treatment of student revolt is very puzzling. As is the rejection of Peter Terson. The fact that the talents of Halliwell and Terson are frustrated while Shaffer and Stoppard arrive straight in the West End should cause unease. Fortunately Terson found one of the two homes for writers at this period: Stoke-on-Trent.

In 1955 Stephen Joseph collected a group of friends to form Studio Theatre Ltd., and his work coincides with that of George Devine at the Royal Court. But where Devine worked in Sloane Square, Stephen Joseph decided to form a new kind of theatre and went to Scarborough where he worked at Theatre-in-the-Round. In 1962 he opened a second company at Stoke-on-Trent where the Victoria Theatre was converted. Joseph's company was originally small (about six actors) with an Arts Council grant to tour widely. It held summer playwriting courses during which, for example, David Campton was helped. It produced James Saunders who, like Campton, had an Arts Council Bursary and Allan Ayckbourn (then called Ronald Allen). Joseph died in 1966, by which time the theatre at Stoke had separated itself, painfully, from its parent. The theatre at Stoke is now run by Peter Cheeseman

---

[4] In 1972 Mercer was working on the screenplay for the film of Saul Bellow's *Herzog* and has a new play ready called *Ducksong*.

who remembers receiving the manuscript of a play in 1963 called *The Runaway* which impressed him, although homosexual incidents made it impossible to perform. He met Terson (b. 1932), discussed two or three possibilities and Terson wrote *A Night to Make the Angels Weep* while working as a games teacher in a small village in the Vale of Evesham. Terson joined the staff at Stoke as resident dramatist in 1966. As a dramatist he admits that he fears sophistication, that he is prolific and that he depends on another man, like Cheeseman, to tell him what to do. Basically he dislikes the loneliness of writing and finds the theatre a good place to work in because it brings a writer in contact with the producer and his actors. It is not surprising, therefore, that although his plays are apparently finished they change during production either in the hands of Cheeseman at Stoke or with Croft at the NYT.[5] These two 'homes' for Terson reflect the two sides of the dramatist and he produces plays which suit the demands of two widely differing companies. Stoke has small, quiet plays, well-knit and usually rural in setting while the NYT has loud, showy, energetic and urban plays. Outside the environs of Stoke Terson is probably known for his plays at the NYT: *Zigger-Zagger* (1967), *The Apprentices* (1968), *Fuzz* (1969) which generally employ social stereotypes, large crowds and choric exposition. Terson is best seen, however, in the Stoke plays, exploring the suffocating nature of the Vale of Evesham and the dangers of change. The NYT plays have become increasingly outlines to be filled in by Littlewood techniques but the Stoke plays suggest complexity or approaches to it.

Thus, in *A Night to Make the Angels Weep* (1964) we find the basic opposition of all his early Stoke plays: past versus present, urban versus rural, hill versus valley. They all contain hints of some impending disaster from some unspecified, possibly non-existent force, a kind of atmosphere in which he is less successful than, say, David Rudkin. But there is also good colloquial dialogue. In 1966 he wrote a documentary,

150

[5] See Michael Croft's introduction to *The Apprentices*.

*The Knotty,* and his most recent play was commissioned by his native Newcastle for a new University Theatre. *Prisoners of War* (1971) has been called a Geordie *Under Milk Wood,* but the title points to the theme that the working classes are prisoners of war, whether the war be national or social, a strain of social comment which had appeared in *The 1861 Whitby Lifeboat Disaster* (1970). Terson admits that he finds being a full-time writer a strain, understandably in view of his output. It is difficult to judge whether his recent work is a consequence of the strain or of the policy of documentaries pursued at Stoke recently. *Prisoners of War* has the usual episodic structure and is comic at the usual sacrifice of shape and character, while displaying the usual theatrical energy.[6]

The main source of new dramatic writing in the sixties remained, however, the Royal Court, which retained its basic characters as a writers' theatre. 18 October 1965 represented a new start at the Court after the retirement of George Devine. The Court was now run by William Gaskill, assisted by Iain Cuthbertson and Keith Johnstone and the season's three authors were N. F. Simpson, Ann Jellicoe and a newcomer, Edward Bond. Gaskill's first response to running the Court was to feel that the zig-zag course between an Osborne play to make money and experimental work like *Meals on Wheels* playing to empty houses was unhealthy. He turned back, therefore, to repertory and changed Devine's slogan—the right to fail—into his own: the right to succeed. His policy at the Court soon gave rise to misgivings. Clearly the Court could not and should not re-enact the heroics of the late 1950s but its main publicity now seemed to come from Gaskill's personal truculence. The original fight over *Saved* was calmed down by Bond himself, but the notorious *Macbeth* of 1966 led to attacks by Gaskill on critics at large, for their insincerity, their superficiality and their desire to make journalistic capital. As several of these critics pointed out they can, and do, often *fill* a theatre, but unless a piece is very bad they have very little power to empty it. Moreover, since Macbeth was played by

[6] Terson dramatised *Moby Dick* for Stoke in 1972.

Alec Guinness, little they could say or do would prevent the production, however bad, from being a sell-out. In 1969 Gaskill was still making headlines, for the wrong reasons, when he offered free seats for the last two weeks of the run of *Life Price,* a play about a child-murderer, by Michael O'Neill and Jeremy Seabrook. This filled a theatre that had previously not been filled, and with young people. If it seemed a good idea there remained the nagging suspicion that those young people could afford to pay for their seats, that the Court was subsidised, that a play that goes badly might, just, be a bad play and that while theatre was free in Sloane Square it was dying outside London.

But Gaskill also backed Bond, Storey, Howarth, Hampton. Devine had founded a writers' theatre in the belief that there was no better way of getting good work out of everybody than a good text. The Court had fought hard on this principle and fighting induces paranoia, traces of which remain today. The 'family' at the Court often behave as if there was a vast West End conspiracy against them and nothing less than complete approval will satisfy. Gaskill's resentments over the treatment of his *Macbeth* made critics feel that they had intruded on his privacy, which is ridiculous. When control passed from Gaskill to Gaskill with Anthony Page and Lindsay Anderson, the Court began to be more outward-looking, recognising that casting has to be as it can and that a theatre dedicated to new plays cannot follow that ideal of a permanent company which has hovered over the Court since 1956. The result has been some splendid appearances at the Court: Gielgud and Richardson, Alec McCowen, Richard O'Callaghan and Diana Dors. How three men manage to run the Court is their secret, but it has been very successful. Gaskill in his report for 1970 can make considerable claims—plays by Storey, the establishment of Bond and the discovery of the dramatist D. H. Lawrence; first plays by Christopher Hampton, John Hopkins, Frank Norman, Wole Soyinka, Arnold Wesker and Charles Wood; the opening of the Theatre Upstairs in 1969 and visits by the Open Theatre (in Jean-Claude van Itallie's

*American Hurrah,* 1967), the Paper Bag Players (1967), the Bread and Puppet Theatre (1968) and a controversial production of Michael McClure's *The Beard* (1968); and productions of classics like *Ubu Roi, The Voysey Inheritance* (1966), *The Soldier's Fortune* (1967), *Twelfth Night* (1968) and *The Double Dealer* (1969). The really important thing is that the Court has continued to foster writers, of which the most controversial has been Edward Bond and, to my mind, the most distinguished, David Storey.

Edward Bond (b. 1935), a Londoner from a working-class background, started writing plays when he came out of the Army. He had written several, and some poetry, before Keith Johnstone, a member of the Court Writers' Group, read his play called *Klaxon in Atreus' Palace* and assured Gaskill (who found the play difficult) that Bond was talented. Johnstone gave a Sunday performance of *The Pope's Wedding* in 1962. The Court then commissioned a play and Bond gave them *Saved* which was banned by the Lord Chamberlain and given club performances in 1965. *Early Morning* was given a Sunday performance in 1968 and in 1969 a season of Bond plays included the first public performances of *Saved, Early Morning* and a new play, *Narrow Road to the Deep North.* The battle over censorship, fought over *Saved,* was repeated with *Early Morning* although Gaskill now complained that he was not merely fighting traditional enemies—the censor, the critics and the property owners—but also the Arts Council, the British Council, the Foreign Office and members of Parliament. As it happened, the Arts Council continued to subsidise the Court, the British Council sponsored a tour of two of Bond's plays and the Theatre Bill was passed.

*The Pope's Wedding* is loosely based, like James Saunders's *Next Time I'll Sing to You,* on Trevelyan's book *A Hermit Disclosed,* but where Saunders concentrates on the Hermit, Bond is interested in the effect the hermit has on the life of a young married couple where the wife has the responsibility for looking after him. The husband becomes obsessed with the enigma of the hermit's existence and finally takes his place by

153

killing him, which is nearer *A Slight Ache* by Pinter than the Saunders's play. As in his next play, *Saved,* Bond is interested in the aimless life of the young couple, a life that accepts casual sex and violence as part of living. When Scopey says that he is going to marry Pat he seems to have disengaged himself from an aimless life, but he then finds he has taken on the hermit, Alen, as well. The fascination with Alen takes up more and more of his time until he loses his job and neglects his wife, though it is not clear whether this fascination rests on a desire to understand why Alen is as he is or to achieve Alen's sense of withdrawal. The same themes of obsessively gloomy family life and narrow opportunities are taken up in *Saved* and the best writing is in these scenes rather than in the more lurid episodes. It was the stoning of a baby (invisible) that caused all the fuss: the mother had reduced the baby to an object because she cannot picture him as a human being and because he is treated as an object the gang can kill him. Whether this works in the theatre—Bond sees it as ritual—is doubtful and the image is much more powerful than the final image—Len repairing a chair—which is supposed to balance it. In his preface, Bond wrote that he was a pessimist by experience but an optimist by nature and he insists that *Saved* is a comedy, that even if the play comes to the brink of despair, some hope gleams through. We are bound to feel, however, that the title is ironic and savagely so. All Bond's work is concerned with the corruption of man's innocence by environment and upbringing, through abstractions like society, morality and order. Bond maintains that when personal freedom is frustrated by external authority it takes an ugly, alternative, course, but he also insists that there is no such thing as instinctual evil, violence or cruelty: take a dog, chain it and it will become vicious—and this is what we do with children. A child denied total freedom becomes devious and we create a chronic defensive state which we call aggression. Bond, however, has no convincing answer as to where, if there is no instinctual evil, evil itself can be said to have originated. He seems to suggest, or allow, that it lies in our

154

consciousness—which would seem to be fairly essential. It is this consciousness which enables us to plan and calculate in ways that no other species can, but since we do not know how to use this faculty properly, it becomes our enemy. He believes that aggression is under control in animal societies and serves a useful function, but in human societies the presence of aggression is absolutely mad. And so it may be, but it exists, has always existed and given human nature probably always will. Bond seems to maintain a faulty view of human nature, or restates the doctrine of original sin and this gives a bias to his work; but no more so than that found in any committed writer.

*Saved* was a transitional play, a compromise between naturalism and the freer form seen in his next play *Early Morning*. Where *Saved* portrays the suffering classes, *Early Morning* looks at those who exert the pressures which 'cause' the suffering. The play takes the form of fantasy with historical labels and as such was neither offensive nor effective. The assertion that Queen Victoria had a Lesbian crush on Florence Nightingale, disguised as John Brown, is obviously a grotesque joke, and we are in the realms of fantasy, free from logic or proof. Therefore the play cannot be said to attack anything. It exists as firmly within its fantasy world as an Orton comedy and, likewise, fails to shake even the flimsiest of foundations. Its disgusting things happen in the context of dream or nightmare, where oral eroticism becomes cannibalism, and infantile sexuality suggests the world of Ionesco and Genet. Or we can try to see it as Bond intended, in social terms. Bond sees Arthur as the development of his central character Scopey and Len. Len cannot see how to act in *Saved* and this failure is brought into *Early Morning* and compared with Arthur who cannot see how to solve the problem of correct political action because he is not entirely himself, being joined to George, the purely socialised version of himself. He can see the nature of Len's predicament more clearly but is still tied-up and Len kicks the clothes over him to illustrate this. In the second act Arthur goes mad under the pressure and follows the law and order line (Victorian) but, if

155

this is the answer, it seems to lead to more and more laws, and if such is the case what is the point of living? Arthur sees that we are all part of the same body, in the same predicament, and by the last act his vision has cleared. He is no longer baffled by excuses and pretences but sees that society behaves like cannibals; this is society's view of heaven and he wishes to escape. The play is written from Arthur's point of view and to develop his character. For Len there was no escape, only an image to suggest that he had not been completely destroyed. But Arthur ends up as a complete person. Society, Bond contends, could not exist unless it destroyed people since a human being was not designed as a tool, part of a mechanistic society.

Such a play begs many questions: society is not simply 'them' and 'us'. According to admirers of Bond this does not matter, as they cheerfully assert that in the theatre what is important is not the abstract validity (John Russell Taylor's dismissive phrase) of the image presented or its power to change our minds but the effectiveness of the image itself; that Bond's obsessions bludgeon us into belief. But what this can mean is not clear; how can image, even in the theatre, be effective if it is not valid or meaningful? Impressive as his plays are the objections to them are not mere dislike; Bond's view of society and animals is what the plays are about and it is contentious.

In *Narrow Road to the Deep North* (1969), which was written very rapidly to serve as a comment on a conference about city planning held in Coventry, in June 1968, Bond moved further away from everyday reality into a parable mercifully free of questions about Queen Victoria. It is a play about the building of a good city, but it is set in Japan at a time when the Westerners first landed. It concerns the city built by an upstart tyrant, Shogo, which is captured by the forces of British colonialism. The play itself is a meditation from the point of view of Basho, a poet-priest, who is going north to seek enlightenment. He finds a baby exposed to die and leaves it. When he returns thirty years later he finds the city built on that spot by Shogo, who may very well have been

that baby. Shogo has grown up evil and resentful because he
was unloved as a child. His tyranny is overthrown by the
Commodore and his Sister Georgina, but she goes mad when a
whole form of her pupils is killed because she will not reveal
the true heir hidden among them. Kiro, refused as a pupil by
Basho has become Shogo's friend and confronted by all this
kills himself just at the moment when a drowning man calls for
help. The man saves himself, which makes it difficult to accept
that a moral of the play could be that active help, not
speculation, is what is needed. If Basho had abandoned the
road—and he learned nothing in the north—and if he had not
been a poet (and selfish for his art), then. . . . The Orientialism
is only a Brechtian device to show us familar problems in a
different light, it does not imply an understanding of Oriental
thought processes. Bond has said that if there is a villain in the
play it would be Basho who might have picked up the child but
this ignores the fact that as a good Buddhist Basho would have
known better and would no more pick up the child than one
should assist a man who is drowning, since to do either might
be interfering with Karma. Also, had he picked up the child
there might have been no need to write poems and when Bond
suggests that we should behave like animals because they have
better manners, he concedes that they do not write plays.

Allardyce Nicoll's comparison of Bond with Chapman is
most persuasive here.[7] Nicoll suggests that the absurdities
arise from a desire to be different which is so self-centred that,
in both writers, the ideas are not fully realised. When Bond
writes that the stoning of a baby is as nothing compared with
the atrocities of our own time (revealing, incidentally a
contemporary preoccupation with numbers) we can agree and
think of concentration camps; but all Bond can offer is the
strategic bombing of German towns. He insists that he wants
to be just a good writer not a social writer although the insistence is safely within his context that all art functions socially;
he admires Pinter and Charles Wood, lives mainly off film
work (for example, Antonioni's *Blow Up*) and sadly admits

[7] Allardyce Nicoll, *English Drama: A Modern Viewpoint* (1968), pp. 151–2.     157

that he writes largely for people who do not understand his work. His latest play, *Lear,* opened at the Royal Court in 1971. Here Bond took Shakespeare's play and its resolution and attempted to make it viable for himself and contemporary society. Cordelia is very much altered and Lear himself appears to learn nothing from the experiences of the play which is generously littered with executions, torture, rape, blinding and sundry other acts of violence. It is not clear whether knowledge of the source play is an advantage or not. Bond has summed up his work as self-education; the plays are 'an examination of what it means to be living at this time', and try to make people recognise their frustrations and use them unaggressively, rather than seeking scapegoats. But it can be objected that Bond has an oversimple view of politics and human nature which disturbs our response to the obvious seriousness of his plays.

David Storey (b. 1933) is a dramatist for whom the word 'traditional' scarcely seems old-fashioned enough. He studied at the Slade School of Fine Arts and has been a professional Rugby player, schoolteacher and showground tent erector, occupations which figure in his novels and plays. After he had written seven or eight novels without success he tried his hand at writing plays beginning, in 1959, with *The Restoration of Arnold Middleton.* But when *This Sporting Life* was published in 1950, after being turned down fifteen times, followed by *Flight Into Camden* (1960) and *Radcliffe* (1963), Granada asked him for a play. He rewrote *Restoration* for them but was unwilling to make certain changes which Granada insisted on and so it was sent to four repertory companies who also turned it down. The BBC showed interest but objected to the hero's attraction to his mother-in-law whom he assaults in the last act, and dropped the idea. When *This Sporting Life* was being filmed Lindsay Anderson, who has been Storey's producer ever since, asked Storey if he had ever written a play and hoped to produce *Restoration* at the Court with Richard Harris in the main rôle. This fell through, and Storey continued to rewrite the play everytime he looked at it until

2. The Roundhouse, Chalk Farm (Winter 1964).

4. National Theatre on the South Bank under construction.

1. The Royal Shakespeare Theatre, Stratford-upon-Avon.

3. The Chichester Festival Theatre.

5. Peter Hall.

6. Peter Brook.

7. Edward Bond.

8. David Storey.

9. Arnold Wesker.

10. John Osborne.

11. Laurence Olivier as Othello, directed by John Dexter.
National Theatre, 1964.

12. Albert Finney as John Armstrong of
Gilnockie in John Arden's
*Armstrong's Last Goodnight.*
National Theatre, 1965.

13. Laurence Olivier as the Captain in
Strindberg's *The Dance of Death.*
National Theatre, 1967.

14. John Stride as Rosencrantz and Edward Petherbridge as
Guildenstern in *Rosencrantz and Guildenstern are Dead* by Tom Stoppard.
The National Theatre production was directed by Derek Goldby
with scenery and costumes by Desmond Heeley, 1967.

15. The Royal Court Theatre in Sloane Square.

16. 1956 production of Osborne's *Look Back in Anger*. Left to right:
Mary Ure as Alison, Alan Bates as Cliff, Helena Hughes as Helena,
Kenneth Haigh as Jimmy Porter.

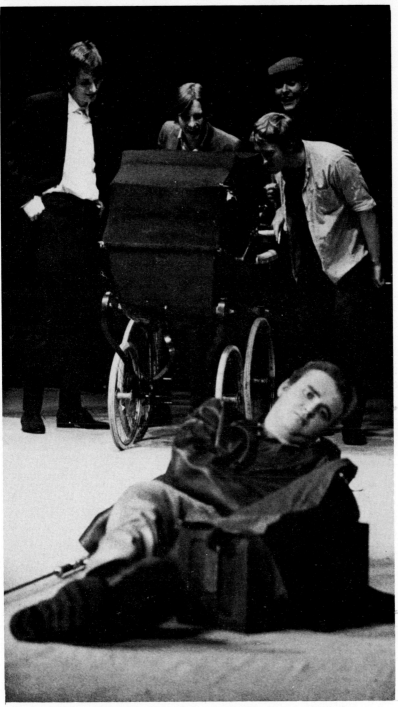

17. The 1965 production of Edward Bond's *Saved* at the Royal
Court with Ronald Pickup, Dennis Waterman, John Bull,
William Stewart, Tony Selby.

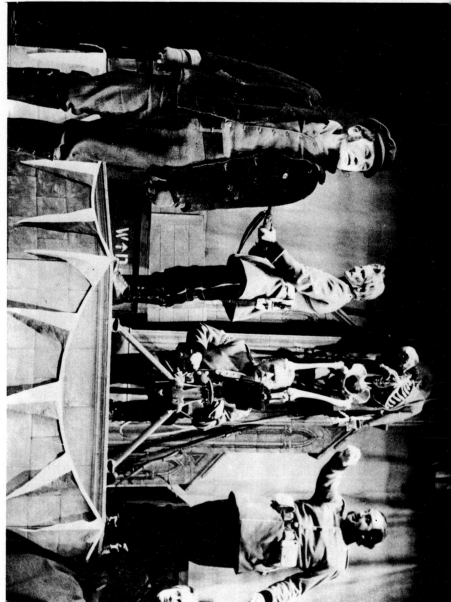

18. Serjeant Musgrave's Dance by John Arden, revived at the Royal Court Theatre in 1965

19. The *Hair* tribe .  *Hair* opened at the Shaftesbury Theatre, London, in September 1968.

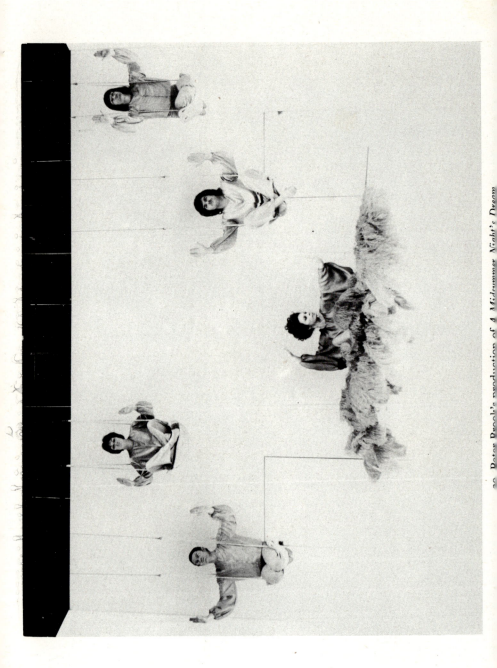

20 Peter Brook's production of *A Midsummer Night's Dream*

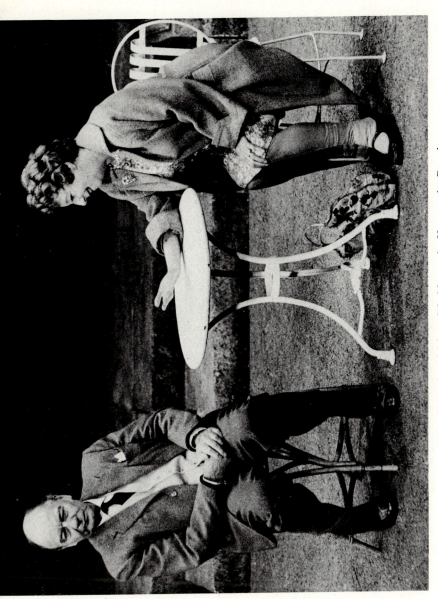

21. John Gielgud and Mona Washborne in *Home* at the Royal
Court Theatre, 1970.

22. A scene from the new 1950s Rock 'n' Roll musical *Grease* at the New London Theatre, 1973.

Gordon McDougal put it on at the Traverse in 1966 and the Court, its interest reawakened, produced it in 1967.

Storey admits that he turns to plays when other forms of creation are blocked and the basic theme of his novels runs into the plays: a man trying to make his life work on two levels: the spiritual and the external—generally with a sense of failure. *The Restoration of Arnold Middleton* sprang from a remark by a friend on seeing a local teacher walking out with his wife and mother-in-law, and the comment: he's knocking both of them off! The hero of the play is a teacher doing a school production of Robin Hood[8] in terms of northern revolt against bad central government. This hero is alienated both from society and his family, and his fantasy life has encroached on real life. Unable to give himself to his wife, attracted to his mother-in-law, he uses the house as a museum for objects, including a newly acquired suit of armour. But he cannot hide in the armour, nor be Robin Hood, so he toys with the idea of going mad, which he describes as 'the one refuge I've always felt I was able to afford'. His restoration by the end of the play from a never very clearly explained breakdown is ambiguous, particularly as his madness appears to have provided no new insights. But the play has immense vitality and has rightly been seen as Hamlet in the West Riding, asking questions such as is he the victim of a dominant mother, and how does his kingship relate to modern suburban life.

This production started Storey writing more plays and since he was having difficulties with a new novel he wrote five or six very rapidly: both *In Celebration* and *The Contractor* date from this period. *In Celebration* was produced in April, 1969 and it shows Storey looking, compassionately, at that thing called human nature rather than using human nature for doctrinaire purposes. There is no sense of ideology or commitment, just love and hate in a family. Three sons travel north to celebrate their parent's 40th wedding anniversary.

[8] There is a school of thought which claims Robin Hood as a native of Storey's Wakefield.

159

Although two are married neither brings his wife. Andy, the eldest, is a dangerous, destructive person who has thrown up his legal practice to become a painter, Colin, the bachelor, is a rather smug, successful, labour relations man while Steven, the youngest, is a teacher who has just abandoned the study of society at which he has been working for seven years and is in a depressed state intensified by the reunion. Colin, a correct sort of man, is unlovable, and Andy's banter conceals a hatred for his mother apparently explained by her having to marry his father, which she saw as a social comedown, and having emasculated his father in the process of maintaining her social pretensions. Ironically that first child, Jamie, died from pneumonia at the age of seven. But finally it becomes clear that Andy's hatred of his mother springs from the fact that she farmed him out at the age of five when she was having another child. The play ends with all traces of Andy's revenge being wiped out by the father.

Storey saw in the three sons aspects of human behaviour which interested him: conformity in Colin, the spiritual in Steven and the revolutionary in Andy, and the drama, initially, comes from the conflict of these three views. But when the sons are faced with a greater reality, that of their parents, and they sense that these parents live their own lives without any views on society except such as are exhibited in their living the play moves into another phase. The form is not in the least experimental, the dialogue energetic, and the basic impression is the unease of these complex, rootless children when faced with the solidity of their parents and the old, hideous (at least by contemporary standards) home: *their* old home. The explanation for Andy's behaviour is, perhaps, too glib, particularly as the mother does not emerge as the kind of monster Andy claims she is, but this, too, serves to intensify Andy's character rather than spoil the play. Storey says that the mother is well aware what is going on all the time, but the major difficulty for audiences in these self-conscious times, and especially at the Royal Court, is to appreciate that the parents' life is not a criticism of anything. It presents itself as having a greater reality than the intellectual, socially-orientated, analytical existences of the children. Beyond this, its narrowness is a kind of criticism, but the opposing rootlessness makes it easy for such narrowness to be the most important thing that the play has to offer.

*The Contractor,* which followed in October 1969, is a difficult play to judge because of its form. During the action of the play a marquee is put up and taken down, involving the people who erect it and the people who use it. The expertise required for this commands respect and may distract us from thinking about the play itself. During Acts 1 and 2 the marquee is erected for the wedding of the contractor's daughter, Claire, to the aristocratic Maurice and the marquee is dismantled in Act 3. As this happens the family drift in and out: Ewbank, the contractor, with money and a temper, his father, with a hatred of machines and a passion for rope, the daughter and a son, Paul who seems to exist only to despise everything his father does. The workmen, too, are a collection of misfits: a man left by his wife, an embezzler, two Irishmen and an idiot, such as only Ewbank would employ or could get to work for him. But the play seems to go no further than this web of mistrustful relationships and leads to no kind of conclusion. It can be characterised as light comedy with suggestions of a not quite realised drift beneath. We feel this, possibly, because the tent motif has appeared elsewhere in Storey's work and readers of *Radcliffe* will not only recognise Ewbank but also remember that it is in a tent that Radcliffe finally achieves his relationship with Tolson. Storey had explored in the novels his own dilemma, the division between appetite, the physical capacity for living in society and the opposing desire to lead one's own spiritual existence. In Machin (*This Sporting Life*) he explored the physical side, looking at the spiritual or feminine aspect in *Flight Into Camden,* and he brought the two aspects together in *Radcliffe.* Here, in a large Gothic novel, reminiscent of the Brontës, Radcliffe, the last scion of a once noble family, goes mad amidst the encroaching housing estate which spawned Tolson.

161

At one point Radcliffe murmurs that he would have liked to live in a castle, or a tent; and his explanation for killing Tolson is that he wanted an absolute, an ideal, an order for things. *The Contractor* captures very little of this; it is not Wesker's *The Kitchen*. Yet it does move into a criticism of Western society and the split between being absorbed by it and detached from it, with themes of violence and madness, suggesting the need for order, and a home. And, perhaps, madness—present in Arnold, Steven and Radcliffe—is the high price that has to be paid for detachment, as Storey's next elegiac play suggests. The image at the end of *The Contractor* of a little white table suggested to him that people could come, sit at it and talk. *Home* (1970) is, technically, his most adventurous and austere play so far. Produced by Lindsay Anderson, with a brilliant cast, it looks a slight play in the sense that nothing happens and very little is said. The four characters are static, returning to commonplaces, sustained by routine which they have elevated into ritual, leaving us to infer the play from what they do not say or do as much as from what is said and done. A play of great, gaping silences it demands strong ensemble playing and enormous attention from the audience. Here the themes of home and insanity converge as an institution provides the only supportable environment for these losers in life. Like *Home,* Storey's next play, *The Changing Room* (1971) really only makes sense in the theatre. In it a rugby team undress, play the game, dress and go home having won the cup. Apart from being the first play to use nudity rather than abuse it, the play requires impressive ensemble work from actors, producer, designer and dramatist, so that here, for once, the perfect balance existed between the parts of a theatrical performance.[9]

The Court has also sustained the talents of various other writers such as David Cregan, Donald Howarth and Charles Wood. Of these Wood is, by far, the most unusual and interesting.

[9] Storey's latest play, *The Farm,* is scheduled for the Royal Court in early 1973; and possibly another, historical play, *Cromwell.*

Charles Wood (b. 1932) belongs to what Peter Brook has called the Rough Theatre, as in Jarry and Spike Milligan, where energy derives from truculence and obscenity. If we associate Owen with Liverpool, Terson and Rudkin with the Vale of Evesham, then Wood, son of actors touring the country, must be associated with the army, and it looks as if being a regular soldier from 1950–5 made the deepest impression on him. His first plays, written for television, all concern the army: *Traitor in a Tin Helmet* and *Prisoner and Escort*. This latter, together with *Spare* and a third play, *John Thomas*, were produced under the title *Cockade* at the Arts, in 1963, at the end of Michael Codron's regime. In the first play a prisoner is being taken by a sadistic corporal and his stupid private on a train where the prisoner, a born victim, meets a sympathetic girl but is revolted when he discovers she had a coloured lover. *Spare* is a mysterious little play set in a military museum where three soldiers are cleaning up and are showered from above by dust. The museum appears to exist as an image of military life which flows on unchangingly as old soldiers come and go. Such plays present difficulties for contemporary audiences since they generally assume that Wood must be anti-army but his fascination for loving detail about the army and a refusal to leap at an easy judgement suggest that although he is anti-war (and in *Spare* even war is allowed as an absurd necessity) he is not anti-army. He is passionately neutral, exploring what makes us behave as we do, as in his third play *John Thomas,* where he looks at a timid man's dreams of power. And since theatre is the second dominant image of his life Wood is concerned with the physical fact of stage and actors in front of an audience and the use of language—over which he has a poet's control— to explore the things he feels deeply about. He begins by entertaining, but having made something appear very funny he then shows it turning painfully sour, as in *John Thomas* where, up to a point, fascism is made an engaging subject.

His television play *Drill Pig* (1964) and the one-acter *Don't Make Me Laugh* (seen at the Aldwych in *Expeditions Two*

(1965)) both explored the contrast between military and civilian behaviour and looked forward to his two major plays *Dingo* and *H*, written for the National Theatre, although only one of them was produced there; and the film scripts for Richard Lester's *How I Won the War* and Tony Richardson's *Charge of the Light Brigade*. The other side of Wood produced scripts for the Beatles' film *Help!* and the English version of Fellini's *Satyricon* and, presumably, it was this side which wrote *Meals on Wheels* (1965) and *Fill the Stage With Happy Hours* (1966). Wood was living in Bristol when he wrote *Meals on Wheels* and decided he ought to write something about Bristol for Bristol. He came up with this farce which the Council renamed 'Muck on a Truck' and banned. The Royal Court produced it but Wood felt, defensively perhaps, that it was out of place there, having been written for Bristol to get angry about rather than in general terms of anger. The real difficulty was in seeing Wood, hitherto a devoted user of army obscenity and observer of army life, turned farceur with social purpose. Or so the play vaguely suggested. At the most charitable assessment it was a muddled play about a man searching for a wife or girl, with a weird family—a sister given to imaginary pregnancies and an aged father and elder half-brother who have to be waited on, hand and foot: hence the title. It was not very amusing and audiences were left with the suspicion, only, that something was being said. *Fill the Stage With Happy Hours,* too, was not about the army, but since it gave a nostalgic picture of life in a small provincial theatre it was also semi-autobiographical, and since the theatre represents another closed community with its own peculiar ways and language, it continued to demonstrate Wood's ear for words and satiric method, here reminiscent of Pinero Wood's return to the army in *Dingo* (1967) was, however, most welcome. Not unexpectedly, this play is an unheroic view of the North African campaign showing soldiers as foulmouthed, callous and sex-starved. A kind of riposte to *Cavalcade,* the weak construction is scarcely noticeable, and Wood rejects martial glory and heroism in favour of a sterile life with mimed masturbation and the pinning of the DSO on the bottom of a bikini worn by a transvestite officer. The play shows a war fought for politicians and ambitious generals; as a character remarks, in 1963 they hadn't heard about the Jews. And, of course, Rommel is portrayed more sympathetically than Monty—a view which life encourages. This, therefore, is an early example of the anti-heroic cliché, but no amount of cliché can dismiss the fact of Belsen. Indeed Wood's treatment of the army and war grows more in line with fashionable bias, and more ambitious. In *H* (1968) he turned to a historical subject, the Indian mutiny of 1857, firmly placed behind a deliberate proscenium arch. His subject, here, could be the dilemma of being both a Christian and a professional soldier although this would hardly be a dilemma in 1857 and, for different reasons, would hardly be so now. Or his theme could be the plight of those Englishmen who loved India and felt rejected by her, or simply a study of military men. The H of the title is General Havelock who is giving a dinner. The party is subdued since they have arrived at Cawnpore to discover that the women and children they came to save have been massacred. H is depressed, but Wood keeps him too passive for a tragic hero or even a good theatrical character, although as a soldier who would not tolerate bad language he makes an intriguing centrepiece for a Wood play. The construction is, once more, weak and the long solo speeches (the subtitle is 'Monologues at the Front of Burning Cities') hinder the play, putting characters in counterpoint but rarely in conflict, while some of the short interludes, if amusing, seem to be there only to give the play life. But Wood's lively use of language marks him out as an interesting dramatist.[10]

The Court's most recent, most praised dramatist is, of course, Christopher Hampton (b. 1946) who, by the age of 24, has had three very traditional plays produced at the Court, was appointed resident dramatist and head of scripts department in 1968 and whose slender output (in every sense)

[10] *Veterans,* starring John Gielgud, was produced at the Royal Court in March 1972.

has been received with little short of ecstasy. With a background of Lancing and Oxford, Hampton cheerfully admits to a life devoid of traumas, privations or other environmental catastrophes, and although he had to wait two years to get his first play produced he was still only 20 when it was. *When Did You Last See Your Mother* was written when he was only eighteen. The plot came to him sitting in a pub and the play took six weeks to write. It was given a Sunday night production in 1966 and sketches out youthful unhappiness in the rather narrow confines of Earls Court. Hampton seems to have felt the need to widen his scope in the next play and reading Enid Starkie's book on Rimbaud provided it. *Total Eclipse* (1968) deals with the well-known passion between Rimbaud and Verlaine, freely drawn on by Brecht in *Baal* and *The Jungle of the Cities* but treated here as a documentary: the destruction of the elder poet's marriage because of his infatuation with a seventeen-year-old lout, in twelve short scenes. Dr. Starkie poses two major questions: first, whether a correct picture can be painted of the poet from the incalculable contradictions and complexities 'and not merely a collection of abstractions loosely strung together', and secondly, can a satisfactory explanation be found for his abandonment of literature at the height of his powers, when he was not yet 20. Hampton presents the 'facts' and leaves it at that, attempting neither answer nor insight into either of these problems. *The Philanthropist* (1970) showed a return to the present day, Oxford and a suggestion of social comment. Hampton has said that he likes the civilised behaviour of Oxford but that, perhaps, civilised behaviour is doomed. At any rate he produces a hero who alienates everybody because he tries to be so good and kind—a sort of Jimmy Porter upside down. In an interview of 1970 Hampton suggested that the only worthwhile philosophical question to ask was whether to kill yourself: which leads on to whether or not to go on writing. The opening scene of *The Philanthropist*—the title should suggest Molière—is a brief discussion between a don and a young playwright who feels his play is being underpraised:

John *(to* Don): Now, what were you saying?

Don: I was just wondering whether the suicide is altogether justified.

John: Oh, I think so. Given the kind of man he is. I think it could be quite powerful. I think perhaps he might put the revolver in his mouth. Then, if the back wall of the set was white-washed, they would use some quaint device to cover it with great gobs of brain and bright blood at the vital moment. And just the two of them sitting there gaping. That would be wonder-ful.

*(To illustrate,* John *puts the revolver into his mouth and presses the trigger. Loud explosion. By some quaint device, gobs of brain and bright blood appear on the whitewashed wall.* Philip *and* Don *sit gaping. Long silence.*

Don: Jesus.

(John *slumps to the ground.* Philip *rushes abruptly from the stage.* Don *gropes shakily for the telephone and begins to dial.)*

*Blackout*

*(The first movement of the 2nd Brandenburg Concerto)*

Regrettably, the Mayfair Theatre appeared not to have the quaint device. From this striking opening the play proceeds through a conventional plot as Philip loses his girl-friend to a novelist and is seduced by a nymphomaniac who stays behind to do the washing up. Philip, who is fond of anagrams, can, we gather, control words but nothing else. At least Ian in Hampton's first play, who also felt inept and was homosexual, was allowed to seduce a middle-aged woman in his bed-sit! But Philip is so afraid of hurting people that he emerges as a charming nonentity, particularly when compared with the cynical novelist who, at least, makes some sort of theatrical impression.

Like Osborne, Hampton transfers from the Court successfully, as Arden and Wesker never did. It is unlikely that he will have to blow his brains out for want of praise, but the comment on this scene—too cerebral—is apt. By comparison with, say, Osborne, Hampton is cerebral, and private to the point of being trivial. His success is another sign of the state of the theatre and the desperation of critics. It is difficult to see

167

why Hampton is so admired and not, for example, Peter Ransley, whose *Ellen* (1971), for all its faults, is more assured, profound and instinctive than anything produced by Hampton. for the Court, so far. But, as Gaskill reminds us in his report for 1970, apart from Stoke only the Court offers a home for the dramatist now, and its accommodation is limited. Theatres are dying, and new writers will have to look more and more to radio and television. Meanwhile, Gaskill, with an astronautical flourish, sees the Court as a launching pad and expresses the hope that some of its rockets will remain in orbit!

One rocket that came from Nottingham, rather than the Court, was Peter Barnes (b. 1931). Barnes had a play called *Schlerosis* (1965) produced at the Traverse Theatre in Edinburgh, and subsequently by Marowitz at the Aldwych, which dealt with the British army using torture in Cyprus. He had been a playwright for ten years and screenwriter for fourteen before he blazed into prominence at Nottingham with his baroque comedy, *The Ruling Class* (1968). 'Blazed' is Hobson's verb and that critic saw this play as proof of 'an entirely new talent of a very high order'. The play won the John Whiting Award for the best play of 1968 and Whiting would have approved, for Barnes is interested, primarily, in verbal fireworks, without falling simply into the tribe of Pinteretti. He worked for a film company as a story editor, writing film scripts which, he says, help to eliminate self-indulgence and make you professional and economical. He aims at 'a very rich texture to the language' lamenting that audiences seem to have lost the ability to listen. We have become, he believes, an image-obsessed society and it is the duty of writers to fight back and show how important words are, to recall to the theatre much of the energy and vitality which has been drained off into cinema and music. He wishes to write comedy that is intensely serious in a theatre that is both a moral platform and entertaining. *The Ruling Class,* therefore, is both tragic and ridiculous. It can be called satiric as one would use the word for *Volpone* or *Measure for Measure* and it looks at society as Swift looked at it. The satire

168

is thus rather religious than political: the first half of the play (formally in two parts, the play was divided into three because of the heavy demands it makes on the leading actor) is New Testament while the second half is Old: the God of Love giving way to the God of Vengeance when the Earl is 'cured'. But as a play it is social in that it is about appearances, how we judge people by their appearance and even by how they speak.

Barnes has subsequently adapted two Wedekind plays for Nottingham with the title *Lulu* (1970) and written two one-act plays, *Leonardo's Last Supper* and *Noonday Demons,* produced at the Open Space in 1969, and continuing the theme of belief and how people believe what they believe. Barnes uses alienation effects (as when da Vinci quotes Dr. Johnson) but his aim is still to create a comic theatre of contrasting modes and opposites. He feels that the basic problem is not in the events which, however improbable, will have happened somewhere at some time, but in finding a style and for these plays he has pillaged all sources from Elizabethan slang to the Bible. He insists, moreover, that the meaning is *in* the lines, not between them, that absolute precision and speed are essential. John Russell Taylor sees a pattern of black baroque comedy linking Barnes with Colin Spencer, David Pinner, David Halliwell and Howard Brenton.[11] They treat material of a certain kind (thus murder; but sex murder or child murder) in a certain way without disapproval and in a comic manner suggesting that life is more complex than ever and that dark fantasy and savage comedy are the most direct and only adequate way of telling the truth without compromise. But this is to look for a pattern among writers—a natural hope for critics who can hardly discuss multi-media experiments in terms of anything other than memoir. Mr. Hobson adds his visit to *The Ruling Class* as the fourth great occasion after *Waiting for Godot, Look Back in Anger,* and *The Birthday Party.* It would be pleasant to end on a note of optimism with Hobson's choice, but the splendours of *The Ruling Class* are, again, of a more intellectually contrived kind. The difficulty

[11] 'The Dark Fantastic', *The Second Wave*, pp. 205 ff.

169

facing any new dramatist is that the New Wave precedes him. Given Shakespeare and any dramatist of that time is at a disadvantage. Given those three plays and even the lurid imagination of Barnes looks academic. John Russell Taylor, in *Plays and Players,* January 1971, lists six dramatists with glib efficiency, under the heading 'New Arrivals'. Their newness is, to say the least, comparative, but his sub-title is most suggestive: Six of a Traditional Kind. It may be that contemporary theatre does not require writers of any other kind. The life of this theatre has now passed into a kind of art which would find the writer who insists on his importance both a nuisance and an irrelevance.

# CHAPTER EIGHT

# Producer's Theatre

The title is probably misleading. In an obvious sense all theatre is producer's theatre since only he is uniquely placed to look at and combine the different parts of what we correctly call production. But in recent times the producer, in various ways, has become dominant in a creative sense. Even as an interpreter his central position gave him considerable power but the prevalent theatrical custom checked this power. In the polygon of forces which makes up theatre—writer, actor, producer, audience and theatre manager—the parts are seldom, if ever, equipollent. In 1950 the actor was dominant and both writers and producers worked within this situation which met the expectations of the audience and was, therefore, fostered by theatre managers. For Aristotle, too, the actor was more important than the dramatic poet. About 1956, mainly under the impetus of the Royal Court, the writer became the dominant force. Whether 'committed' or 'absurd', dramatists laid down careful indications of how a play should be performed, and seemed careless of such matters as the shape of the stage. The new seriousness which replaced the old elegance may have called for a new kind of actor and producer, and met the demands of a new kind of audience, but essentially such dramatists used these to get over ideas.

About 1956, however, both Theatre Workshop and Stratford suggested other ways of serious theatre. It was

Littlewood's intention to train a different kind of actor and reach a wider audience. Her theatre looked Brechtian[1] and called for a scenario rather than a playtext. But if her work was clearly seminal it relied, like Brecht's, more upon the forcefulness of Littlewood than anything else. The situation at Stratford was more unusual since that theatre had a fixed number of plays which it was the company's function (and many think privilege) to perform. But this very 'limitation'—the need to go on doing the same plays—left producers with little scope outside actual production. Shakespeare's plays have always been fair game for the vivisectionist[2] and during this period we can trace a development from lead actor to a collaborative approach in which the producer, naturally, becomes the dominant force. If the result is often reminiscent of eighteenth-century burlesque Shakespeare, it must be remembered that from 1660–1843, when only two theatres had the royal patent, other theatres were obliged to turn straight plays into operettas, adding mime and music, however irrelevant. The movement at Stratford, particularly noticeable in plays done in sequence, has been a deliberate attempt to show to modern audiences Shakespeare, our contemporary.

Thus, by 'Producer's Theatre' we really mean that significant part of recent theatre in which the producer plays a more than usually dominant rôle, in which interpretation becomes creation; where there is either no text or where the text is used merely as the beginning of a production—much like the script of a film.

Writing in 1950 Tynan lamented that although England could boast a succession of great actors she had not produced one *homme du théâtre* (a Diaghilev, Copeau, Stanislavski or Meyerhold) and he could find only three outstanding producers. Since then, there has been Peter Daubeney,[3] and

---

[1] It is not clear how far Brecht's own plays were given the improvisation treatment, and in any case it was Brecht the producer who supervised it.

[2] See Benedict Nightingale's 'Shakespeare Is As Shakespeare's Done', *Theatre '71*, pp. 154–68.

172     [3] From 1945 Daubeney has brought over to England a distinguished list

one of those producers, Peter Brook (b. 1925), has more than fulfilled Tynan's judgement of him as the most mature and exciting producer in England, combining the invention of Guthrie with a continental delicacy. Brook, called the 'youngest earthquake' by Sir Barry Jackson, already had, at the age of 25, a list of memorable productions. Tynan lists *Man and Superman* and *King John* (Birmingham Rep), *Loves Labours Lost, Romeo and Juliet* and *Measure for Measure* (Stratford), *Huis Clos* (Arts Theatre), *The Brothers Karamazov, Men Without Shadows, The Respectable Prostitute* and *Dark of the Moon* as well as *Boris Godunov, La Bohème, The Olympians* and *Salome* at Covent Garden.

When Brook left Oxford he directed an ENSA show and then moved to Birmingham Rep and Stratford. He was ballet critic for *The Observer* in the late forties, and became director of productions at Covent Garden in 1948 where his ideas for revolution in opera made little headway. His first London production was *Dr. Faustus* in 1942 and he made his film debut in 1953 with *The Beggar's Opera*. Olivier was MacHeath, the music was adapted by Bliss and the libretto written by Christopher Fry; this last was disappointing and may explain, partly, why the film was a box-office disaster. In 1955 Brook directed Olivier in *Titus Andronicus* and 1956 saw the Brook–Scofield season at the Phoenix Theatre, with *Hamlet, The Power and the Glory* and *The Family Reunion*. In the same year Brook also directed *Cat on a Hot Tin Roof* in Paris and has, since then, divided his time between England and Europe as well as between drama and opera. It was possibly in Paris that he became really familiar with the work of Artaud. 1957 saw the controversial production of *The Tempest* with John Gielgud and when Peter Hall succeeded Glen Byam-Shaw at Stratford in 1960 Brook, with Michel Saint-Denis, went there as a director. Subsequent important of productions: Brecht's Berliner Ensemble, the Moscow Arts Theatre, the Living Theatre and the talents of Bergman, Feuillère, Koun, Svoboda Smoktunovsky and Jerome Robbins, as well as running the World Theatre seasons at the Aldwych; but he is a talented importer rather than an impresario.

173

productions are *King Lear* (with Schofield) (1962), *The Physicists* (1964), *The Marat-Sade* (1964), *US* (1966), *Oedipus* (1968) and, continuing his reputation for visual brilliance and cleverness, *A Midsummer Night's Dream* in 1970.[4]

Brook is an outstanding producer poised uncertainly between interpreter and creator. He is, of course, an inveterate enemy of what he calls the Deadly Theatre (which, by his own account, consists of usherettes, stage curtains, theatre buildings, programmes and bars) and he welcomes Cruelty, the Happening, anything to waken people up. This assumes that people, after a hard day's work, wish to be kept on their toes. But he is wise enough to recognise that the effect of violent shocks wears off and ask: what follows? He himself has not been idle in the giving of violent shocks. His production of Peter Weiss's *Marat-Sade* was described as 'the most visually exciting, brilliantly produced and magnificently acted load of old cobblers ever seen in London'. This is a clue to his art. Given Weiss's inferior play, with its Brechtian tricks and instant philosophies, he sensibly turned it into an excuse for production and if the result had little to do with drama it was blatantly theatrical.

*US* (or *U.S.*) in 1967 showed the same technique with a veneer of social purpose. Brook has argued that there is no shared view of Vietnam in England, only a shared confusion and that if his production was clumsy this was to be expected because no one had written plays about Vietnam. The show begins, therefore, as a condemnation of dramatists for not writing on such a burning issue. Having decided to do it and lacking a script the company had to write one, so what was seen was a work in progress, with a formal freedom but also lacking coherence, objectivity and balance. It was, apparently, splendid moral therapy for the actors who progressed from banal opinions to shame at their own prejudices while working on it. The show was anti-American because, here, America is committing atrocities in our name but, if the show were to be

[4] He turned it into an 'aluminium pantomime'. The phrase is Benedict Nightingale's and is, it must be admitted, a minority judgement.

done in Moscow (and Brook seems to think that it could be done there) the company would, of course, have to deal with the Viet Cong because Russia is backing North Vietnam.

Brook followed this with a production of Seneca's *Oedipus* at the National Theatre in 1968. Since Seneca wrote the play as an exercise and not for performance the choice seems perverse. Artaud admired Seneca, but, more crucially, perhaps, Jean-Louis Barrault had just done Seneca's *Medea* at the Odéon. The text was used as an excuse for fusing Brecht and Artaud. Brook aimed at alienation by having the characters as actors only, the costumes deliberately unhistoricised and the play recited as a concert performance. But he employed the whole auditorium by chaining the chorus around it, in the audience, moaning and wailing to suggest a primitive rite, uninterrupted by intervals. But it is questionable whether ritual can work for unbelievers who have come for entertainment, or even thrills. The solution appeared to be a deliberate drift towards sexual images and shocks culminating in a large, inflated, golden phallus which appeared at the end—to trendy applause or embarrassment.

Brook, whose career has been described by J. C. Trewin in *Peter Brook* (1971), has always been a producer who decorates the theatre. He early achieved a reputation for being 'clever'—which is an ambivalent word. His work is notable for invention and visual excitement, sometimes at the expense of the play and sometimes, as in the case of *Dark of the Moon* (1949), turning a poor play into a wonder. He can make the less perfect play a thrilling experience; but, as with Littlewood, a good play sometimes interferes with his intentions, and particularly his continual need to make theatre relevant. Thus, whether correct or not for Seneca, the sexual images and shocks of *Oedipus* were right for the times.

Such things could not have existed while the Lord Chamberlain ruled the theatre; nor, for that matter, could producers have employed improvisation since he required to see a text which, once passed, must not be deviated from. Ironically it was the dramatists who fought the battle with a

175

Lord Chamberlain who stood as the last barrier between a theatre which would require dramatists and a theatre which would not. For the real battle, once more, was with Sire Le Mot in a medium which is perilously poised between spectacle and literature. Tynan heralded the death of the word at the Edinburgh Conference of 1963—significantly with a naked lady. Many words have been used to point up the uselessness of words as a means of communication, and if this is understandable in the cinema it is less so in the theatre where even Artaud conceded that words had a place. But the producer's theatre of recent years has been close to what Artaud envisaged. A look at the list of plays that he wished to stage suggests that they were little more than pretexts *for* staging. Craig and Appia had stressed the importance of lighting, gestures and music before Artaud (and when, in the theatre, can they ever be forgotten?) but Artaud sought to use the theatre as the beginning of a radical transformation of society itself. He chose the image of the plague because during the plague order collapses, authority disappears, anarchy prevails and man demonstrates all those impulses which normally lie buried deep within him. Language would be needed for this kind of theatre only for incantation, as part of the emotional colouring. Artaud's disorder implied the laying aside of all formulae, ideas and theories. Total Theatre of Cruelty, based on Artaud's principles, looks novel until we remember Grand Guignol.[5]

Artaud's techniques have been applied in England to the theatre of ideas, or documentary theatre, thus confirming social purpose but overlooking the plague image. Such theatre was given impetus and respectability by the success of Joan

[5] Founded in 1897 in a former chapel in the Rue Chaptal, it survived the First World War successfully. Originally the two emotions—horror and laughter—were kept apart and an evening of Grand Guignol consisted of two tragedies and three comedies in alternation. Seasons of Grand Guignol were organised at the Little Theatre (1920–2) with Sybil Thorndike and Lewis Casson appeared in macabre dramas drawn from the French programmes. There was another, shorter, season at the Granville, Waltham Green in 1945. The Grand Guignol in Paris closed in 1965, its aims and methods largely taken over by the legitimate theatre.

Littlewood in *Oh, What a Lovely War* (1963) and can be seen in various forms including Stoke (where it is used to revive a sense of community) and small groups like Albert Hunt and the Bradford Theatre Group. Hunt worked with Brook on *US* before going to the Regional College of Arts at Bradford (Yorks.) where he restaged the Russian revolution in the streets in 1967 and, more recently, *John Ford's Cuban Missile Crisis* (1970). What unites Hunt and Peter Brook is an antagonism towards Deadly Theatre and a desire to make relevant or be relevant depending on whether you are producing Shakespeare or collating your own script.

The trouble with documentary theatre is that that is precisely what it cannot be. Its producers insist that if accuracy and the dissemination of information were intended then the theatre would be competing, unequally, with films and television. The facts have been *chosen* and *used* as symbols with deeper meanings, and they are assembled to convey the deeper meaning, bringing back social purpose, and the people, into the theatre.[6] In fact the opposite may be true, and they preach only to the converted. Such a theatre looks to Piscator for inspiration, and it was Piscator's theatre in West Berlin that staged *The Representative* and *In The Matter of J. Robert Oppenheimer* suggesting the equation: popular theatre = political theatre = propaganda theatre. But Artaud intended theatre to be cathartic not an alternative to a Left-Wing demonstration. His short-lived Théâtre de la Cruauté staged a version of *The Cenci* (1935), a tale of incest and murder, which brought into the theatre some of the power of Goya, Breughel and Bosch.

Whatever form and whether in the streets or theatre

[6] The idea of a People's Theatre, which is bound to be self-conscious, probably dates from the French Revolution when poets were called upon to celebrate the events of the Revolution, with no pretence at impartiality or conflict of ideas. Rollin published *Le Théâtre du Peuple* in 1903 and Fermin Gémier became the first director of the newly created Théâtre National Populaire, formed to oppose the idea of theatre as a place for the privileged classes. The most interesting experiment was the Théâtre d'Action International in 1932 under the directorship of Leon Moussinac, which was inspired by the work of Piscator.

177

buildings such activities could only take place after the disappearance of the Lord Chamberlain's licensing powers. It did seem odd that dramatists were censored when practically anything could be danced or sung. A dramatist naturally resented having words or scenes removed which he considered organic and necessary, particularly when the logic behind such deletions was often arbitrary or apparently foolish. Edward Bond's *Saved* at the Royal Court precipitated a court case, with Olivier and Lord Harewood as defence witnesses, and although the Court was found guilty it was conditionally discharged in 1966. In the same year the House of Lords proposed a Select Committee to review the law and practice relating to the censorship of plays and the Commons agreed. This Select Committee reported in June, 1967 and the Royal Assent to the Bill was given in July. It became law on 28 September 1968. That year a completely naked Helen walked across the stage at Stratford in *Dr Faustus* but the end of censorship was celebrated by the delayed first performance of the American musical *Hair* which convinced both sides of the rightness of their arguments.

For the first fruits of liberty were far from being linguistic. It soon became apparent that the fight for the right to say certain words had become a fight to portray the actions the words described. Nudity and sexual intercourse, of various kinds, were the immediate results and neither is capable of much dramatic extension. Kenneth Tynan mounted the first sex show for the commercial theatre, an evening of elegant erotica produced in America and called *Oh! Calcutta!* (1969). He wanted, he said, to explore the area of human sexual response on a social rather than an individual scale. But, as Wesker pointed out, the opportunism of such a show encourages as well as satisfies the need for mere novelty. Tynan claimed that critics who said they were bored meant that they were shocked, and that until the show had been seen in London the sexual aspect would continue to be over-inflated. Only when saturation point had been reached would the law of diminishing returns take over. It remains to be seen whether or not sex *has* a law of diminishing returns. *Oh! Calcutta!* opened at the Roundhouse in 1970 under the direction of Clifford Williams before it transferred, appropriately, to one of the theatres of Paul Raymond, the strip-club king. Tynan thought it would be interesting to see how pornography would develop in the hands of first-rate writers and scripts were contributed, anonymously, by Jules Pfeiffer, John Lennon, Peter Nichols, Joe Orton, Sam Shepard and a prologue by Beckett. Unfortunately, pornography does not seem to encourage first-class writing. The production was reviewed, with extremely discreet photographs, in the September issue of *Plays and Players* where the critic (female) found it natural, attractive and not in the least erotic. She claimed it was a breakthrough although the audience was 'of course middle class, middle aged and middle brow'. Which hardly suggests breakthrough. The same critic pointed out that the evening was not erotic because 'whether from stage-fright or the temperature, the male members of the cast were resolutely unaroused'. But if we take it that a theatrical performance is an imitation then a real erection would surely remove it from the artistic context? It is unfortunate that a male erection cannot be acted: it either is or it is not: if it is not then the point of the action is missed and if it is we are no longer watching an actor. Moreover the suggestion of real sex (which has been made, and, in America, performed) might lead to wider demands for realism: blinding *(King Lear)*, castration *(The Balcony, Mann ist Mann, Heloïse and Abelard)* not to mention death, childbirth and, most difficult of all, love. Gillian Hanson, in *Original Skin* (1970) dismisses this as a cliché argument, citing the war in Vietnam as our real blood and death, which is hardly a decent analogy. There is nothing very new in this. Henry James, in 1877, remarked that at the Prince of Wales's Theatre it was a point of honour to have nothing that was not real. This, he added, made the scenery somewhat better than the actors and, if carried to its logical conclusion, would lead to Romeo drinking real poison and Medea murdering a fresh pair of babes every night.

What is new is that the problem hinges on sexual activities which in turn raise moral problems and a great deal of heat. On a practical level the new situation has caused problems for Equity which, together with the managers on the Theatres National Committee, was obliged to lay down six points to protect actors not merely from prosecutions that might arise but also from abuses of the profession during auditions, casting and performance. But our objections can only be in terms of mimesis. If we say that it is better to leave such matters to the imagination we may, indeed, be prescribing pornography. On the other hand the code of decency which allows something when it is necessary is a circular argument since, given box office pressures and the spirit of the times, a dramatist may well feel obliged to make such scenes necessary. Tynan's advocacy apparently knows no bounds. He has said that he would have real intercourse performed on the stage. Having been 'liberated' with masturbation, cunnilinctus and sodomy many critics have suggested that we could proceed to more interesting things, and there is no reason to think that they would not find an audience.

Marshall McLuhan may be right when he speaks of nudity as 'the richest possible expression of structural form' but as a box office draw it does not always cater for such aspirations, as well as imposing obligations on the acting profession: witness the brief inclusion of nudity in a dull costume drama like *Heloïse and Abelard*. Where the gross sexuality of the Greek theatre was used for comic relief, nudity at the moment is serious and awed. Hugh Leonard summed up the problem in his review of *The Dirtiest Show in Town*—the theme is pollution. He complained that the imitation of the sex act here was a mockery far removed from love, that the difference between nakedness in a stripclub and a theatre was only a matter of pretensions, and, most importantly, that when one is introduced to a naked lady it is not easy to concentrate on her merits as a conversationalist. Eroticism, in short, is a single-minded pursuit which murders other emotions.

180    But the attack is not on our morals, or even those of our

servants. It is against the deadly theatre of the middle-aged which is no longer relevant to our democratic, permissive times, and on the writer who, by producing a text, confines the spontaneous in a form which, by tomorrow, must be irrelevant. Just as Gordon Craig found stage directions useless and, indeed, impertinent, now producers feel the same way about texts, even when by Shakespeare. Remembering the long declamatory speeches of French classical and boulevard drama we can sympathise with Artaud's wish to eliminate words as much as possible, but he would not have reduced them to slogans. Experiments like those of Brecht were rooted in the twenties but dadaism, surrealism, cubism, no plot, character or meaning has ultimately produced what Laurence Kitchin calls the International Style: emphasis on feeling and a conspicuous neglect of the mind. This can be seen in Marowitz's *Hamlet,* Grotowski's *Faustus* and Brook's *Lear*—all extreme versions of Brecht's method with *Coriolanus.* Tynan calls this theatre totalitarian and apocalyptic. If essentially an irreverent theatre it tends to take itself very seriously. This is not to say that Brook's attack on the Deadly Theatre is not sincere. It is certainly very timely: new writers, new movements, much experimentation and yet theatre audiences dwindle and at a time when there are no longer the easy excuses of cinema and television. But Brook's three examples of living theatre are very significant: Cunningham, Grotowski and Beckett—for, as he points out, all three are alike in several respects: small means, intense work, rigorous discipline and, almost as a condition of existence, they are theatres for an élite.

Such élitist theatres must run counter to the idea of popular audiences. And this is the basic dilemma of producer's theatre. It is inspired by social purpose and the desire to reach wider, more popular audiences which, it is claimed, the theatre has lost somewhere in its history. But the finest theatre appears to be élitist. The difficulty is to reconcile discipline and mass theatre. Brustein has called theatre for the masses the third theatre, as opposed to commercial and subsidized theatre, and

181

has recorded his disappointment that in bringing the people back to theatre it has so rapidly become arrogant, sloppy and glossy. *Hair* is an excellent example of the pressures which success can bring. When the show transferred to Broadway it was restaged in 1968 and Brustein correctly predicted that the commercial theatre would soon be besieged with imitations. The book and lyrics of *Hair* were by Gerome Ragni and James Rado, music by Galt McDermott and the production was originally part of Joseph Papp's programme to make Shakespeare contemporary. But the restaging for Broadway was by La Mama's Tom O'Horgan and was followed by Rochelle Owens's *Futz*, a tale of ungratified desires in a rural community of Christians which tries to destroy its one innocent member, Cyrus Futz, who is in love with a sow. The effect of this show was to put the audience firmly in the rôle of Peeping Tom but the next stage was total participation with the Performing Group in *Dionysus in 69* where everyone was asked to join in sexual activities, which would have surprised the Greeks who saw Dionysus as a source of frenzy and irrationality.[7] The use of Euripides was slight and an excuse for events the Greeks would not have understood and for the Group to show off; which only, as Brustein sadly remarked, revealed that they had lives of considerably less significance than one has a right to expect in the theatre.[8]

The first English performance of *Hair* took place on the day the Lord Chamberlain ceased to function as theatrical censor and, like *Look Back in Anger,* it captured the mood of the

[7] Which could lead to sex, but, as Brustein remarks in *The Third Theatre*, p. 74, the Greeks associated the erotic principle with Aphrodite. This may be a little pedantic. Aphrodite was certainly the goddess of love and licentiousness to whom prostitutes were dedicated. She was the mother of Priapus of whom even she was ashamed and who is now tactfully referred to as the God of the Gardens. The parentage of Dionysus is as disputed as his birthplace, but although he is principally the god of wine (cf. Bacchus) he is certainly a phallic god. Because of his relationship with Polymnus he is often depicted (says Clement of Alexandria) with naked posteriors seated upon an upright wooden phallus.

[8] See 'From Hair to Hamlet', 'A Theatre Slouches to be Born', and 'The Democratisation of Art', by Brustein, *The Third Theatre* (1970), pp. 60–77.

moment: hip culture, drugs, Marcuse and Cage's indeterminacy. But the written material had been completely submerged beneath O'Horgan's effects which were kept up with such febrile desperation that the slight nature of the show escaped notice. Most of the tricks were from Underground Theatre emerging and surprising an audience unfamiliar with them but basically what Marowitz (not exactly an old-fashioned critic) called a certain hippie mindlessness lurked beneath the lurid surfaces. As for the nudity, this was palpably a tool of publicity, timid and minor in an otherwise expansively extroverted entertainment. The London success encouraged the formation of a touring company which took *Hair* through the major cities of England in an even more diluted form reaching audiences in a way that *The Beard*, say, at the Royal Court could not. It has had its successors. A rock version of *Othello* opened in Manchester in 1970 and transferred to the Roundhouse. It was very much a work in progress which, in the pop world, is a virtue but is apt to suggest to a theatregoer that he is attending rehearsals at a price. Nevertheless it is this protean quality which suggests the legitimate parent of this commercial product: the Happening.

There have always been Happenings in the theatre. In the Middle Ages they were called Marvels and their charm rests on their calculated impermanence and deliberate spontaneity—which cannot co-exist with the long run as enjoyed by *Hair*. Spontaneity is also paradoxical since if the happening is to have form there must be deliberation on someone's part. Two points of view are possible on the Happening. The *avant-garde* theatre view is that theatre, beyond keeping classics alive, as in a museum, may have no function in the future: though such a usefulness has its own importance. Or, one can agree with Tynan (in 1971) that if theatre becomes prohibitive, economically, then do theatre-in-the-round which is cheaper, or stage a happening which is even cheaper, but is 'a pathetic alternative' to theatre. Tynan maintains that there is a distinction between the intentional and the fortuitous: the fortuitous is life, but when the intentional intervenes in the fortuitous the result is art. If such a distinction is ignored then you have a form of theatre so indistinguishable from life as to be non-theatre.

Allan Kaprow describes the various kinds of 'happening' by pointing out that, unlike the arts of the past, they do not have a structure (*i.e.* a beginning, middle and end): happenings are open-ended, fluid, in which nothing obvious is sought and therefore nothing won except the certainty of a number of occurrences to which one is more than usually attentive.[9] Happenings exist for a single performance, or, at most, for a limited number, and then are gone for ever. They are essentially theatrical although they occur in contexts other than the theatre, and there is no separation of actor and audience. There is no script, and if words have to be used they may or may not make sense and can have, anyway, only 'a brief, emergent and sometimes detached quality'. Such an element of chance is not found in traditional theatre. Kaprow prefers the word 'chance' to 'spontaneity' because it suggests the element of risk in every happening, whereas traditional art always aims at making it good every time. Chance must not, however, be taken to mean chaos, for Kaprow seems to claim that there is some organisation arising from the creators; which suggests that a little practice makes chance less chancy. The important things are impermanence and inclusiveness; happenings must be perishable.

Their source is probably Kurt Schwitter's formulation of Merz (1920)—'a stage event that would embrace all branches of art in one artistic unit'. American Happenings seem to have been more like extensions of sculpture and painting than drama. In 1956 Allan Kaprow converted an exhibition of collages into an 'environment'—the Penny Arcade—while Claes Oldenberg was creating environmental mess—calculated rubbish tips—in an attempt to transmute ordinary objects into something new and rare. Words can have little importance because the physical is there to be looked at

[9] ' "Happenings" in the New York Scene', *The Modern American Theater,* ed. A. B. Kernan, 1967, pp. 121–30.

in a different way and from that different way a new meaning occurs. We are, by now, speaking and thinking of theatrical events which are more life in general than art: as Cage has said, theatre takes place all the time. But the disappearance of the line between life and art has interesting consequences. There are economic problems in an art form that is deliberately ephemeral and that finds the whole idea of audiences odious. Moreover, as Peter Brook acutely observes, a Happening is always somebody's brainchild, and producers tend to get caught up in their own obsessional symbols, like the old custard pie comedy.

In September 1964 an American Group called the Living Theatre fled America and performed *The Brig* at the Mermaid Theatre. They were a collective undertaking united by a common view of society and a way of acting, and they were exciting. They prepared the way for experimental theatre such as Joseph Chaikin's Open Theatre, the La Mama troupe, Jim Hayne's Arts Lab., Marowitz's Open Space and Ed Berman's Ambiance. The Living Theatre were brilliant as a performing group—the actors were always inferior to the production—but they have over the years begun to require their audiences to accept the mechanics of performance while concentrating on a new group relationship. The result in practice has been a deterioration of their art and an increase in hysteria. A happening, after all, as Brook reminds us, is simply an occasion, and going to the Opera in a dinner jacket is as legitimate as wearing beads in a cellar. This challenge to organised theatre is an old one. Rousseau, in his *Lettre sur Les Spectacles* (1758) distinguished between professional theatre (artificial) and community pleasures and dances (natural). The only possible excuse for a theatre was in a large town where it might distract some people from committing crimes. Since rural people lead happy and contented lives theatre would only be a disruption. However, they were to be allowed some dramatic pleasures, but not gloomily enclosed in a dark cave (*i.e.* a theatre); simply 'plant a pole crowned with flowers in the middle of a square, assemble the people, and you will have a

185

festival. Turn the spectators into a spectacle; make them the actors themselves . . .'.

Clearly the most serious challenge of happenings is less to the building, and more to the principle of mimesis. Theatre as illusion—whether under the identification theory or the alienation theory (of either Brecht or Ionesco) is now questioned as the basis of drama. Recently Happenings themselves have begun to be replaced by 'Actuals'. Here analogies are drawn from anthropology between primitive societies and parts of our society, particularly the young. An actual is the theory of the happening restated whereby art becomes an event as opposed to an event becoming art. The Aristotelian concept of mimesis has always dominated theatre and it insists that art comes after experience, suggesting the separation which is now to be abolished. An example would be Ralph Ortiz's *The Sky is Falling* which required the slaughter of mice and chickens and the participants doused in blood; this precipitated discussion and became an allegory of Vietnam. Clearly this reaches back to Artaud's view of theatre as the double of life rather than an imitation of life. But when the anthropologist points to the Heheve ritual (every performance takes twenty years to prepare) we must, surely, be still imitating the Elema tribe in New Guinea; imitating their ritual rather than discovering the ritual for our time and society.

The final irony of collaborative theatre which, in formal terms, is the end of producer's theatre as opposed to the anarchy of Happenings, is that the producer is eliminated too. Thus the Stables production in Manchester of *Dracula* had seven authors and the power lay with the compiler just as Peter Brook's production of *The Tempest* (1968) relied on Brook (and the audience's understanding of the text) before it could be understood. But such collaboration has led to the new actors' theatre. But actors' theatre now means actors in the plural, an ensemble, as opposed to actor's theatre in the singular which was identical with writer's theatre since that theatre provided rôles for singular actors. This new form is

186

discussed by David Caute, inspired by having his play boycotted by actors in Stuttgart because it would have given comfort to a bourgeois audience. Group conclusions, as Caute points out, are often predetermined by the character of the concluders:

The writer's remoteness from the theatre does have its value. Seclusion allows him to dwell on fundamentals, to give the work unity and a coherent development. His architectural imagination operates in a mind's eye undistracted by the immediate paraphernalia of show business. The writer alone can provide the structure of words and situations which joins the audience to a world they recognise. He rescues the theatre from its in-built tendency towards narcissism, towards making the medium the message. And even if the text is never finalised, even if there are improvisations and new departures during rehearsals, a plausible framework will usually survive. Without the guiding hand of the writer, the theatre is all too often a red-hot vacuum.[10]

Miss Littlewood was always inviting the actors to rise up and take over the theatre. If this was not just a rhetorical flourish she must have realised that if they did, she, as much as wicked managers and dramatists, would have to go.

Eric Bentley pointed out two things. First, that however well Wagner's Gesamtkunstwerk (or Schwitter's Merz) may work in opera it is less successful in drama. Whenever drama subordinates words to other media, such as music or dancing, it invariably trivialises those things without much improvement to the drama. Secondly, if we assume the orgy theory to be true, there must have come a time when the frenzied horde split into two groups one of which became voyeurs, later called spectators. And, at a later date, there must have been a time when there was no orgy at all, only talk about orgy: drama finds itself as it finds its voice.[11]

However sincere, exciting, relevant and imaginative much of this theatre has been, the emphasis on feeling has tended to be

[10] 'Actors' Theatre', *The Listener,* 3 June 1971.
[11] Bentley, for example, describes the playwright as 'the forgotten man of the modern stage' in his Foreword to *The Playwright as Thinker.*

simple-minded; it preaches to the converted in fragmented minority theatres and it will not tolerate argument or dissent. In inviting audience participation, and seeking relevance, Producer's Theatre attacks the Wagnerian atmosphere of reverence, and tolerance of a great deal of bad acting and foolish drama. But audience participation always leaves the audience at a disadvantage since it has not rehearsed *its* reactions. Theatre is not life, it is, in the words of Frank Marcus, 'an artificial, created, moulded reality with a moral point'. As for physical participation, Tynan properly insists that audiences have civil rights, too. We might wish to be only psychically involved and it is presumptuous to assume that those of us not physically involved are asleep. This may, of course, be a generation point of view, from a dying race of voyeurs. Frank Dunlop's conception of the Young Vic was aimed at discovering whether there was a special form of Young People's Theatre, probing the widespread belief that those who came to puberty after the Bomb are a different kind of human being. For the rest, we recall Quince's reply to Snug:

Snug:  Have you the lion's part written? Pray you, if it be, give it me, for I am slow of study.
Quince: You may do it extempore, for it is nothing but roaring.

# CHAPTER NINE

# The Living Theatre

Sartre, staging the first play he ever wrote as a prisoner in Germany, saw what theatre ought to be: a great collective, religious phenomenon. If it was this in the time of Sophocles and Shakespeare it can rarely be so in our fragmented lives, but the changing shape of the theatre over the last twenty years at least testifies to its continuing life. And Sartre's choice of drama as a preferred means of expressing *une littérature engagée* reminds us that drama, even now, must be a collective experience. The focus of that experience has shifted. In 1950, actor's theatre, given suitable material by the writers of the time and sumptuously produced, provided heroic rôles to display the elegant capacities of a large number of remarkable actors. This was a time when going to the theatre was an occasion, a glamorous, if largely escapist theatre which matched the needs of a post-war generation who asked for little more than colourful entertainment. A rising generation of actors, producers and writers felt the need to use theatre to come to grips with the realities of life in the 1950s, a need echoed in those who were just beginning to go to the theatre. This socially-conscious time required dramas which commented upon the experience of living, in terms of either metaphysical anguish or political questioning. Dramatists wrote plays which met this demand, creating heroic rôles, albeit in a minor key. But whether their relevance was metaphysical or political the dramatists were concerned with the physical nature of theatre only in so far as it was necessary to create the play and its ideas. Producer's theatre, however, aware of technological changes as well as moral alternatives looked for ways in which performance could be more effective, and exploit the methods and manners of contemporary theatre. Producer's theatre, therefore, caused or coincided with two developments: the changing pattern of theatrical activity in Britain and the changing shape of the theatre building itself. Social relevance was hardly appropriate in buildings which maintained the old class distinctions through the price of a ticket, and stood as architectural reminders of an older, irrelevant kind of theatre. Like the dramatists, but in a more technical manner, producers were interested in the relationship between audience and actor. An attack on theatrical conditions was inevitable.

Stephen Joseph, for example, argued that in building new theatres we should avoid the proscenium arch stage which was more suitable for opera than drama. The new dramatists needed new theatres and new shapes and he expressed the view that if we had a wider variety of theatre buildings then we might bring in a wider and more varied kind of audience. Such new shapes would, moreover, be economical to build and run and would abolish the conventional seating arrangement where you could pay a great deal for a bad seat. The proscenium arch, he argued, separated the audience from the action, and even where actors had a technique for projecting a play they could soon reach the point where it was impossible to remain true to the conventions of the play and be both visible and audible. Melodrama, with its emphasis on spectacle, for which the older theatres were built, could now be better achieved in the cinema.[1] For Joseph, theatre-in-the-round was the most radical solution. The open-end stage, least unorthodox from an audience's point of view, can develop no new methods of acting or production, while the arena stage (as at Chichester) is suitable for large productions before large

190

[1] 'Arenas and All That', *Twentieth Century,* February 1961, pp. 108–18.

audiences. Theatre-in-the-round, however, demanded new techniques of presentation, since the projection of the play should be effective in all directions. Thus the actor assumed a greater responsibility, and would be encouraged to improvise.[2] The writer for such a theatre would either be less important or totally immersed in the project. Joseph concluded that there was no best stage shape. We need all kinds and it would be a pity if his name were to be mentioned only as an advocate of theatre-in-the-round.[3] But theatre-in-the-round, itself, presents difficulties of vision particularly when an actor blocks out the stage by standing in front of part of the audience. Under such conditions the proscenium arch stage, being a picture stage, has its advantages, particularly as it is now possible to build theatres which require no supporting pillars. It is also possible that acting methods, acoustics and television work have turned actors into mere speakers scarcely audible even in small theatres. The current hysteria against the proscenium arch may very well overlook the possibility of natural selection in architecture; and, as Wesker once remarked, an actor can enter and leave one as easily as any other kind of stage. The debate continues. In 1969 Sir Bernard Miles attacked the design of the new theatre at Sheffield, describing its thrust stage as a theatrical freak. He was joined by Olivier and Sir John Clements and attacked by Peter Cheeseman, Plater, Terson, Rudkin, Campton and Ayckbourn. Impressive opposition but all, of course, united by the common factor of work at Scarborough and Stoke, in theatre-in-the-round. It may turn out to be only a matter of fashion although, once a theatre is built, ratepayers will expect it to last for some time. In 1599 the child actors (Hamlet's 'little eyases') performed their plays indoors at Blackfriars in a theatre which looked very much in the direction of the proscenium arch and attracted fashionable playgoers. Thus the

[2] Illegal at the time Joseph was writing and seen by him as a device to prevent actors and writers from expressing their views.
[3] See, for example, his views on theatre subsidy, in his last book, *New Theatre Forms* (1968).

revolutionary theatre of Elizabeth I was rejecting the open stage and moving in the opposite direction to the theatre of Elizabeth II. And Whiting had a point when he deplored the cult of intimacy and the loss to the theatre of the power of the remote, the isolated figure.

This debate on stage shapes could only take place, obviously, in the context of theatre building. In a sense Wesker's Golden Cities were springing up as local theatres: Nottingham under John Neville, Stoke under Peter Cheeseman being striking (and, significantly, controversial) examples. That local theatre has its problems can be seen from the career of these two theatres, and the earlier example of Coventry. The Belgrade was conceived as part of the massive redevelopment of the city in 1956 and opened in 1958, subsidised by the corporation. Like all local theatre it has to rely on audiences who will not put up with too much experiment. It gave Wesker a chance, but with a grant from the Royal Court, and did excellent work under Bryan Bailey until his death in a car crash in 1960. But the fortunes of these little civic theatres are more than usually prone to change. Possibly the most striking venture was the building of the theatre at Chichester, but its initial close relationship with the National Theatre under Olivier ensured that it worked, and continues to work under Sir John Clements, in the spirit of the West End. Others have followed, including Sheffield; but the controversy highlights one problem—intimate theatres cannot provide a home for touring productions.

The editor of *Plays and Players,* in his New Year Message for 1971, complained that we were in danger of becoming, theatrically, two nations. He meant, of course, the split between traditional theatre and *avant-garde* theatre. Had he written from any point outside London he would have known that Britain has always been, theatrically, two nations. The high concentration of theatre (and subsidy) in London is both inevitable and perpetual but it raises qualms. Two documents appeared about this time which surveyed the theatrical scene. The first was the report of the Arts Council Theatre Enquiry,

*The Theatre Today* (1970) and the second, John Elsom's *Theatre Outside London* (1971). This latter, in spite of its title, was really an excuse to challenge and denounce the findings of the former document.

The Arts Council enquiry, undertaken in 1967 and completed by the end of 1969, was to report on the causes for concern in the 'confusing spectacle of theatre in Britain', and discuss the fact that 'London theatre is having a difficult time economically and aesthetically' while, outside London, private-enterprise theatre was 'on its last legs, physically run down and morally disheartened'. The report disclosed that the number of touring theatres had shrunk within the last forty years from 130 to approximately 30 and many had for long been 'transit camps for a miscellaneous procession of speculative productions which in recent years have been scarcer and seedier and decreasingly profitable'. In fact, this report had been overtaken by events by the time it was published and its support of touring programmes was largely belated. National companies not only show a reluctance to tour but they could not provide sufficient product to justify the maintenance of large, unprofitable buildings to accommodate them. Moreover, the New York habit of previews has proved a cheaper solution to the problem of getting a show ready to open. Thus John Elsom, in his Cook's tour of provincial theatres, is more in touch with the characteristic pattern of theatre: local, subsidized repertory theatre. It is characteristic, too, of the volatile nature of this kind of theatre that some of the information on buildings and companies was out of date when the book was published.

Elsom begins with the premise that theatre is either on the brink of a renaissance or disaster depending on how we interpret the facts. Taking the basic axiom that theatre should serve the community he points out that this statement raises three questions: theatre = ?, serve = ? and community = ? As he suggests, according to the definition of these three terms, the statistics will prove renaissance or disaster. He himself seems to be in favour of renaissance, commenting that local theatre

193

has come into its own: witness the fact that since 1961, as a reviewer, he has had to go outside London. He points towards Derby Man who is faced with an embarrassment of theatrical riches; provided he has a car. Given this enthusiastic support of local theatre (which is easier if one lives in Kensington) the book develops into an attack on the Arts Council report's recommendations which strongly supported the touring system. Elsom favours the local community arts centre and naturally sees no reason for touring theatre. He recognises that such local institutions face the difficulty of keeping the audience they already have as well as gaining a new one—bridging the generation gap—but he seems undismayed by the example of Dundee. There, the theatre was burned down in 1953 and the company moved into a new hall nearer the University. When the administrator was asked what happened to the old audience he replied that they had been killed off.

This sounds more like changing audiences than bridgework. Furthermore, when Elsom moves into children's theatre, which is fashionable nowadays,[4] we must ask why educate audiences if they are to be killed off by the next theatre shape? In short, Elsom emerges in favour of improvisation, participation (but not particularly from old audiences), relevant theatre shapes and the usual subsidy on an analogy with libraries. What he fails to acknowledge, among other things, is that local theatre does not provide the same product as London and such theatres are inadequate to house opera, ballet and the National Theatre.

The question of subsidy, both national (and heavily concentrated on London) and local is vast and vexed. The bourgeois audience sensibly tended to see theatre as just another commodity to be bought and sold but the contemporary point of view is that theatre is, or ought to be, as

[4] Of course children's theatre is not new. The first was probably in Paris in 1769. Improvisation and drama in schools have been advocated for some time; see, for example, Edmond Holmes, *What Is and What Might Be* (1911) and the Perse Playbooks of 1911. The modern trend is away from drama, however, in favour of improvisation.

much a part of life as the health service and education. The usual comparison is with libraries, as we have seen, but a copy of *Hamlet* will be identical in Halifax and London, whereas productions of the play are hardly likely to be so. It is not inevitable that London will be superior but there is a general tendency for it to be so. Clearly theatre cannot survive without subsidy but it may be that subsidy stultifies as well as stimulates, particularly when the local ratepayer can keep a close eye on how the money is being spent. Marowitz's cries for subsidy in *The Guardian*—since fringe theatre and underground theatres are the laboratories where research for the industry takes place—are beguiling; but what industry would subsidise laboratories the professed aim of which is the destruction of the industry?

Community drama, too, poses problems. In the first place it suggests community. This may be true for Alan Plater, since Durham miners have preserved a sense of community to almost ghetto-like proportions, but Peter Cheeseman, at Stoke, produced documentaries strictly based on historical fact in an effort to induce a sense of community. And Plater has been quick to recognise the dangers of this local drama:

It is good to see full houses prepared to look, eye to eye, at theatre which reflects, and does not evade, their own experience. But there is a danger of introspection and parochialism and while most of these shows are many times more adventurous and gutsy than much West End fodder it may be that the next job is to use their collective experience without being seen using it.[5]

Elsom concludes his survey of theatre outside London with a rhetorical flourish (like the Arts Council report!) describing the theatre as a place where different levels and types of culture can meet, quarrel peacefully and marry; which is hardly the Dundee experience. In short, he preaches tolerance but practises and supports intolerance of those habits and manners which do not match his idea of the spirit of the seventies. In this, too, he is characteristic. It is this intolerance which is the

[5] Introduction to *Close the Coalhouse Door*.

195

most saddening aspect of the view from 1970. Looking back over the last twenty years we can see a burst of energy, vitality and creation in a period of brilliant confusion. British theatre had a decided advantage in coming to European influences when those influences had achieved their proper ends, but it continues to work under the disadvantage of being what Raymond Williams calls 'split theatre'. Thus small theatres with uncertain futures take risks and produce excellent work the best of which is then absorbed into traditional theatre. usually in a diluted form. The established theatre, after a slow start, has shown itself recently very adept at absorbing the new and the shocking, witness the way in which it has turned *Hair* into family entertainment.

The main impression, then, is of tension between subsidised giants (careless in their ever-increasing subsidy) and nervous commercial theatre, with a great deal of life on the fringe or underground. It is mostly in this last area that healthy attention is being paid to development and theatrical experiment as well as a great deal of mindless *avant-garde*. This is only to be expected. It must be remembered that *avant-garde* is an attitude rather than a style, testing and exploring possibilities which finally, if successful, become conventions and are assimilated into traditional theatre which continues to show predictable forms of entertainment. There are no compelling reasons for believing in the Romantic cliché that art is improved by starving in a garret, nor that subsidy will inevitably produce good work. Of these three parts 1970 saw a more than usual polarisation; between what, for simplicity, we can call the young and the old, the experimental and the traditional.

The Royal Court venture, *Come Together,* ironically emphasised this. Neither side had a spoon long enough to sup with the other devil. And how could they? The new theatre aims at ending the conventional actor–audience relationship, the use of dialogue as the principal means of communication, and such a theatre, if it can speak at all, will do so only in terms of abuse. Producers who wish to strike a balance between tradition and experiment have a problem which, so far, they have not solved. The great plays of the period are all inward-looking, like *Home* and *The Friends*. Such plays, like Pinter's *Old Times,* show a retreat into private worlds away from social and political issues, towards a poetic nostalgia, and a lament, as in *Time Present,* for graces of a past lost in a mean time. British dramatists, of course, even when overtly committed, had always used private examples of feeling. Arden is an exception and the coldness is as frightening as his recent silence. Now, home is a lunatic asylum and Wesker's final image is a corpse dominating the stage.

Such dramatists are growing old, and in any case, as John Russell Taylor points out, between 1950–70 the revolution has been in the theatre rather than in drama. The absence of any reasonably common form seemed promising, but its liberating power led to waves of fashionable emphases, the most important of which was production as an end rather than the means. Developments have taken place, and mainly through these new ideas and new relationships with the audience which producer's theatre has created; but such occasions are very susceptible to exploitation and it is not always possible to see whether the Emperor has any clothes on.

Moreover, drama is no longer restricted to theatre. From the point of view of financial rewards the film scenario promises more, while television reaches a far greater audience, immediately. Both, however, distract the audience from words in favour of images and each is a finished product. Each helps audiences to come to the theatre with less prejudices about form but it would still seem to be the duty of the writer and producer to unite the audience around the thoughts and emotions of the performance. Facing the consequences of the new freedoms the writer or producer usually opts for the mixed form, dark comedy, which allows him every liberty. But changing sides can be painful as well as exciting, and leaving the theatre with no conclusion can seem like an anticlimax. As Eric Bentley reminds us, if the optimistic conclusion suggests that nothing need be done, and the pessimistic conclusion that

197

nothing can be done, the open end is bitter, leaving only repercussions, one of which might be that the author's ideas were half-baked. But, however strong our nostalgia, we cannot recreate the theatre of Sophocles or Shakespeare, who worked at the centre of a culture with the insights of that culture. Comedy would seem to be our only defence against the disintegration of society and within ourselves, particularly as the time is unpropitious for heroes and tragedy. Our reassurance may come from the fact that the dividing line between comedy and tragedy has not been as clear as criticism implies; comedy has never meant simply laughter and a happy ending.

Such liberty of forms has produced, then, a period of labels, as if labelling could solve the problem: Angry Young Men, Kitchen Sink, New Wave, Theatre of the Absurd, Theatre of Cruelty, Theatre of Fact, the Happening, Total Theatre; a large number of 'isms' and various slogans like 'the people', 'Multimedia' and 'relevance'. There has been a great deal of talk about finding an audience by going out into the streets to meet the people. To lose an audience looks like carelessness; but what, exactly, is meant by 'the People'? How, for example, are we to take Alan Plater's complaint that the workers do not go to the theatre: 'school-teachers rather than lorry drivers, and dressed for the occasion'. The theatre has been preoccupied with multi-media performances often overlooking the fact that someone has to be in control. Debussy once complained that Nijinski was just watching his music go by. The theatre has been preoccupied with making things relevant: which is a contradiction in terms.

1956 saw a luminous accident in the history of British Theatre. As Steiner points out, the major dramatic poet rarely lives alone: Aeschylus is followed by Euripides and Sophocles; Marlowe by Shakespeare, Jonson and Webster; Corneille by Racine; Goethe by Schiller, Kleist and Buechner while in 1900 Ibsen, Strindberg and Chekhov were all alive. Looking backward from 1970, 1956 was clearly such a point in time but who, on 1 January 1956, could have foreseen this?

Looking forward into the 1970s presents the same blank aspect. Fortunately the historian is not required to be a prophet, and in the theatre the conclusion in which nothing is concluded is entirely appropriate. In all its aspects the theatre is still basically concerned with the relationship, as Ruby Cohn expresses it, between the rôle and the real. As it changes, it lives, as it lives it must change—as Mrs. Telfer recognised in that under-rated play about the theatre, *Trelawney of the Wells:*

Telfer: *(pointing to the Green-room)*: And so this new-fangled stuff, and these dandified people, are to push us, and such as us, from our stools!

Mrs. Telfer: Yes, James, just as some other new fashion will, in course of time, push *them* from their stools.

Venice–Manchester, 1970–2.

# The National Theatre

The history of the creation of the National Theatre is a kind of morality on the place of the theatre in national life. The first suggestion for this institution was put forward in 1848 by a London publisher called Effingham Wilson and the idea was supported at various times by Arnold, Harley Granville-Barker, William Archer and Winston Churchill. Barker and Archer formed the Shakespeare National Memorial Committee in 1910 but when Barker revised his book of 1903 in 1930 nothing had been done. Barker, prophetically, suggested the South Bank as a site. In fact a site was purchased in 1937 opposite the Victoria and Albert Museum and George Bernard Shaw turned the first sod. Building was delayed by the war (1939–45) and negotiations with the LCC led to an exchange for a new site on the South Bank. In 1949 the National Theatre Bill passed through both Houses of Parliament empowering the Government to contribute up to one million pounds but leaving the precise date to the discretion of the Chancellor of the Exchequer. In 1951 Her Majesty the Queen laid a foundation stone. Unfortunately it was decided the following year that the National Theatre should occupy another and better site and in 1956 Tynan was lamenting that nothing had happened since 1949 save that a single stone had been regally laid and, by mischance, in the wrong place. However, in 1958, Laurence Olivier was appointed a trustee of the National

Theatre and in 1960 the RSC were invited to join the Joint Council and create the amalgamation of the Old Vic and the RSC in a National Theatre. This idea was rejected by the Treasury in 1961 until the LCC entered the discussions when the Chancellor agreed to reconsider a scheme for rehousing Sadlers Wells in an opera house under the same roof as the National Theatre. In 1962 the RSC withdrew from the project, a National Theatre Board was appointed and it was agreed with the Governors of the Old Vic that that theatre should become the temporary home of the National Theatre while a Board was established to supervise the building of an Opera House and Theatre on adjoining sites. Olivier was appointed Director of the National Theatre and the inaugural production of *Hamlet* took place in 1963. The architect Lasdun was appointed that same year and after a campaign of 115 years the end was in sight. In 1966 a decision was taken by the South Bank Board to proceed (!) with a theatre at a capital cost of £7$\frac{1}{2}$ million (estimated) with the Government and the LCC each committed to providing three and three-quarter million pounds. By July 1967 the Government was stating that it would not contribute to the cost of the Opera House and the GLC was refusing to contribute if the Government did not. This stalemate was resolved by the decision not to build an Opera House on the South Bank and it was therefore proposed to build the National Theatre on a site immediately downstream of Waterloo Bridge in lieu of the site next to the County Hall. In 1969 Sir Robert McAlpine moved on to the Princess Meadow site to build a National Theatre.

Meanwhile the company has been performing in cramped conditions at the Old Vic and in theatres leased for a summer season in the West End. When the National Theatre occupy their new home on the South Bank in 1974 (?) Lord Olivier will become Life President and will be succeeded by Peter Hall.

Postscript: In September 1972 it was announced that, because of the building workers' strike the January opening in 1974 had been abandoned and that the earliest date for the first production must be February or even March.

# Select Bibliography

Not enough people seem to be aware that we have a British Theatre Museum at Leighton House, London, W.14. This institution was suggested in 1955, came into existence in 1963 and is already a useful repository of theatre material. Since the regrettable end of *Encore* in 1965 there has been no comparable replacement, but the following theatre magazines continue to appear: *Modern Drama, Tulane Drama Review* (now called *The Drama Review*) and, in England, *Gambit* and the monthly *Plays and Players* (which claims to incorporate *Encore, Theatre World* and *Play Pictorial*). In 1971 Methuen's brought out *Theatre Quartery* which should fill the gap.

Many of the books in this bibliography have their own comprehensive listings which enlarges the scope of this select list.

Artaud, Antonin: *The Theater and its Double,* New York, 1958.
Barnard, G. C.: *Samuel Beckett,* London, 1970.
Banham, Martin: *Osborne,* Edinburgh, 1969.
Bentley, Eric: *The Playwright as Thinker,* New York, 1955.
   *The Theatre of Commitment,* London, 1968.
   (ed.) *The Theory of the Modern Stage,* London, 1968.
Billington, Michael: *The Modern Actor,* London, 1973.
Blau, Herbert: *The Impossible Theatre,* New York, 1965.
Bradbrook, M. C.: *English Dramatic Form,* London, 1965.
Brecht, Bertolt: *The Messingkauf Dialogues,* London, 1965.

Brook, Peter: *the empty space*, London, 1968.

Brown, John Russell: *Theatre Language*, London, 1972.

Brustein, Robert: *The Theatre of Revolt*, London, 1965.
  *The Third Theatre*, London, 1970.

Carter, Alan: *John Osborne*, Edinburgh, 1969.

Coe, R. N.: *Beckett*, Edinburgh, 1964.
  *Ionesco*, London, 1971.

Darlington, W. A.: *The Actor and His Audience*, London, 1949.

Doherty, Francis: *Samuel Beckett*, London, 1971.

Donoghue, Denis: *The Third Voice*, Princeton, 1959.

Elsom, John: *Theatre Outside London*, London, 1971.

Esslin, Martin: *The Theatre of the Absurd*, London, 1968.
  *Brief Chronicles*, London, 1970.
  *The Peopled Wound: The Plays of Harold Pinter*, London, 1970.

Grossvogel, David I.: *Twentieth Century French Drama*, New York, 1961.

Fowlie, Wallace: *Dionysus in Paris*, London, 1961.

Guicharnaud, Jacques: *Modern French Theatre*, New Haven, 1967.

Hanson, Gillian: *Original Skin*, London, 1970.

Hayman, Ronald: *John Whiting*, London, 1969.
  *Gielgud*, London, 1971.

Henderson, J. A.: *The First Avant-Garde 1887–1894*, London, 1971.

Kitchin, Laurence: *Mid-Century Drama*, London, 1960.
  *Drama in the Sixties*, London, 1966.

Ionesco, Eugene: *Notes and Counternotes*, London, 1964.

Joseph, Stephen: *Theatre in the Round*, London, 1967.

Charles Marowitz (with Tom Milne and Owen Hale) [eds.] *The Encore Reader*, London, 1965.

Nicoll, Allardyce: *English Drama: A Modern Viewpoint*, London, 1968.

O'Connor, Ulick: *Brendan Behan*, London, 1970.

Pronko, L. C.: *Avant Garde*, London, 1962.

Ribalow, H. U.: *Arnold Wesker*, New York, 1965.

Shattuck, Roger: *The Banquet Years*, London, 1969.

Steiner, George: *The Death of Tragedy*, London, 1961.

Styan, J. L.: *The Dark Comedy*, Cambridge, 1968.

Trussler, Simon: *The Plays of John Osborne*, London, 1969.
  *The Plays of Arnold Wesker*, London, 1971.
  *The Plays of John Whiting*, London, 1972.
  *The Plays of Harold Pinter*, London, 1973.

Taylor, John Russell: *Anger and After,* London, 1969.
*The Second Wave,* London. 1971.
Trewin, J. C.: *Peter Brook,* London, 1971.
Tynan, Kenneth: *He that Plays the King,* London, 1950.
*Tynan on Theatre,* London, 1964.
Wellwarth, George: *The Theatre of Protest and Paradox,* New York, 1964/70.
Wesker, Arnold: *Fears of Fragmentation,* London, 1970.
Williams, Raymond: *Modern Tragedy,* London, 1966.
*Drama from Ibsen to Brecht,* London, 1968.
Worsley, T. C.: *The Fugitive Art,* London, 1952.
Worth, Katharine J.: *Revolutions in Modern English Drama,* London, 1973.
Wulbern, Julian H.: *Brecht and Ionesco: Commitment in Context,* University of Illinois, 1971.

The National Theatre issued a pictorial record covering the years 1963–71 in 1971, and the Arts Council Report, *The Theatre Today* (1970) makes interesting reading. The following collections of essays are useful:

*Contemporary Theatre,* Stratford-upon-Avon Studies No. 4, 1962.
*Modern Drama* (edited Bogard and Oliver), 1965.
*Modern British Playwrights* (edited John Russell Brown), 1968.
*The Playwrights Speak* (edited Walter Wager), 1967.
*Theatre in the Twentieth Century* (edited R. W. Corrigan), 1963.
*Experimental Drama* (edited W. A. Armstrong), 1963.
*Aspects of Drama and Theatre,* Sidney, 1965.
*Theatre '71* (edited Sheridan Morley), 1971.